Welcome to the *EVERYTHI[NG]*

These handy, accessible books give you all you need to tackle a difficult project, gain a new hobby, comprehend a fascinating topic, prepare for an exam, or even brush up on something you learned back in school but have since forgotten.

You can read an *EVERYTHING®* book from cover-to-cover or just pick out the information you want from our four useful boxes: e-wisdoms, e-ssentials, e-alerts, and e-questions. We literally give you everything you need to know on the subject, but throw in a lot of fun stuff along the way, too.

We now have well over 100 *EVERYTHING®* books in print, spanning such wide-ranging topics as weddings, pregnancy, wine, learning guitar, one-pot cooking, managing people, and so much more. When you're done reading them all, you can finally say you know *EVERYTHING®*!

E-WISDOM

Important sound bytes of information

ESSENTIALS

Quick handy tips

ALERT

Urgent warnings

QUESTIONS?

Solutions to common problems

THE

EVERYTHING

Series®

Dear Reader:

You are about to embark on a life-altering journey. By picking up this book, you've already taken the first step toward inviting more positive energy into your life.

When I first took on the adventure of feng shui, I naively thought that moving some furniture around was all I had to do in order to apply the ancient Chinese principles of this practice. I thought all I really needed to do was move my water fountain to a different corner of my living room to increase the flow of greater prosperity into my life. I was wrong. Feng shui is about so much more than such selfishness—it's about shifting the old mindsets that have blocked you from your greatest potential. It's about making positive changes in your life in order to be in more perfect flow, harmony, and balance. It's about recognizing and respecting your place in the Universe.

Today you are beginning to open your mind to the world of feng shui and all its magnificent wonders. You'll move some furniture, but you'll also remove clutter from your environment and cleanse your mind, opening yourself up to new opportunities to create a better, happier, and more balanced life.

Writing this book has brought me closer to peace and harmony than I've ever been—and it's brought me new opportunities in the form of helpful new people. One of those people, feng shui consultant Kris Halter, whose introduction and tips grace and bless this book, is now a friend with whom I feel a strong connection.

There are no accidents. You will experience positive growth on your own new path using the ancient wisdom of feng shui. This book has changed my life for the better. May it do the same for yours, starting right now!

Katina Z Jones

THE
EVERYTHING®
FENG SHUI BOOK

Create harmony and peace in any room

Katina Z. Jones

Adams Media Corporation
Avon, Massachusetts

EDITORIAL
Publishing Director: Gary M. Krebs
Managing Editor: Kate McBride
Copy Chief: Laura MacLaughlin
Acquisitions Editor: Allison Carpenter Yoder
Development Editor: Christel A. Shea

PRODUCTION
Production Director: Susan Beale
Production Manager: Michelle Roy Kelly
Series Designer: Daria Perreault
Layout and Graphics: Arlene Apone,
Paul Beatrice, Brooke C. Camfield,
Colleen Cunningham, Daria Perreault,
Frank Rivera

Published by Adams Media, an F+W Publications Company
57 Littlefield Street, Avon, MA 02322 U.S.A.
www.adamsmedia.com

ISBN: 1-58062-587-8
Printed in the United States of America.

J I H G F E

Library of Congress Cataloging-in-Publication Data
Jones, Katina Z.
The everything feng shui book : create harmony and peace in any room /
Katina Z. Jones.
p. cm. -- (An everything series book)
Includes index.
ISBN 1-58062-587-8
1. Feng shui. I. Title. II. Everything series.
BF1779.F4 J66 2002
133.3'337--dc21
2002003930

This publication is designed to provide accurate and authoritative information with regard to the subject matter covered. It is sold with the understanding that the publisher is not engaged in rendering legal, accounting, or other professional advice. If legal advice or other expert assistance is required, the services of a competent professional person should be sought.

—From a *Declaration of Principles* jointly adopted by a Committee of the American Bar Association and a Committee of Publishers and Associations

Illustrations by Barry Littmann and Kathie Kelleher.
Interior photographs by David Shoenfelt.

*This book is available at quantity discounts for bulk purchases.
For information, call 1-800-872-5627.*

Visit the entire Everything® series at *www.everything.com*

Contents

Dedication

For Zoe Yaceczko,
Our new Chinese daughter
who brings blessings
and good fortune
and to Hong Wen Bin
for blessings already bestowed.

Acknowledgments

Special thanks to all who helped in the making of this book: Kris Halter, feng shui consultant, for sharing her lessons and inspirations; David Shoenfelt, for his fabulous photographs; Allison Carpenter, my patient and enthusiastic editor at Adams Media; Frank Weimann of The Literary Group International; Elaine DeRosa for much-needed editorial assistance; John Yaceczko Jr. (the best husband on the planet) and Mary Lou Lund for their love, guidance, and support.

Introduction

By Kris Halter, Feng Shui Consultant

When I teach feng shui, I always begin with an acknowledgment. I tell my students, "I am teaching you what you already know. I'm just reminding you that you know it!"

But what is feng shui, and how will it change your life? Translated literally, *feng shui* means "wind" and "water." It is a language of symbols that focus on the individual and relates everything in our space to our conscious and unconscious minds. It encompasses the forces of nature and the energies within and around us. What you learn when you practice feng shui is how to work with your intentions in ways that attract the best things into your life, while simultaneously showing you how to disperse or eliminate the negative things.

Feng shui practice teaches us to be sure that the things we cling to are the things we really want in our lives—because what we create in our homes symbolizes how we feel about ourselves. Feng shui does this using the *bagua* (an ancient tool) and simple psychology.

If feng shui is so simple a concept to employ in our lives, why does it at first seem so difficult? Many of us live our lives on autopilot—at an unconscious level. Feng shui teaches us to be active—to be conscious participants in our lives and our surroundings.

Feng shui has its roots in ancient Chinese culture, and the Tao teaches us about the interconnectedness of all things. Only when we truly grasp this concept are we able to experience life with open eyes. Not until we are ready to surrender the outcome of things do our lives begin to shift in positive, often amazing, ways.

For example, when my friend Katina asked me if she could photograph my home for this book, initially I felt guarded. I mean, it's a very big deal to open yourself and your life to the whole world! Did I really want to do that?

Since I often pay attention to my gut feelings, and advocate doing the same for my clients, I looked within: there, deep inside, was excitement. But I had let the critic in me start to object, bringing fear to the surface and covering my excitement as though with a blanket.

In order to get to the true answer, I had to get to that silent space between my thoughts where true knowing exists. So I meditated, and before I went to bed that night, I asked for guidance in my dreams as to the course of action I should take with this book. Usually when I do this, the answer appears in my dream—but not this time.

Instead of a dream, I awoke with only the word *Pegasus* in my mind. "Pegasus?" I thought. I wasn't even sure what the word really meant.

Intrigued, I ran down to my computer and typed the word *Pegasus* into my favorite search engine. Of course, I learned all about the winged mythological creature on several of the Greek mythology Web sites. But then

I dug a little deeper, and here is what I found: "In modern times, Pegasus is seen as the symbol for immortality of the soul, and as the carrier and protector that guards the spirit in its journeys to the astral plane."

I had asked for this information to come to me in my dreams!

The passage continued: "Pegasus is the power of the creative spirit in all of us. He is the symbol of the muses, of inspiration, and of the beauty we bring to our lives and the lives of others. It is said, if you are drawn to Pegasus, then he is calling you to create . . . in any form you choose. Create, and share your expressions of beauty."

Wow. I had my answer. But here's where it really becomes interesting.

I told Katina it was okay to go ahead and schedule the photo shoot. When David Shoenfelt, the photographer, showed up to photograph the examples of feng shui throughout my home, we exchanged the usual introductions and small talk. I asked David where he lived, and he began to describe his neighborhood. There is a landmark by his house, a sculpture by a well-known local artist, and I recalled having seen it. Imagine my surprise, though, when David suddenly said, "Oh, yeah— that's Pegasus!" It was the name of the sculpture!

So, how is this story relevant? Feng shui teaches us to trust our intuition, to listen to what feels right, to pay attention to ourselves and our experience. It is so much more than simply moving furniture or hanging a crystal. It's the intention behind hanging the crystal that's most important.

Be clear about your intentions. Write down what you want most in your life—beyond material things, and encompassing such life-strengthening desires as more fulfilling relationships and better health—so you can focus more intently on bringing it to fruition. Use feng shui to set your attractive power and energies into motion.

Once you begin working with feng shui, you will be able to give up "neediness" in favor of attracting prosperity, health, and happiness—the abundance of the Universe can be yours through conscious living. The amazing thing is that once you give up your want and need for something, you will open up every ounce of your being to real (and powerful) abundance. It's a difficult concept to master, and one that goes totally against the powerful need for instant gratification, but I promise that once you do it you will change your life forever.

May you be filled with wonder and awe as you begin your journey through this ancient Chinese wisdom. Apply this art to your living space and learn to use it to support your personal ambitions, reflect your values and aesthetics, and remind you of your dreams. Your home reflects to the world your own feelings, hopes, and dreams—display them proudly to yourself and the Universe, and you will be richly rewarded.

Kris Halter can be reached through her Web site at *www.mindfuldesign.net*.

CHAPTER 1

The Basics: Goals of Feng Shui

From its literal translation, *feng shui* means "wind and water." Wind moves the invisible life force of feng shui, chi, and water retains or cultivates it. An ancient Chinese system, feng shui teaches people how to create harmony between nature and man-made structures. The belief was that this "intentional harmony" would ultimately balance out the world, bringing peace and prosperity to all.

The Mother of Invention

Thousands of years ago, in southern China (a rich, fertile region ripe with mountains, rivers, valleys, and farms), the art of feng shui was born out of necessity. There was a definite need among the people to determine the best and most auspicious places for their homes, altars, and burial grounds. The burial sites were particularly important to the people, since they relied heavily upon the energy of their ancestors for everything from good crops to spiritual guidance and assistance with prosperity.

To these primitive yet wise rural people, everything spiritual and ethereal had its earthly correspondent in nature—and everything in nature could be carefully "directed" to assist in the achievement of earthly goals. What were (and are) those goals? Simply put, to achieve a positive flow of energy, a balance of yin and yang, and an interaction of the five elements.

QUESTIONS?

What is feng shui?
Feng shui means, literally, "wind and water." The practice of feng shui relates to the positive flow of energy through your indoor, outdoor, and spiritual surroundings. It isn't just about moving furniture around to attract wealth!

Although we are many miles and several centuries away from the original feng shui "masters," we share a common belief today that external factors affect our internal landscapes, whether for good or ill.

We know that there are invisible cosmic forces that govern all things—man, nature, and the Universe—and the main goal of feng shui is to learn to move gracefully within this flow. It's definitely not a religion, and it's not about moving some stuff out of your house so you can go get more stuff. In feng shui, it's the energy, or *chi,* that counts most, followed by good intention and personal integrity. It requires an open mind, but also one that can take an objective and honest look at its surroundings and be ready to give up in order to receive.

Do you need to practice the principles of good feng shui in every single room of your house? No, you don't. But remember—the more you create using feng shui principles in your life, the better your overall results are likely to be.

What is chi?
Chi is the Americanized phonetic spelling of *qi*, the force of life that flows through objects and nature in general. Chi flows through your life, and your surroundings. The goal of feng shui is to direct chi in a more positively flowing manner.

The Feng Shui "Schools"

Today, there are many schools of feng shui, and many different methods that practitioners use to help others move their possessions and elements in the right direction. But there are only three basic schools of feng shui.

Form School

The Form School began in rural southern China and focuses on the lay of the land (i.e., landforms), water formations, and the topography of the land. Practitioners of this school will generally spend most of their time evaluating the lot your home is situated on and the relationship of each area of your home to the land surrounding it.

Compass School

In northern China, where there weren't as many hills, the Chinese devised a more scientific method of finding the right directions for homes, people, and possessions: They created a compass called the *luo pan*. Many places in the world use this method, but because it requires the use of a compass and some mathematical prowess, many Westerners find it too difficult to use on their own. If this school is appealing to you, your best bet is to find a practitioner who is skilled in the Compass School—attempting to use the compass on your own could result in inaccurate readings or results.

Black Hat (or Buddhist) Sect

Founded by Professor Thomas Lin Yun, the Black Hat Sect (or School) synthesizes Buddhism, Taoism, shamanism, and folk wisdom. It encourages anyone who practices feng shui, professional or novice, to rely heavily upon his intuition. The only feng shui tool a Black Hat practitioner uses is the bagua, since much emphasis is placed on intuition and intention. In the Black Hat Sect, if it feels right, it probably is—as long as there is a positive, healthy flow of chi. Black Hat also incorporates the Zen practice of meditation.

(*The Everything® Feng Shui Book* will focus more on the Black Hat Sect of feng shui, as it is easier for the novice to effectively follow and implement in his surroundings.)

The Balance of Yin and Yang

The concept of yin and yang, the eternal opposites, is common to all schools of feng shui study and practice. Chances are, you've even heard the saying, "It's a yin-yang thing." But what exactly are *yin* and *yang*—and how do they work in the world of feng shui? In their simplest sense, they represent two opposing yet complementary halves of a whole—the duality of the Universe.

"Yin" is the female energy, which is soft, nurturing, flowing, passive, and contemplative. Its direction is north, the numbers associated with it are even, and its universal correspondent is Earth. "Yang" is the male, or aggressive, energy and is bright, solid, and creative. Yang represents odd numbers, the southern direction, and the energy of Heaven. Together, the two symbols form a whole circle and the complete Universe—but each has a dot in it of the other's energy, meaning there is some yin in yang and some yang in yin to complete the whole picture.

The symbol of yin and yang shows us that we should seek the natural balance in all things, and that all things, both natural and man-made, naturally gravitate toward this balance. The same is true in human beings, all of whom contain a little of the opposite sex's energy in them. How many times have you heard someone say, "Wow, that man is really in touch with his feminine side!" or "She has a male strength about her"?

What people are really responding to when they say things like that is the complementary nature of energies in another that set them apart or help them to achieve admirable feats—well-balanced people are admirable!

Yin is earth energy (feminine, passive energy), and yang is heaven energy (masculine, dynamic energy). The yin-yang symbol is round, continuous, and complementary—both energies are needed in balanced form to create wholeness. Neither is better than the other.

With yin and yang, the object is to keep the balance as,—well, balanced, as possible—to not have rooms or living spaces that are too yin or too yang. The mission of feng shui is to seek out that balance in each room so you can help yourself feel grounded or centered in your living environment.

The Five Elements

A key to understanding feng shui is learning the five elements (fire, earth, metal, water, and wood) and discovering how they relate to one another in ways that mimic nature. As in nature, there are both creative and destructive cycles, and here's the "magic formula" for each:

- **Creative cycle:** fire creates earth, earth creates metal, metal creates water, water creates wood, and wood creates fire.
- **Destructive cycle:** fire melts metal, metal cuts wood, wood moves earth, earth muddies water, and water puts out fire.

SSENTIALS

Good feng shui takes some time to get used to—and to take effect. Give your efforts some "breathing time" before you start expecting miracles. The best feng shui practitioners will tell you that some results will feel instant, while others will take time and perhaps even some refining.

The Chinese believe that the Universe is heavily influenced by this positive and negative (yin-yang) interaction of the five elements. A room that uses good feng shui placement has a balanced use of each element—and is not too heavy on any one element. Too much of one element (especially a powerful one like fire) can make a room feel oppressive and can actually block the chi of the home's inhabitants.

Elemental Qualities

On a symbolic level, the elements represent order and the influence of the Universe in nature and all things, including humankind.

But let's look more closely at the qualities associated with each element for an even deeper understanding:

- **Fire** represents emotions and corresponds to the color red. Fire energy is pure yang—strong, assertive, and dominant. In objects for décor, real fire elements such as candles or oil lamps can be used to represent the fire element in a room—or you can use symbolic items like a red star, red fabric, or even red flowers.
- **Earth** relates very much to the physical plane of existence. In people, earth types are grounded, organized, and very practical in all matters. They are quite levelheaded and hold harmony very dear to their hearts. Earth elements that can be used in décor include soil in a potted plant, yellow and brown items, or rectangular objects like a flowerbed that fits on a windowsill.
- **Metal** energy pertains to mental activity and thought processes. Use metal objects like metal picture frames, lampposts, sculptures, or clocks in a room to represent this pensive energy. Symbolically, you can use round items that are silver, gold, or white in color to represent metal. Just remember that the closer the object to its natural element, the stronger the energy of the object in your home. The more symbolic you get, the less powerful the object will be in positively affecting your home situation.
- **Water** relates to spirituality, reflection, and meditation. There is always an air of mystery with water elements. To incorporate water into your home, use clear glass vases or pitchers with fresh water, glass or

clear marble stones in a dish or bowl, or anything black (since black is the symbolic color of water). You can also add the water element to a room with a water fountain or aquarium.

- **Wood** relates to intuition and the feeling of "knowingness" inside us all. Wood people are strong yet flexible, trusting their inner voice to lead them to the next project or situation safely. Best to use real live plants in your home décor to represent wood; bamboo sticks are especially considered in feng shui to be auspicious, or full of good luck. Anything green will symbolically create the wood element in your home.

ALERT

Begin your feng shui process with a clear idea of your intention. Everything about your process should be geared toward the positive, from your initial attitude to the finishing touches. Never begin on a negative note (i.e., with a plan to use feng shui to ward off evil neighbors).

Each of these elements is represented on the bagua (see "Feng Shui's Energy Map" on page 8). The most important thing to remember about the elements is to keep them balanced—don't worry if you don't understand it all, yet. When we go room by room later in the book, there will be plenty of good examples!

Sensory Connection

Also key to the principles of good feng shui is the need to balance appeal to all of the senses. After all, the senses are considered to be the human manifestation of the five elements. But how can you accomplish a balance of these energies in your home? Here's an example of how it can work. You will have a well-balanced living room if you include items that appeal to each of your senses: a scented candle (smell), soft pillows on the sofa (touch), fresh fruit in a bowl (taste), soft music or a water fountain (sound), and an interesting, dynamic piece of artwork hanging on one of the walls (sight).

Every room of the house can use this kind of attention to achieve or maintain its balance of the senses. Don't be afraid to think a little unconventionally, too—you can incorporate taste into your bathroom "spa" experience by mixing up a fresh fruit smoothie to sip on during your luxury bath.

Feng Shui's Energy Map

If feng shui is a way of life, then the bagua (see diagram on page 64) is the road map for getting to all the great places you want to be in life. Each of your endeavors is represented in a corner of the octagon—and each corner also has its corresponding colors, elements, and energy.

Used correctly, the bagua helps you to determine the preferred locations for all of your beloved possessions—and ancient Chinese wisdom holds the belief that when we place items carefully and with intention, we clear away the blockages of energy that can hold us back from success. In other words, it's how you keep your stuff that determines how well you do in life.

The Tool

Simply translated, bagua means eight-sided figure or octagon. It comes from a book of ancient Chinese wisdom called the *I Ching,* or the *Book of Changes.* The *Book of Changes* is a method of divination that contains insightful and profound teachings in the form of trigrams, which are symbols pertaining to business, life, and the ways of nature and the Universe. The *I Ching* reveals the flow of nature as perfect balance (yin-yang) and harmony.

Each area of the bagua has a connection with the main aspects of your life: career, helpful people (who assist in creating opportunities and good luck), children/creativity, relationship/marriage, fame/reputation, wealth/ abundance, family/community/ancestors, knowledge/self-cultivation, and health/well-being. In feng shui, all of these "channels" are affected by both positive and negative (or blocked) energies; the goal is to keep the energies as positive and flowing as possible.

Go easy on yourself and your surroundings at first. Assess your current living situation with a positive checklist rather than a guilt-ridden list of what's wrong. Remember to stay positive throughout the process—this includes being positive toward yourself!

As a tool, the bagua is placed over your location so each area of your home or business has meaning. For example, one area represents wealth, and another, partnership. As these sections of your location represent areas of your life, you have the potential to transform your life situation when you activate them in alignment with your clearly stated intention.

The Sections

To use the bagua, you need to place it (either physically or using your visualization ability) over the main entrance to your home with the career side aligned with the front wall. The area of career is always at the front of the location; this means that your front door is usually in knowledge, career, or helpful people.

- **Career** represents how you serve community and family. This part of the bagua demonstrates your expression in the world of work, whether as an employee, entrepreneur, or volunteer.
- **Helpful people** represents teachers, mentors, helpers in life, friends, angels (as spiritual "helpers"), and opportunities brought through chance meetings. It is sometimes called the "Gate of Heaven" and is the method by which luck comes into your life.
- **Children and creativity** represents all children and the incubation-like process of creativity. The creative process is key to your personal, spiritual, and psychological growth—and absolutely critical to your career success if you are a writer, artist, or creative type.
- **Relationship** represents the important relationships (including marriage) of the inhabitants of the house. For a business, it represents the partners involved in running the business. The relationship corner is where you'll want to support a present relationship or conjure a new one by placing things in pairs.

- **Fame** represents reputation, image, and how others see us in the world. Our ability to generate fame and success in business and in life depends heavily on the integrity of our intentions.
- **Wealth** represents the "ka-ching" factor in our lives, or our ability to earn, keep, and grow money. But it can also represent abundance in all things, not just the material.
- **Family** represents a loving, supporting family well rooted in ancestry. It also supports your interaction with your community of friends with whom you share gather and may similar interests. If the location is an office, it supports a community atmosphere and people working in harmony.
- **Knowledge** represents wisdom and the ability to acquire new knowledge. This area also supports a total path of self-knowledge and spiritual awareness. In this area of the bagua, self-help books are quite welcome.
- **Health** is in the center of the bagua and the center, or "heart," of your house. It represents the individual and collective health of all living beings—including pets and plants—in a building such as your home.

Place the bagua over geographic areas in your house (either over your whole floor plan or just room by room), then look at its corresponding life endeavor. As a map of sorts, the bagua will help you determine the most auspicious locations and décor to help you achieve your life's goals. Remember, you don't have to practice feng shui in every single room, but the more attention and mindfulness you give to each part of your surroundings, the better the results will be.

Feng Shui and Chinese Astrology

Another tool that helps you find your place in the world of feng shui is Chinese astrology. By taking a look at a chart of Chinese lunar years and their corresponding animal signs (much like Western astrological signs), you can get a clearer picture of who you are. When you see which element is attached to your sign's particular birth year, you can easily determine which elements you most need in order to keep yourself in good balance.

Once you look at the Sign Finder chart (Appendix C), you can learn more about the basic qualities and characteristics of your animal sign. It's a fun way to incorporate your own characteristics into your feng shui projects throughout your home, work environment, and surroundings!

E-WISDOM

Balance the yin energies (feminine, curving, nurturing, dark, soft, earthy energy) with the yang (masculine, active, angular, sharp, heaven, and sun energy) to achieve a balance that will make you feel most comfortable in a space.

Here's a quick look at the yin and yang of each sign in the Chinese zodiac:

- **Rats** are charismatic, progressive leaders with quick wits and smooth social skill (yin). On the yang (or negative) side, they can be power-mongers who are prone to letting greed rule their decisions.
- **Oxen** are strong, morally aware, and conscientious (yin). They are loyal, dependable, sincere, and hardworking. Stubbornness and narrow-mindedness are their yang qualities.
- **Tigers** have yin courage, pride, and bravado. They are the eternal optimists—energetic, enthusiastic, and even lucky. On the yang side, they are sometimes impatient and impulsive.
- The **Cat** (sometimes Rabbit) is wise, diplomatic, and good at assessing people and situations (yin). But they can also be snobs who have tantrums when they feel jealous (yang).
- **Dragons** are born leaders with lots of the yin pioneering spirit. They can be flamboyant and confident and often do things in a big, grandiose way. Their negative yang qualities are bossiness and a quick-tempered nature. They can pout when they don't get their way.
- **Snakes** are private, almost mysterious creatures in the Chinese zodiac. They are full of wisdom, insight, and quiet determination (yin), but can also be possessive, manipulative, or "biting" in their ways (yang).

- **Horses** are cheery, extroverted, and often popular people (yin). But they can also have a short attention span that holds them back from achieving all they can in life (yang).
- On the yin side, **Goats** (or Sheep) are the gentle, peace-loving home-bodies of Chinese astrology. Yang qualities make them fussy and persnickety, insecure and hermitlike.
- **Monkeys** are the most fun-loving of all the animal signs. They are funny, creative, and imaginative (yin). On the yang side, their mischief can wreak havoc on relationships, and they can appear superficial and uncaring.
- **Roosters** are reliable, honest, and plain speaking (yin). They can be quite industrious, focused, and sociable, but they can also be blunt to the point of rudeness, ruffling feathers with their yang qualities.
- **Dogs** are devoted, loyal, and helpful to family and friends (yin). They are unselfish, trustworthy, and resourceful. On the yang side, though, they can be pessimistic worrywarts.
- **Pigs** are the beloved servants, the quintessential "followers" of the Chinese zodiac. On the yin side, they love to bring joy and happiness to others. But the yang of it is that they are often gullible and naïve, misled by others who set out to deliberately deceive them. Good thing they forgive easily, too.

Using Chinese astrology to incorporate your own personality into the feng shui of your home and work environments can be a positive—and enlightening—thing to do before embarking on a total overhaul of your design or décor. But don't get too hung up on the specific qualities of each sign—it's the corresponding elements that will mean the most to you in feng shui.

Does Your Home Reflect Your Life?

What does your home say about you? If you try to view your home through the eyes of a stranger, considering the arrangement of each room, the amount of clutter or the lack thereof, the colors, the textures, the scents and sights, what do you think your home reveals?

1. *How much clutter is in each room of your house?* Is the clutter reflective of your personality? A friend's teenage son defends the piles of clothes, books, papers, and other odds and ends in his room as providing comfort and security for him. "It's who I am," he says defiantly when asked why he seems to enjoy this environment. If clutter truly reflects who you are, don't worry about it. But if you feel embarrassed by it, or, worse, constrained; if it prevents your living comfortably, keeps you awake at night, or prevents you from thinking clearly or creatively, then you should take steps to eliminate the clutter and allow the chi to flow freely.

2. *Conversely, are your rooms too spare?* Are the walls white and bare, the furniture sterile, the space too pristine? Are guests afraid to sit or move about freely for fear of making a mess or disturbing the arrangement in some way? Do you cover your furniture with plastic or rush to place coasters under every cup and glass? In other words, are you projecting unfriendliness and a "keep out" mentality to others? This is fine if you truly do not want guests showing up on your door-step. However, if you are having trouble attracting friends to your home or keeping them there long once they arrive, it could be because the starkness of your décor or the sparseness of your furnishings is pushing them away.

Work on one room or area of your house at a time. Do not try to feng shui your whole house in one weekend—it takes plenty of "reflective time" to consider your actions and to determine the changes that will feel best.

3. *Is your home completely open to your children, or have you relegated their toys, books, and other possessions to only a room or two?* Is there anything at all that is welcoming or comforting to children in the living room, the dining room, the patio, or the den? Allowing them even a little space throughout the house and a place for them to play in most, if not all, of the rooms gives children the comfort of knowing that the home is theirs, too. Providing child-sized furniture and allowing

a few toys in even the neatest and most sophisticated of rooms tells others that there is room in your life and your heart for something much more important than material possessions—your children.

4. *Is your home open, airy, and filled with light, or packed with possessions, close, and dark?* Are the colors rich and vibrant in the rooms where you spend your waking hours and soft and relaxing in the rooms where you sleep or unwind? Can chi move easily through your rooms and hallways? Do you demonstrate awareness of the bagua in how your furnishings are arranged? Can the flow of energy in your home be improved by making minor adjustments in one or more rooms, or even in the yard or garden?

Once you become aware of the principles of feng shui, you will see that it is not difficult to change aspects of your home and property in order to improve energy flow and open up your life to the positive results that will follow!

Good Vibrations Energy Audit

When you first embark on your feng shui journey, it's a good idea to conduct an "energy audit" to determine areas of clear and blocked chi. Here's a quick checklist for assessing the chi in and around your home:

1. *Is the path to your front door open, curved, and inviting?* Do you use your front door to enter your home, or is a side door favored? In good feng shui, your doorway should be clear and unencumbered. Too much clutter (even in the form of too much foliage) can block energy from reaching your door.

2. *Are staircases easy to access—but not in direct line with doorways?* Does your front door open to a staircase that goes up or down? Chi comes in through your front door and should be able to move through your house slowly for maximum benefit to all living in the home. If your staircase is in direct line with the front door, the chi rushes up the stairs and back out of the house—especially if there is a small window at the top of the staircase. Hang a crystal to slow down the chi.

3. *In your living room, does the air feel stagnant?* That's a good sign that the energy in the room is blocked. Open some windows or use a ceiling fan to circulate the chi in the room—and bring some life back to the living room.
4. *Do the hallways seem open and airy?* Are there piles of clutter stacked in a hallway "loading dock" (i.e., waiting for a move to storage that never seems to happen)?

Start with a Clean Space

Before you begin the process of changing your home's energy, be sure to begin with a space clearing. If weather permits, open windows to get the chi moving. Physically clean the space you will be working on. Dirt and dust symbolize stagnant chi—and that must always be cleared first!

Clearing and Enhancing with Intention

Light a candle (pure aromatherapy type), diffuse pure essential oils, burn incense, or use a smudge stick (a tightly wrapped bundle of herbs and wood) to clear a space. Just be sure that whatever you use is in its purest form. Unfortunately, there are a lot of products on the market today that claim to be pure aromatherapy that are, in fact, full of artificial fillers and additives.

Play some music. A wonderful drumming or chanting CD would be great, but use what you love! It doesn't have to be meditation music to "speak" to you—and there's nothing like a little Tina Turner or Rolling Stones to get the chi moving!

Always begin with a close look at your intentions. What do you want to accomplish? What are your goals, and which are most important to you right now? What action are you preparing yourself to take?

Now you're ready for step two, which is intention. Remember your intention as you're placing the appropriate enhancement or cure in a particular sector. Keep this intention clearly in your mind. Open your heart to your highest good. Embrace the possibilities, and most important, trust your process.

The final step involves reinforcing all that you have done—giving more power to your enhancement or cure. This is the part where you meditate and offer blessings or thanks to the Universe through a process the Black Hat Sect of feng shui calls "The Three Secrets":

1. *Mudra* (hand gesture) is often the position of prayer, with both palms together, fingers pointing up. Hold your hands to your heart.
2. *Mantra* (prayer) is the prayer or blessing you are most comfortable with. It could be as simple as "thy will be done," or maybe a simple prayer you've written on your own. Whatever the case, recite it nine times. Nine is an auspicious number in feng shui.
3. Visualization of your specific intention. As you are reciting your mantra and holding your hands in the mudra position, hold your intention in your mind's eye the entire time, as though it has already been accomplished. Use affirmative statements along with this visualization (i.e., "I have already created space for love in my life" or "I am surrounded by a loving family").

Chances are, you'll feel uplifted and ready to take on the world when you're finished with these steps. But don't forget the last step of the whole process: Let go of the outcome—and trust the Universe to do its work!

The Eight Remedies or Cures

Adding remedies to a specific area where the chi seems to be blocked is the best way to open up the energy to its greatest good. In feng shui, there are eight basic remedies or cures:

- *Light*—includes lighting, mirrors, candles, and reflective surfaces.
- *Sound*—wind chimes, bells, metal mobiles, and hollow bamboo flutes. Anything that sounds harmonious (such as music or chanting) can also work well as a cure.

- *Color*—Red and black in particular can be used to stimulate flow of chi.
- *Life*—Living objects, such as pets or plants, can also get the chi moving in your home or surroundings.
- *Movement*—Flags, ribbons, banners, fountains, wind chimes, weather vanes, or hanging crystals are cures associated with movement.

FIGURE 1-1: Get It Going
Crystals are quick, easy cures for areas where the chi appears to be stuck. Round, multifaceted ones work best; avoid hanging crystals with sharp edges.

FIGURE 1-2: Slow It Down
This lovely garden statue's primary purpose is to represent the missing relationship sector of the owner's backyard, but it also slows down chi so that sector gets enough energy. (It is particularly auspicious that there are two cherubs in the statue, since relationships depend on at least two people.)

- *Stillness*—When chi moves too quickly, you need to slow it down with still objects such as statues or large rocks.
- *Mechanical/electrical*—This can mean machinery, but be careful that your electrical items don't overstimulate the chi. Too much energy defeats the purpose of a cure.
- *Straight lines*—Best here to use scrolls, swords, flutes, bamboo sticks, and fans.

Harness the subtle power of feng shui and its cures to move yourself in the right spiritual direction. Your feng shui mantra should be: Trust the Universe. Trust your intuition. Let go of the outcome. Give thanks for all that is.

E-WISDOM

Remember the universal law of prosperity: What you put out into the Universe is what you will get back. Want greater abundance in all things? Your own positive attitude is the real starting point.

Using Total Feng Shui

Learn to "mindfully move" the items in your environment that are creating obstacles in your life. Obstacles are not only physical items such as a couch, table, or computer, but also the mental "clutter" that keeps you from practicing mindfulness and holds you back from achieving your greatest potential in life.

Now, roll up your silk sleeves, put on some soft Chinese bamboo flute music, and get started!

CHAPTER 2

Slaying the Clutter Dragon

I t starts out rather innocently—a few things that you bought to decorate your home (or yourself)—just a few "nice things" that you couldn't pass up. Then a pattern begins—a few more bargains you couldn't refuse, a closet filled with clothes you might still wear when you lose those last five pounds, an attic full of things you haven't seen in twenty years . . .

"Just in Case"

The mighty clutter dragon has reared its ugly head—and fire begins to breathe down your neck, usually in the form of a spouse or family member who says, "Hey, are you starting a junk store in here? Let's clean this stuff up and move some things out of here."

"No!" you cry. "I'm keeping that in case I need it later!" But when is later, especially when you find that you are keeping clothes you've had since the ninth grade that you will never, ever wear again?

Simplify, Simplify

The Chinese are correct when they say that a cluttered house is a cluttered mind. Chinese tradition says that the more things you own, the more problems you will have in life. Think about it: When you were in college and had basically nothing, wasn't life simpler, too? So, why do you think all of the "live simpler" books have sold well in the last five years? We all seek a simpler life, yet many of us still have basements, attics, and family rooms filled with clutter.

E-WISDOM

What you don't own, owns you. What you resist persists.

—Zen saying

Slaying the clutter dragon is actually an easy thing to do—all it takes is a new perspective, a new way of taking a hard look at yourself and honestly assessing what you truly need in life.

The American Way

A woman who has recently been to China has the best travel advice for almost any trip: "Don't pack more than you can comfortably hold in a carry-on bag. Americans are notorious for packing more in one large suitcase than an entire Chinese family typically owns!" She, of course, was not aware of the feng shui significance her advice imparted. But the truth is, most Chinese families (except for the fabulously wealthy) have a very limited need for things. They tend to have only the most necessary, basic items on hand: a bed, a couch, a kitchen table, some dishes, and silverware. Seldom will you see more than one of anything in their homes.

The need for many things is purely American—and it can easily go from just a bad habit to a fixation that is difficult to get over. Look at the success of eBay, which lists more than a million items for sale by their owners on a daily basis. That's a lot of stuff!

Keeping things that are broken, useless, or obsolete is not practicing good feng shui. In good feng shui, everything you own should provide some kind of service to you—otherwise you will become a slave to it.

It seems unavoidable—every day, people are inundated with more and more opportunities to buy things that will supposedly enhance their lives. The overwhelming accumulation of stuff just seems to happen, but the reality is that you have much more control over your excesses than you think. Western culture has placed such an emphasis on materialism that people actually believe they need more than they do.

Every day, it becomes harder and harder to simply accept life as it is right now, at this moment . . . and to back down from the infinite opportunities to "improve" it. Practice saying "no" to things for one day, and you'll see what conscious effort it requires!

When Your Cup Runneth Over

Most people believe that he who dies with the most toys wins. Watching TV commercials for a day will show you just how possession conscious people can be! In a decidedly unscientific experiment, a few hours of television included seventeen commercials that said viewers were absolutely nothing without the right hair color, the right car, the right home, and all the best new toys and foods. The public is hit with similar images repeatedly throughout the day in everything from radio shows to billboards and shopping cart ads.

How can you tell if you've attained official pack-rat status? Look for the telltale signs:

- Bookshelves are overstuffed receptacles for many things, only half of which are actually books.
- Clothes overflow from your closet and land in piles on the floor, chair, treadmill, or dressing table.
- Kitchen "junk" drawers are filled so high they do not shut properly.
- Pantries are full of food you no longer like or eat.
- Medicine chests are filled with old or expired medications.
- Garages and attics are catch-alls full of things you keep "just in case" you need them someday.
- Desks are crammed with papers so old you are no longer sure of their need or meaning.
- You have a collection of broken items you are keeping to fix later, when you have time.
- You keep anything long past its shelf life or usefulness.

It might be a good idea to do a clutter check before embarking on a fresh new journey through feng shui. The previous list identifies common trouble spots. Find the clutter traps in your environment, and consider that clutter in specific areas of the bagua can affect your life. Copy the list, and use it at the start of each new season. Take a good look around, regularly, to be sure you're not creating blockages in your life by adding clutter in areas where you definitely don't want or need it.

What Clutter Really Means

Author Karen Kingston (*Clear Your Clutter with Feng Shui,* Broadway Books, 1999) says the process of clearing clutter in your home environment is actually the process of releasing, of letting go emotionally. When you begin to clear the clutter in your home, you also begin to release old attachments to things that no longer serve you or bring you joy.

Clutter 911! Are You Addicted to "Stuff?"

Can it be true? Are you really hooked on stuff? If you're uncertain, here are five ways to tell whether you have developed a hardcore clutter habit:

1. You can't pass up the great prices at garage sales, church bazaars, dollar stores, bargain basements, and other "deals" and "steals," regardless of how much space the items consume in your home and how little you use them. Half the time, you can't find them or don't even remember having them until you look for something else, clear out a closet, or, worst of all, buy a duplicate and discover the original when you're putting the new one away!

2. You've run out of room: Your closet is filled with clothes you think you're going to wear when you lose or even gain a little weight, or that will come back into style eventually. Your medicine cabinet overflows with expired lotions and potions. Your desk drawers are overflowing with ancient paperwork. Your dresser is stuffed with mismatched socks, worn-out underwear, and other items that you rarely use or no longer fit your body or your lifestyle. Your attic and/or basement are littered with boxes and bags of items that you haven't looked at in years. You may even have unopened boxes from the last move or two!

3. Your excuse for hanging on to everything is that you never know when you might need it—even though, if you did actually need it, you probably wouldn't be able to find it. Whatever "it" is.

4. One of your joys in life is bargain-hunting on the Internet. Nothing quite like acquiring someone else's discarded junk, is there?

5. You collect other kinds of "stuff"—the nonphysical kind. For instance, you make too many time commitments to others and have no time left for your family. Or, you haven't cleared out your e-mail or your voice mail in awhile. Maybe you eat more than your body needs.

Thankfully, there is a cure for addiction to "stuff," and it's simple—but it's not easy. You must say no to acquiring more useless things. Don't expect to achieve this new goal all at once. Just as with a twelve-step program, you'll have to take it one item and one day at a time. Stick with it, though, and you'll be well on your way toward healthy chi!

For instance, you might be keeping an old pair of tennis shoes that you wore on a favorite date, but since the relationship ultimately didn't work out, keeping the shoes is hanging on to something that is no longer part of your life. Such tendencies can possibly hold you back from a rewarding new relationship, since, psychologically speaking, you are holding on to the past.

When you begin to clear away years' worth of clutter from your attic, you may be amazed by how much stuff from your past has been holding you back from your future. Since the attic represents higher goals or aspirations, it's no wonder you may feel like you haven't achieved all you were capable of in life. That's what good feng shui does, though—it makes you start making conscious decisions based on your true intentions.

Fear and Hoarding

Don't underestimate the power of fear. As you walk through piles of old clothes, record albums, books, and knickknacks, you may ask yourself why you've been keeping all of these things for so long. Did you expect to use them again one day? Not likely. Instead, you probably hadn't felt ready to relinquish your past due to your uncertainty regarding your future.

Between changing jobs, repeated moves, or various stages of marriage, the possibility of not having enough to survive is a very real concern. Individuals in a state of continual change often take comfort in emotional hoarding, collecting things to pacify a soul that is yearning for love, for the kind of satisfaction that money can't buy. Often, they don't realize what they are doing until they have so much stuff in their homes that they can hardly breathe! Of course, if you can't breathe, neither can the chi. For good feng shui in your home, you must take a good hard look at yourself and your needs—and purge the items that no longer serve you.

QUESTIONS?

What is emotional hoarding?
Emotional hoarding is the collecting of things to satisfy the soul's need for comfort, security, love, or other intangibles that money can't buy.

Incorporating feng shui into your lifestyle and mindset is an ongoing process. It may be years before you realize that you are happy, secure, and certain. Continually evaluate where you are and what you need, and soon you will face the clutter dragon. You will know that it is definitely time for a major purging, both physically and psychologically—and what a fabulous feeling it will be to finally liberate yourself from your fears or failures of the past!

As you take a deeper look into the psychological ties you've had to the past, don't forget to check out the other clutter traps in your home. Think about clutter in the garage, basement, hall closet, and even in your car! Looking more deeply at the situation, what can you learn about your clutter patterns? Lots of interesting things. For instance, the clutter in your basement symbolizes some uneasiness in your family situation, since the basement in feng shui is symbolic of family and strong foundations.

The best litmus test for elimination of clutter is to look at each item and ask yourself, "When was the last time I used this?" If it was more than a year ago, it's probably not an essential item in your life—it might be of better use to someone else.

Clutter in the garage can signify an outward manifestation of a psychological difficulty in leaving your house every day—or in coming home. If you block yourself out of your garage with clutter, you might ask yourself what it is you are having difficulty returning to in your home life. Conversely, if you are a real homebody and barricade yourself into your garage with clutter, maybe it's time to consider starting a home-based business so you can spend more time at home—in a healthier manner.

The key to dealing with clutter is to be able to take these kinds of hard looks at yourself, your needs, and your motivations in order to find out why you are keeping what you are keeping. Once you understand your motivations, you can eliminate the clutter for good—and greatly improve your inner sense of well-being in the meantime!

When you really listen to others talk about their clutter (not that they would call it "clutter"), you may notice that their attachment to it almost always has its roots in a fear of not having enough to survive. Although many of these people were born after the Great Depression in the 1930s, their parents carried (and passed on) a "poverty consciousness" based upon their own experience and worries during their family's struggle for survival.

Emotional hoarding is not limited to possessions; the same principles of feng shui clearing apply to the "clutter" people pack into their bodies. It's no accident that overweight people suffer from the same emotional issues as other types of hoarders. There's an eating correlation to the psychological worry of not having enough. What's really interesting is that when hoarders and clutter-a-holics begin to practice good feng shui and relinquish their piles of clutter, many also begin to lose weight!

Prosperity and Abundance

A central aspect to the study of feng shui, and metaphysics in general, is the concept of continual abundance. In prosperity consciousness, as it is also called, the more you give the more you are open to receive. There is no such thing as, "I may need it someday," because as soon as you give something away, you create a space for whatever is new and needed at the moment. If you give in to the worry about never having enough, you will create a life in which you never have enough.

Instead, reframe your thinking to accept yourself where you are now in your life. You will always be prosperous because you will attract positive abundance. It's such a simple concept, yet difficult for most to master without consistent (and committed) practice. It may take several years to look at yourself, and your life, from this perspective on a regular basis!

E-WISDOM

One who knows enough is enough will always have enough.
—Lao Tsu, *Tao te Ching*

One of the basic laws of metaphysics is that what you put out to the Universe is what you will receive back. So, if you tell the Universe that you are poor and unhealthy, that is the life you will create for yourself just by your own limiting mindset. Anyone who's ever read any of Dr. Wayne Dyer's books knows that the real magic of life is in your own beliefs about what you think you can achieve. If you haven't read *You'll See It When You Believe It* (Avon Books, 1990), do yourself a favor and check it out. It will help you understand even more about the process of creating an abundant life—one that is enriched and supported by your practice of good feng shui!

Dealing with a Clutter-a-holic

The piles sit on the floor, are tucked (or stuffed) under the bed, or are balanced precariously in a corner. You want to clean it up, but there's a problem: It's not yours; it's somebody else's pile of clutter. What can you do?

Here are a few hints for dealing with a clutter-a-holic:

- Approach the person in a friendly, congenial manner and offer to help him or her put the items away. People are fiercely protective of their things, so don't just start putting things away, or (worse yet) start pitching them in the trash can. Respect your partner's or family member's need for some privacy—and ownership.
- Try to get to the root of the problem by asking some simple questions: "Does this still serve a purpose for you? Does it bring you joy or have special meaning? If so, we can find a special place for it. If not, maybe we can donate it so that someone else can use it."
- Take the lead by becoming a positive, shining example. When you clear your own clutter, you may actually inspire those around you to be tidy, too. If your kitchen table is stacked high with mail or projects, a lunch box or an extra set of keys won't be noticed. If there's nothing on it, however . . .
- Create opportunities for storage solutions by placing a "collection container" in each room. If there is a designated place for clutter collection, the clutter will become part of a more organized thought process—the first step toward elimination!

Staying positive and solution oriented will go a long way toward clearing the clutter quickly. It is important that you not interfere too much with others' purging process, especially if they seem reluctant at first. Inspire them by setting a good and lasting example of a person who is free from the binding nature of "too many things." It's just like Gandhi said: "You must be the change you want to see."

The Looks of Books Should Be Top Shelf

Ah, books! Isn't that another word for "heaven"? Whatever your weakness is—from CDs to hats, scarves, coats, or knickknacks—how do you keep them? Are they as well organized as you might like them to be, or do they seem to multiply every time you go shopping? (Tip: Organizing lots of small collectible items is a similar process for all things, whether they be CDs, accessories, or best-loved short story collections.)

More than any other item in your house besides clothes, books can mysteriously seem to propagate when you are not watching carefully. You might think that because you are surrounded by books in your home, nothing could make you happier, right? Well-organized books might.

ESSENTIALS

Provide clear passageways to the heart of each room . . . you don't want to trip your way through your house, as symbolically this will represent a struggle through life. Remember: If you're stuck, the chi will be too!

As it is, many of your books are in stacks on tables and on the floor, next to your bed and next to your favorite chair. Although you derive great comfort merely from having the books, you do not so much enjoy tripping over them or having to hunt one of them down. Nor do you enjoy buying the same book again because you can't find your copy or—worse!—you actually forgot that you already owned it! Most importantly, all that disorganization blocks chi in your space.

Bibliophiles (yes, you, too—aren't you reading a book right now?) can benefit from the philosophy of feng shui that impels them to clean up the clutter. Unlike your purging of the overflowing junk in your closets, though, you might not want to give away any of your books, even the ones that have been sitting on shelves unopened since the Carter administration. You might consider you and your books "bound for life," as it were.

You can, however, organize your books. You *can* eliminate the haphazard stacks on various surfaces and find nice new homes for your books. In short, you *can* arrange your numerous friends in various parts of your house in such a way that not only will you find them more easily, but you also may be even more compelled to read them!

Try the following suggestions for organizing your collection of books (or whatever):

- **By category, and even by bagua.** In the bedroom, one person may keep her spiritual and metaphysical books in the knowledge corner. Another may have all her love poetry and romantic fiction in her romance corner. You could keep your business management and financial advice books in your wealth corner. Texts relating to your work can be kept in your office, or books relating to your hobbies can be shelved near where you engage in those hobbies. Store cookbooks in the kitchen, contemplative books in the sunroom, and entertainment books in the den. This kind of organizing not only is easy, it could become addictive!

- **By personal connection.** You can keep the books that are most nostalgic, comforting, and interesting to you in your bedroom.

- **By alphabet.** Some people swear by this method. Individuals have been known to extend this approach to the spice bottles in their kitchens and the medicine bottles in their bathrooms. If you find this approach relaxing, by all means, knock yourself out! But if this method will only cause you stress, or, worse, lead you to delay the whole project because of the time involved, then please find another way to deal with your clutter.

- **Get rid of books that no longer serve you.** Have some good books that really helped you through a rough time in your life, but which you no longer need? Consider giving them to someone you know who might benefit from their wisdom—or sell them at an online auction or garage sale. Give old books new life!

Your collections bring you joy—for whatever reason. Remember, then, that the only way for them to serve you is by being accessible, uncluttered, and in a position to optimize their roles in your life and home.

The "Good Chi Garage Sale"

Having a garage sale is a great (and auspicious) way to begin your journey into the world of feng shui. By selling excess clutter of your own and your family's, you not only free up your living space, you also fill it with good chi and a few extra dollars.

If you decide to hold a "Good Chi Garage Sale," be sure to price everything to go. Assign rock-bottom prices so that you are sure to get rid of most of your stuff in one day. Then use the power of feng shui to position your soon-to-be-former belongings to sell, sell, sell!

Bring out the Bagua

Group like items together, and then place them on tables that are slanted a little in order to activate the flow of energy around them. We want these items to radiate their energy to bargain hunters—not get lost in a huge pile of stagnant energy that is blocked by tables crammed together!

Place your most valuable items for sale on a table in your wealth corner—right near your checkout table, in the upper left corner of the bagua, if you want. The highest-priced items should be in the wealth corner to attract their best buyers.

ESSENTIALS

Once a year, have a "feng shui clearing" garage sale. Get rid of any items you no longer use, like books, kitchen gadgets, CDs, and videos. Donate whatever doesn't sell to charity.

You will greatly increase the profitability of your Good Chi Garage Sale if you follow the bagua octagon in the placement of the goodies you're offering for sale. For instance, place old photo frames in your family corner (on the far left or east side of the bagua, beneath the wealth corner) to attract shoppers who might want these photo frames to house pictures of their loved ones. For added impact, slip in a picture of a family from a magazine.

Books, videos, and old bookshelves should be placed on a table or shelf in the knowledge corner of your "Good Chi" bagua, just below the family section. Line the middle entrance of your driveway with old office furniture, equipment, or accessories, since this is the career corner. It also has the corresponding elements of water and ancestral energy, so things that pertain to those elements can also be included in this area of the garage sale. Along with the career-oriented office stuff, you might also toss in some pool toys (or an old pool itself!), as well as that ugly old lamp that your dear departed relative left you. You've probably been keeping it out of a sense of duty—but while it may not go well with your décor, believe me when I say it will find a home somewhere else. Your benefactor would be happier if she knew her lamp was being used rather than tucked away collecting dust in your attic!

To the right of your "career" entrance is the helpful people corner of your Good Chi Garage Sale bagua. The elements that correspond to this corner are the heavens and travel, so here is where you might display old suitcases, photos, or posters of faraway places. You might also include any religious objects such as statues or icons.

E-WISDOM

Often people attempt to live their lives backwards. They try to have more things, or more money, in order to do more of what they want so that they will be happier. The way it actually works is the reverse. You must first be who you really are, then do what you need to do in order to have what you want.

—Margaret Young

The children's department of your garage sale should be located in the west corner of this bagua, just up from the helpful people corner. This is where you will offer all the toys your kids no longer play with and the clothes they no longer wear. In most garage sales, these are the items that get sold and resold the most! Since the corresponding element to this area of the bagua is metal, you can also include metal items such as bicycles, candlesticks, and kitchen gadgets.

Old wedding gifts you didn't use would be a good fit in the marriage corner. This area of the bagua is in the top right, between the children's area and the fame corner. You can also put pottery and earth-related items in this section, since the corresponding element is earth. Pictures of landscapes can be placed on the ground, leaning on the tables that hold the pottery and other earth-related items. If you are going through a divorce or just coming out of a failed relationship, this would also be a good place to get rid of old gifts and reminders!

The fame corner, which will be dead center in the south corner of your bagua, is the ideal place to sell anything that elevates the attractiveness of the individual (with the potential to bring fame and fortune). Remember those designer jeans you bought just in case you'd lose ten pounds? Hang 'em up here with an enticing price tag. How about the exercise equipment you bought from those famous thin people on TV? Dust it off and move it to this corner for your garage sale. And don't forget that the element that corresponds to fame is fire—making this an ideal corner to feature candles, mirrors, and fireplace tools.

Useful to the End

All of these tips may make you tired at the thought of having a garage sale. You might think you're going to a lot of extra trouble to attractively position stuff you are looking to dump anyway. But keep in mind that your possessions can serve you even as they depart your company. In other words, let your things bring you good fortune in the form of positive money energy while they are leaving your home to offer new life to another's home.

Accept the fact that you were not even using many of these items in the first place. Remember that the goal is to give up the things that no longer bring you happiness or represent who you are now, at this moment. Take a deep breath; then let go of this old, stagnant energy!

Of course, not everything will sell at your Good Chi Garage Sale. Whatever doesn't sell you must remain committed to clearing, so remember to put those items in a small pile and call the Goodwill truck immediately after your sale is over. There should be nothing—seriously, nothing—left once you're finished with a feng shui clearing like this one.

When cleaning your house, don't forget dirt and dust traps such as windowsills, molding, chair rails, and light fixtures. Dust and dirt hold chi down.

Other Kinds of Clutter

Okay, you've cleared the clutter in your attic, garage, and basement. The rest of your home is sparkling clean—and ready for some feng shui, right?

Not necessarily. There are other kinds of clutter besides physical clutter—and though they are not as obvious, they can create obstacles in your life nonetheless.

- **Time clutter** occurs when you fill up your schedule with too many commitments, and then have too little time left over for your family or social life. You should always leave "open" time to allow for new opportunity, learning, or growth through experiences.
- **Mind clutter** happens when you allow your brain to fill with thoughts, worries, and concerns about the future. To alleviate this kind of clutter, you should consider journaling. Writing down your thoughts is a positive, healthy way to get worries and other forms of mental clutter out of your mind and into a safe, directed place.
- **Electronic clutter** is another insidious form of clutter that can block chi. Think about it: At this moment, you probably have uncleared voice mail and e-mails, or a hard drive you haven't cleared since 1995. You should clear as much as you can in your "virtual" world on a daily basis, especially if you are using any of the items in a home office setting. You always want as much of your chi to be as open and flowing as possible.
- **Food clutter** is always worth a second look. If you are consuming more than your body needs, or keeping more food than you or your family will ever eat, you are exhibiting traits of a food hoarder. Constantly throwing away uneaten food that has spoiled is another

sign. Food and dietary feng shui is worthy of its own book, but for more on the subject, see Chapter 7, "The Well-Balanced Kitchen."

Clearing your mind—whether it's cluttered by worry, food, or overbooking—is necessary for your personal chi, and a very healthy thing to do. If journaling seems like it might take too much time, try a "Thoughts and Worries" jar with little slips of paper containing your concerns. What you're doing, of course, is giving your anxiety clutter another place to live. Another way to meditate, after you're more comfortable with the concept of purging that which doesn't serve you, is to get into a quiet space, breathe deeply, and mentally hit the "delete" key in your brain to rid yourself of negativity!

Clearing the Air

The most important thing about clearing clutter of all kinds is to recognize that it is necessary in order to wipe your energy slate clean, so to speak. You want to start rearranging your home and surroundings in the most positive, unaffected way possible—and clutter blocks any and all good energy from flowing positively through your personal environment.

One note of caution: If you're not feeling well or not in a positive mood, don't do your space clearing just yet. Wait until you feel better so that you can offer the best of your energies to the task.

Once you've eliminated the clutter dragon from your life, you are ready to remove stagnant, unhealthy chi from your surroundings. There are many ways to do this effectively.

Some people begin this process with a fresh stick of lavender incense, although many feng shui practitioners use a smudge stick to do the same thing. Choose whichever better suits your mood. Lighting the incense and holding it in your hand, walk through every room in the house to send out the negative energy and welcome the positive into your environment. You may choose to say a little invocation, or prayer, to accomplish this: "Negative energy, be on your way. Positive energy, begin flowing today." You can create one that works for you—there are no hard-and-fast rules except being mindful of the purpose of this exercise.

Begin with a clean house and body, and with clear intentions. What do you want to clear away, and what do you want to positively attract with new energy? Be clear about these things before beginning, and you'll have a better result.

QUESTIONS?

When do you do a space clearing?
Space clearing will be most effective if you do it on a regular basis, such as when each new season arrives or whenever you've made any kind of change in your life. Be sure to bless the change, your space, and all who enter it from that moment forward.

Some experts think you should only do a space clearing in complete silence, but you may prefer to use some soft background music, especially if it complements your intention. For instance, if you want more adventure in your life, why not choose a CD with Native American music? If you want more spirituality, use a new age CD that awakens your awareness. Finding music that speaks to—and encourages—your goal is a powerful experience; yours can be just as empowering. Just remember to think about your intention, about what you want to achieve. Be mindful of your choices so they serve you or your purpose.

In terms of aromas, you can use incense, or you can light scented candles and sprinkle some mineral sea salt (a universally recognized purifier, much like baking soda) in trouble areas where the chi has been blocked. Consider using a little sea salt in your attic (or your previously identified clutter trap), around the toilet (for good pipe clearing), and in the doorway, since so many energies travel to and from there. If you find yourself falling into old traps and habits, use your trouble spot checklist to determine which areas might need a little sprinkle of sea salt to clear unwanted or stale energy.

One final suggestion as you clear space in your now clutter-free domicile: Place a statue of an angel or a Buddha in the helpful people corner of each room in which you perform a space clearing ceremony. This will give you added protection—and enhance the positive chi in each room as you bless and move forward!

Before you begin to feng shui your home, always start with a space clearing. Open the windows to get the chi moving! Light a candle, diffuse pure essential oils, use a smudge stick, play music . . . these will help clear the energy in the area.

Where We Go from Here

Your clutter is gone and your clearing technique (emphasis on *your*) has given your home fresh new energy. Now, you are ready for the moment you've been waiting for—the chance to put the ancient art and practice of feng shui to work for you.

Begin by taking a good hard look into the mouth of chi in your home—the front doorway. Let's go inside now!

CHAPTER 3

Let Feng Shui Guide You

Ah, the joys of owning your own home—of having your own space in the world. Yours to cultivate; to meditate, to live and grow in. What can be more empowering than your very own corner in the "Great Bagua" of the Universe?

Go with a Purpose

Finding your dream home can be a wonderful journey in and of itself—but it can be made even more interesting by using the principles of good feng shui to find the home that can bring you the best in an abundance of health, wealth, and general prosperity. In feng shui, your dream home represents all that you can be or achieve in life. It is your humble beginning—ripe with possibility for a brighter future.

Whether you are building it from scratch or making an older home yours for the first time, it pays to plan ahead to maximize the amount of good chi you start with so that you can avoid costly remodeling projects later on down the road.

Spend a lot of time thinking about your goals and how your home can help you achieve them by creating the best launch pad into a world of fantastic new opportunities.

The future begins at your front door.

The Lay of the Land

As all great journeys begin with a single step on the path, so your feng shui journey begins with the path to your home—the land that it is built on.

Finding a decent lot can be a journey all its own, but using feng shui principles can make it easier to find your little corner of the Universe.

There are several things to consider when looking at land:

- Is the direction facing the way you would like it?
- What was on the land before it went up for sale?
- What are the neighboring spaces like?
- Does the road that leads to it wind and curve, or is it a straight path that would lead right to your front door? (Tip: The curved one is the one you want!)
- Which way will the sun come in to illuminate your home every day? Is there good exposure to sunlight?
- If there are any hills, what direction do they face?

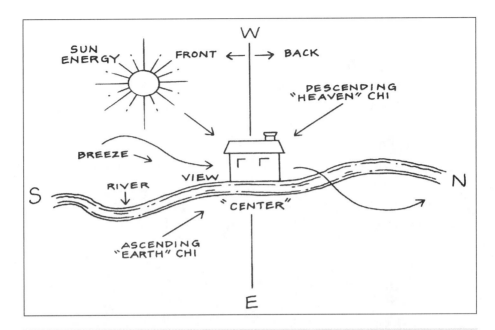

FIGURE 3-1: Yard Diagram (side elevation)
The ideal home location will maximize the flow of every kind of energy.
In this example, the house is located in the center of the property, facing
south. The hill to the north brings dragon energy down from heaven (and
guards the rear). The hill leading up to the front of the house carries chi
from the earth.

Working with a good feng shui practitioner from the start of your homebuilding project can also help you to determine the most auspicious land
to build on. If you want the best results, you should hire a practitioner
from the get-go. The practitioner should be in each and every meeting
with the architects and builders to ensure that you are doing everything
humanly possible to build a house with the best intentions!

Building the Feng Shui "Dream" Home

When you've found the land that is in perfect balance with your chi,
the next stage is to work with a builder who can help you create the feng
shui home of your dreams. But not all builders are devout feng shui

followers, so you might do well to contact the Feng Shui Institute (refer to Appendix D). Ask for a referral of a feng shui–oriented builder in your area.

After you've done that, you have lots of planning and many decisions that need to be made:

- Is the land you've chosen ideal for your dream home? Is there suitable water nearby—and are there small, rolling hills that give your property a flowing feel?
- Have you checked out the land's history to be sure it's not stigmatized (more on that later)?
- Does the actual design of the home meet with feng shui principles of flowing chi? Are the doors, windows, and hallways arranged in such a way that chi is not made to rush?

Be mindful of the energy of energy when building your new home. Too many electrical outlets encourage a steady and constant barrage of electrical current. Place as few as possible along the walls of the home—and put plastic covers over outlets that are not in use.

Have you chosen a yin-yang balance of elements in your building materials? For instance:

- Does the final design match your intentions? If you wanted a peaceful retreat of a home, has the design really reflected this need, or did it turn out to be more than you bargained for?
- Have you matched the bagua to your blueprint to be sure that there are no "missing corners" in the home?

Building the ideal feng shui home can be an exciting and often enlightening experience for you and your family—but the bottom line is that you must feel comfortable with the outcome. Just because something looks like it's right from a feng shui standpoint, it may not be comfortable for your family. Modify the design where needed and in the ways that most comfortably match your intention and lifestyle.

You already know what you really want—go for it!

Knowing When You Are Right

People just learning about feng shui often want to learn how to know whether a new home has good or bad energy—or how to know whether a specific house is the right one for them. Sometimes just saying "Trust your intuition" isn't enough for people who are struggling with their vision of the perfect home.

You need to realize that you already know what is best for you. Maybe you haven't verbalized it yet or focused on it enough to manifest it into being. But manifest you will, especially after you are really clear about everything you dream of having in your dream home.

Whoever is taking active part in your search for the dream home— and will be an active inhabitant of it—needs to first identify what is important. Create a mental "checklist" that includes everything you are looking for in your special new home. You may not be sure, at the beginning, where this dream home is located, but your realtor will help with that. All you need to have is the dream.

QUESTIONS?

Do strong fences really make good neighbors in feng shui?
They can, but you can use natural elements such as pine trees or bushes as privacy walls, too. If your neighbors send out too much negative energy, hang a small mirror at the top of your fence, positioned so their negative vibes are reflected back to them.

If there is one thing that you are especially clear about, don't sacrifice it for expedience. You may look at several houses, you may be tempted, and you may even make an offer on a home that is "almost but not quite." When your offer is not accepted, you may be sad or frustrated, but remember that it wasn't the right house for you, and the perfect one will come.

You won't necessarily know beforehand what the sign will be—you will know it when you feel it. With an awareness of feng shui to guide you, you may also recognize its use in the home for sale. Is there a wind chime in the front doorway? A Zen fountain in the living room? What about soft flute music playing when you see the house for the first time? It won't take long for you to make your decision—it will feel right.

FIGURE 3-2: Mirrors
Reflect negative energies of bad neighbors back to them by strategically placing a mirror in your yard. This can be an effective cure to ease hostilities.

You must have clarity of intention—you need to be aware of what you are looking for—before you can trust your intuition. You already know what kind of house you really want. All you have to do is visualize it and be clear (with yourself or your partner and your realtor) about what you see as the ideal home. Dreams can come true—and there are no accidents. If you practice this carefully, you will manifest the home of your dreams—and you may even wonder why you didn't start earlier.

FIGURE 3-3: Yards
If you are moving into an older home in an established neighborhood, you may have to work a little harder to soften the lines of your home or yard. Some brick walks, for example, encourage rushing chi. A path of stepping stones that curves out into the yard adds a water element. The path will slow down chi and will encourage you and your guests to take your time, too.

The Feng Shui Home Hunter

Okay, so maybe you're not interested in building the perfect feng shui house—for you, a prebuilt home will do just fine. Can you still apply feng shui to the blueprint of an already existing house to turn it into the home of your dreams?

Sure you can. When you're out house hunting, pick up a copy of each home's floor plan—and place the bagua diagram right over it. Now you're ready to assess each home's chi!

On the floor plan, when you approach the front door, is the door area open and unencumbered? If not, is it a situation you can easily remedy?

ESSENTIALS

If you have a missing area in the bagua of your home, hang a crystal or a mirror in the space that would be closest to it to symbolically enlarge the space and include the "missing" room. You can even do this in each of the rooms in your house.

Is the main staircase directly in line with the opening front door? If so, can you easily hang a crystal there to slow down rushing chi? Look at the living room. Is it large enough to accommodate a curved grouping of chairs and a small sofa to create a living room with energy and life? Are bedrooms going to be easy to arrange for you and your children or guests? Can you position each bed properly according to feng shui principles?

What about the kitchen? Is it located in a favorable location? (See Chapter 7, "The Well-Balanced Kitchen," for more details about the best layout and location for the kitchen in your new home.) Are there enough bathrooms for the whole family—and are the bathrooms located in auspicious places (such as away from the kitchen and not above the front doorway)?

If you have decided you would like to have a den or home office, is the room best suited to this endeavor large enough to accommodate your desk at an angle that keeps your back from facing any open doorways?

E-WISDOM

Meditate to connect with the "feel" of your home; then approach change in a positive yet instinctive manner. Don't get hung up on hard-and-fast "rules." The Dalai Lama said, "You must learn all of the rules in order to know which ones to break." Follow your heart, and your intuition.

Take a good look around each house you visit, and be sure to record your gut instincts or intuitive feelings as well. A house can look like it is perfect, but feel somehow inadequate for your needs. Ultimately, you know what's best for you and your family. Remember one of the golden rules of Black Hat Sect feng shui: If it feels right, it probably is. If it doesn't, it probably isn't. Follow that rule as you hunt for the perfect new home.

Don't forget to consult the professionals, either. Your realtor can be a good source of information about each home you are interested in, since it's likely he or she has already seen each property beforehand. If you can, try to work with a realtor who understands the basic concepts of good feng shui.

Use Feng Shui to Sell Your Home

Home buyers are wise to use the principles of feng shui when looking at homes, and as interest in feng shui grows, this is increasingly the case. In light of that, savvy home sellers should highlight or amplify whatever feng shui strong points their home may feature to capture the attention of these home buyers. Possible strengths of your home include the chi of the neighborhood; the direction in which your home faces; the influence of the five elements—fire, water, wood, metal, earth—on your home's location; and the power of water and its significance in relation to the property.

If your home conforms to the following principles, it allows for proper energy flow:

- The front entrance does not face the upstairs stairway.
- The front door does not have a view of the back door.
- There are no heavy beams in the rooms, especially bedrooms.
- It does not rest on a triangular plot of land.
- It is not at the end of a cul-de-sac (which traps bad energy).
- It is beside a gentle stream or it boasts a pond.
- It has an unobstructed view of the night sky.
- The site faces open space to the south.
- The front of the house is slightly lower than the back.
- There are no large trees or bushes obscuring the front door and preventing wealth from entering.

If you follow feng shui principles as much as possible within your home, in terms of furniture arrangement, clearing away clutter, using décor appropriate to the space (calm for bedrooms and bathrooms, for instance), appropriate lighting, and even pleasant aromas, it will entice both the homebuyers who are familiar with feng shui and those who are not. Simply by generating a sense of comfort and peace and projecting a warm, welcoming atmosphere within your home, you will enhance the home's appeal and value, which can only expedite the sale.

Space Clearings and House Blessings

Native Americans healed their stigmatized land by giving gifts of tobacco and corn back to the earth and performing a ceremonial dance on the land to free it from negative energy. The Chinese believe in clearing the negativity through feng shui cures such as ringing a bell or clapping hands to dissipate the negative energy (or, more typically, stagnant chi).

When you move to a new home, take a stick of lavender incense and do a house blessing to make peace with your new environment. It's a way of acknowledging the past of a place while welcoming it to its future. You should also do a space clearing every time you make a major change to the home in the form of a remodeling job or building a new addition.

Space clearing feng shui expert Denise Linn says there are actually four steps to clearing a space:

- **Preparation.** This is where you prepare yourself and the space by making both as clean as possible. It's basically starting with a clean slate.
- **Purification.** Beginning with a brief prayer to ask for guidance in your endeavor, assess the room's energy, and then use whichever space clearing tools you feel most comfortable with (bell, clapping hands, incense, or chimes).
- **Invocation.** In this step, according to Linn, you are putting power behind the purification of the space by adding a blessing. "May the

Great Creator bring peace and bestow blessings upon all who enter this space," is one example. You can use your own invocation instead, but remember to be mindful of the purpose.

- **Preservation.** Here, you are sealing in the new, good energy by creating a focal point for it such as a Zen water fountain in the corner of your living room. This fountain would be dedicated to preserving the good energy simply by your focused intention. Or, you can set up a permanent home altar to seal in new energy for the greater good.

Before you buy a home, take the time to look into its history. You can look through old tax records to find out who the previous owners were, and old newspaper indexes to discover what became of them and how well they did in the rest of their journey on this planet.

If you find a home that has any kind of stigma attached to it, it doesn't mean you can't live there or that it will be bad luck to you—all you need to do is arm yourself with the knowledge of its checkered past, light up some incense sticks (preferably lavender, which makes peace with unsettled spirits), and perform a land healing/space clearing to reclaim the space's positive attributes.

QUESTIONS?

What if the land you're interested in has a troubled past?
"Cure" the land to make it suitable for building. On land where anything tragic has occurred—and perhaps left a negative imprint—perform a land healing. Land healings should also be performed for homes built on ancient burial grounds.

Be sure to bring in as much positive energy as you can with formerly wounded homes, since they are a bit higher maintenance from a feng shui/energy standpoint. Carefully balance the yin and yang energies and the five elements; then be sure there is as much open, flowing chi as possible in and around the home to encourage the healing new energy of you and your family.

Moving Considerations

Once you've found a new place, you'll need to prepare yourself for the "big move"—and what better way than to use feng shui to help?

The first order of business is to pack up the things that you definitely want or need to take with you (as much as you can without disturbing your daily life, of course!). Then you can get a good look at what's left—and what you might want to leave behind.

Moving is the ideal time for removing clutter (refer back to Chapter 2 for tips on dealing with clutter and for organizing a Good Chi Garage Sale). This is a new chapter in your life, so it's entirely appropriate that you get rid of some old things and buy a few new items!

If you suspect that a new item has negative energy attached to it, you can do a clearing by ringing a bell near it or by encircling it with lavender incense. Say a brief prayer to release the negative energy from the item. It's a good idea to do this with antiques, too, unless they have your own ancestral energy attached.

As you get rid of old possessions, release your attachment to them by thanking them for their years of good use. Remember the Zen saying that possessions are never really yours until you can give them away—and then send them off to their greater good for another person who might need them. It may sound like a lot of ceremony over nothing, but you wouldn't believe the attachments that some folks have to stuff they no longer need—and everyone needs closure, don't you think?

One final moving tip: You can arrange your boxes according to each room—and then by bagua, if you really want to stay focused on your feng shui intentions as you move into your new home. Organizing things this way will encourage you to begin placement with intention from the start—and get you off to an auspicious beginning in your new home!

Put out the Welcome Mat

You've moved into your new home—and it's everything you dreamed it could be. You've hung the welcoming wind chime, put out the welcome mat, and sent invitations out to all your friends for your housewarming party. What could be better than a home blessed by people important to you?

One thing that could definitely make it more interesting would be to make it a "Feng Shui Housewarming Party." Why not use feng shui as a theme to get everyone thinking more mindfully about their own homes as they help you warm your new nest?

Start with a flowing fountain placed at the entrance of your home—next to a small table on which you can have laminated cards with your home's bagua on it. Starting with the entrance at the career sector of the bagua, your visitors can take a feng shui tour through your home—breaking the ice for some and giving them plenty to talk about as they investigate the meaning you've instilled in each corner.

Place everyone around the dining room table according to the bagua as well—and let each person represent an area of the bagua by telling a story about themselves relating to the sector they're sitting in. For instance, the person seated in the family/ancestors section of the table can share a family story while you are dining at the table; the person seated at the career section can talk about what she does for a living.

Be sure that you tell anyone who's set on bringing a housewarming gift to wrap it in red, since this is considered the best color for gift giving in Chinese culture. Red envelopes are most often used for gifts in China.

Don't forget that when you make new purchases and incorporate them into your home, you should do a space clearing ceremony to welcome the new addition!

To further enhance the feng shui mood, you might serve Chinese food and include some chrysanthemum tea. Create yin-yang trivets from cork and craft paint for added effect.

Show a movie about Chinese culture that features some of the principles of feng shui, too. If you need a suggestion, try Ang Lee's *Eat Drink Man Woman,* a wonderful tale about a father who still cooks Sunday meals for his daughters despite the chaos in their lives. It offers a terrific glimpse into modern Chinese culture and philosophy.

For those who like to play games at housewarming parties, you could hold a "Count the Cures" contest, with the person who can name the most cures in your home winning a prize (in a red envelope, of course!).

QUESTIONS?

What is a cure?
Remedies or enhancements will "cure" an area where the chi is blocked. The eight basic cures are light, sound, color, life, movement, stillness, mechanics, and straight lines (see Chapter 1).

Another fun (and important) activity would be for your house-warming guests to take part in your space clearing ceremony. Give each of your guests a small stick of incense, and ask them all to write a brief blessing for what they hope you will accomplish in your new home. As you go from room to room with the lighted incense, ask guests one by one to read their blessing. Although your guests may be shy, the sharing of wishes can be a wonderful way of bringing in positive new energy—bestowing you with the blessings and good wishes of all your dear friends.

You don't *need* to do all of these things to have a fun and intellectually stimulating housewarming party. The important thing is to have fun and enjoy the fact that you've worked hard to make your new home as well balanced as possible. Who knows—maybe you've inspired your friends to do the same in the process!

Feng Shui 911: Call in a Pro

You can learn and apply many principles of feng shui on your own. Its personal and individual nature makes incorporating it into your life a do-it-yourself transition. However, there are many situations that call for a feng shui expert, some of which are noted in these pages. If such an instance arises, you need to know what to look for when hiring a professional.

As with other kinds of professions, credentials are very important, and so is the rapport you have with the expert you select. To determine whether your specialist is right for you and will meet your needs, determine the following:

- How long has the consultant been practicing feng shui?
- Does he or she have a feng shui degree or other relevant certification?
- What individual, school, or program taught the consultant, and how many years did the consultant study?
- Does the consultant continue to take classes or pursue other kinds of continuing education in feng shui?
- What general philosophy and school of feng shui does the consultant lean toward—Form, Compass, or Black Hat Sect (Buddhist)?

The differences between one consultant and another emerge in approach. A consultant may use a compass and be highly scientific and methodical, or the individual may rely primarily on his or her own intuition, spirituality, and creativity. It is best to choose someone whose approach most closely matches your own attitudes and preferences. You will be living with the effects of decisions the consultant makes and the advice he or she offers, so it's important to be highly compatible in your outlooks.

Not only will you need to ask questions of the consultant, but the practitioner may also have some for you. These include:

- What do you intend to do with the space in question?
- What is your history in relation to the home or particular part of the home with which you are seeking assistance? (This probably will include information on where you were before you moved into your current home and how your current home compares with the former.)
- What do you know about the history of your home, its previous occupants, and why they no longer live there?

- What was your reaction on seeing your home for the first time?
- What was your original vision for your home or the particular room in question?
- Did you attempt to realize this vision, and, if so, how? What were the results?
- How have your life and the lives of your family members been affected by living there? Good experiences? Bad experiences? What were they?
- What have you enjoyed about living in your home, and what, if anything, disturbs you about it?
- What, specifically, do you desire from your home or in your life while living in your home? Any major life goals or dreams that you would like to realize that might be influenced by where you live?

The more you know about yourself, your home, and the feng shui consultant you select, the more effective the outcome will be!

ESSENTIALS

A feng shui consultant should help you create an environment that fosters balance inside and out. Use your power of choice: Screen consultants to ensure mutual understanding and compatibility before you sign a contract or make any final decisions.

Smaller Spaces

What if your little corner of the Universe is just a small rented space that you have chosen to live in temporarily? Is feng shui still important when you're only going to be there for a little while? It definitely is. In feng shui, there is no such thing as "for a little while"—every space, no matter how small or large, can benefit from the principles of this ancient wisdom.

In apartments, you will need to use many of the cures discussed throughout this book in order to remedy tight corners and keep the chi flowing, but you should be able to apply the bagua as you would in any other space.

In apartments, other residents tend to come and go frequently, changing the energy often. Because you share this space, you may benefit from a regular, monthly space clearing.

Vacation properties might benefit from having more emphasis on the yin side of décor—in other words, you might use more of the softer colors and fabrics to decorate your vacation space in order to derive the best rest and relaxation you have come to the space for in the first place.

QUESTIONS?

Is it possible to apply elements of feng shui to an automobile?
If you spend a lot of time in your car, incorporate some basics: Clear clutter regularly; cut your driving anxiety by playing soft, stress-free music; and hang a crystal from the mirror to move energy around your vehicle.

Remember that feng shui is applied through approach and intent, so it doesn't matter whether you own your space or simply make it your own. With feng shui, good chi can come in small packages—and that definitely applies to apartments, condos, and vacation homes!

CHAPTER 4
Dramatic Entrances

I n feng shui, your front door is many important things: It is the mouth of chi and the gateway of energy as it enters your home, but it is also the window to your world, the passage through which all others see you.

All Paths Lead to Your Door

Making a good first impression is important in feng shui—but in feng shui, it's not about impressing others as much as it is about mindfully projecting the picture of yourself that you want the world to see. You control how others perceive you—and if your front door is a mess of overgrown shrubbery, piles of junk, and a rusty old mailbox, others will perceive you as an unhappy, overwhelmed person whose decision-making skills are not the best.

SSENTIALS

Make sure that all the elements of your entrance are represented by shape, color, or actual element. Ensure that the shrubs are cut back, leaving a clear walkway. You want a meandering path leading to your front door; this avoids what we call "rushing chi."

When you mindfully project a positive image of yourself to the world around you, your front door radiates warmth, abundance, peace, and togetherness. It exudes a feeling of welcome energy while it attracts new possibilities, since it also represents new opportunities to attract abundance and prosperity to yourself and your family. It is the conduit through which chi can enter and spread its healthy qualities throughout your home and its immediate surroundings.

But before anyone—including opportunity—can get to your door, they must walk the path that leads to it.

The Long and Winding Road

The path to your front door can be made of many materials, including wood, stone, or brick. The important consideration in feng shui, however, is the configuration. Your walk should be designed for its representation of "meandering stream." In other words, rather than having a path in a straight line that "beats a path" to your front door, you'll ideally want a path that slows down rushing chi and allows visitors to stop and smell the roses a bit.

You could have small bushes, shrubbery, pachysandra, or even delicate flowers such as geraniums or violets welcoming visitors to your home. Just be sure to keep the flora healthy and well tended.

Whatever plant you choose to adorn your walkway, know that, aside from pure aesthetics and beauty, it will serve the purpose of slowing down the chi even more along the winding path. It will also represent your intentions, just as the seeds of your thought do. Whether you are planting red California poppies for fame and recognition or marigolds for better health, planting specific flora can help you stay focused on your life's goals—and can help you to literally grow your intentions from seed to reality.

Some feng shui practitioners warn against roses due to their thorny nature, although you may think of them as good yin-yang because of their soft petals and prickly thorns.

Consider the house that has the inauspicious configuration of the straight-line path leading to its front door, further complicated by the fact that a busy street dead-ends right at the beginning of it! If you happen to have a straight path leading to your door, rather than tear it out and replace it with a winding one, you could simply plant more bushes or shrubs—and position them in a meandering, flowing path around the straight line of the actual walkway. It's a simple way to enhance the feeling of the meditative, meandering path to your door. You could also plant a tree or, better yet, a line of pine trees as a natural barrier in the front yard to block some of the energy from rushing to your door.

In feng shui, no particular positioning is inherently bad—just challenging. You might have a very short front walk but a long driveway, and that's all right because you can connect the two by positioning rocks in a "faux path" that connects and makes for a much longer and auspiciously winding path to the front door. Challenging doesn't mean impossible!

What if you live in an older neighborhood that features very well-planned, straight paths to your door? Is this rushing chi? Certainly it is, but it can be slowed by planting some bushes in a curved pattern along the path and by hanging a wind chime at your front door. How about placing two potted plants on either side of your front door as well? Good idea. Be creative, but always be mindful of how the path feels. If it feels like the energy is rushing to your door, it probably is and should be addressed.

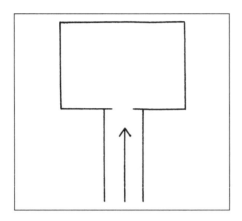
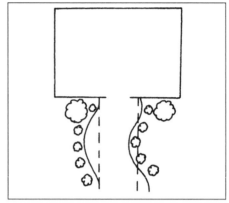

FIGURE 4-1: The Challenge
This walkway is challenging because its straight, direct path creates an arrow that "attacks" the house with rushing chi.

FIGURE 4-2: The Cure
Correct the fundamental flaw by positioning a path of rocks in a curved, waterlike pattern along the sides of the walkway, and by anchoring the door with a pair of potted plants.

If you use a side entrance to the house rather than the front door, you can treat it as your main entrance, especially when placing the bagua there as a starting point in feng shui. If you live in an apartment with a nonprivate entrance, you can still create a personalized pathway to your door by placing a small wind chime in front of your door or by placing a small potted plant just outside of it.

Accentuate the Positive

If you want to show the world that you are ready to receive any prosperity the Universe might want to send your way, you can show it symbolically by adding the water element to your front yard. You could have a nice, big water fountain in the middle of a pond—or you could stay on the simple side and have a small birdbath. Whatever you decide to use as your water element, be sure the water is directed toward your house rather than away from it, since water in feng shui equals wealth, and you don't want your wealth to be draining away from your house. You want to attract more wealth, of course!

ESSENTIALS

A free-flowing path to your front door is good, positive use of chi. If your path isn't a winding one, consider arranging rocks around it in a more winding pattern to slow down the chi; a straight path speeds the flow of energy (chi) right to your front door in an unhealthy manner.

There are a few other feng shui considerations in the front yard to be mindful of as you create a meaningful first impression to the world. For instance, a wind chime next to the front door is considered to be very auspicious because it serves three purposes: first, it lets people know where you are; second, it protects you by detecting when others are near; and third, it spreads good chi to all who come to your door.

As a final touch, consider placing a few potted yellow or red plants on either side of the front door, since that will extend the chi sideways a bit and spread it around your entire front door area.

The Key to Your Front Door

The quality of chi in a house is directly related to its ability to flow in freely through your front door. This is why your door's "feng shui" name is "the mouth of chi," because it feeds chi throughout your home. Simply put, it's the only way for the good chi and all its wonderful energy to enter your home and enrich your life.

Metaphysically speaking, your door is a major center of attraction in your home. It's symbolic of all that you wish to attract or let into your life simply by opening the door. As you look at your front door right now, what are your intentions—and does your door really let opportunity walk in?

Place a wreath with a red ribbon on your front door, to show that you're open to new opportunities. Place yellow and red flowers along the path that leads to the front doorway. These things will give life to this very important space we call the mouth of chi.

Give lots of thought to how you treat opportunity if and when it does come knocking at your door. Create an inviting doorway that attracts what you most want by sending out the appropriate message to the Universe. If you want a new love relationship, place a wreath with a pink ribbon on it on your front door, and be sure to plant shrubs or trees in pairs by your doorstep. If you want wealth to start pouring in, put a penny under your welcome mat to send out the message that money is welcome here.

Setting the Stage

Make sure your doorway is open and clutter-free. You don't want opportunity to trip and fall over your stuff—that would be bad feng shui, of course. Keep it freshly painted, clean, and free of debris, and you'll open the path for greater things in your life. If the front door is anything less than clear and clean, you'll always feel like opportunity is passing you by.

Keeping your doorway clear serves another good purpose aimed at helping you reach your goals: It allows people and new opportunities to find you in the easiest, clearest way possible.

If you don't often use the front door of your home, make it crystal clear which door you intend for others to use. However, if you want new opportunities to come to you, it is strongly advised in feng shui practice for you to go in and out of your front door every once in a while to strengthen your intention.

Be sure that all mechanical items near your front door is in working order. Lights should be working, hinges should not squeak, and the doorbell should ring in a way that pleases you and your visitors. If you don't have a doorbell, you can improvise by hanging a small bell on the doorknob or a wind chime near the front door. The important thing is to have a pleasant way of being notified when opportunity presents itself.

FIGURE 4-3: Better Than Bells
Wind chimes are easy feng shui cures, and they serve the dual purpose of letting people know where you are located!

What color should your front door be if it's how you project your image to the world? Red front doors work best; the Chinese believe that red holds the most power and energy, making it most auspicious for a door that projects power and authority. Show your strength!

But what if red just isn't your favorite color for a front door? You can use variations of the color—anything from burgundy to purple or even a lovely shade of mauve. You may lean toward a deep, mauve-ish purple for your front door if red just seems a bit too forward for your personality. Purple is still a color of power, and it has greater significance when it comes to wealth—maybe that's the color for you!

The color of your door should stand out from the other colors of your home's exterior. This draws even more energy to your front door, since it can then become the focus of your entire entranceway.

Making an Entrance

Once you open the door, note whether it opens nice and wide. You'll want it to so your opportunities have the most room to enter your home. If your door is too tight or is blocked by inside, you might discover that your opportunities are also limited. Keep your door wide open during the day so the maximum amount of light can come in, and also to signify to the world that you're ready for new and wonderful things to happen!

E-WISDOM

In many ways, your doorway is the window into your soul. If passersby see clutter around your doorway, or a view obscured by large trees or fences, what is the message to them? A clear, inviting doorway means a happy, cheerful, and open spirit dwells within.

If your door opens to a straight path leading back out of the house via a back door, you have the feng shui challenge of rushing chi to contend with, so create a few boundaries along that path to slow down the energy and allow your opportunities to linger a spell. You can place a small water fountain near the front door, or perhaps a pillar with a plant on it in the hallway. If it is big enough to divert your eye's attention, it's big enough to slow down the chi. You can also use a screen or a wind chime to slow down the energy.

Another common problem with respect to the front door is the issue of a bathroom on the second floor directly above the front door. Although this is not favorable because it puts you in the position of "flushing" opportunities back out the front door, it can be corrected by hanging a mirror on the ceiling of the entranceway below. This symbolically pushes the energy that comes in through the front door back down into the room—and keeps the flushing of the upstairs toilet from interfering with the good chi below!

If the front door creates issues with clutter for you due to daily "disturbances" such as mail, boots, coats, and the like, you can keep a good handle on the clutter by creating a designated space for such items. Ideally, you'll have a closet nearby for the clothing-related items; then all you need is a small desk or wall basket for your incoming mail. But you can keep it there only until you sort it accordingly—no month-old bills allowed, because these represent unmade decisions, which is stagnant chi.

SSENTIALS Want to welcome more friends to your door? Hang a wind chime outside, next to your front door. Wind chimes move freely through the air—positively affecting and circulating good energy.

The Bagua at Your Doorstep

At first glance, the bagua may seem to be only a plan—it gives you direction for placing tangible items. Beyond that, however, it has deeper meanings. Remember that everything with the bagua begins at your front doorstep.

Kris Halter, feng shui consultant, said, "When you align yourself to the natural energies in the universe, you feel a sense of balance and harmony. When you don't, the opposite happens—and you're working against the natural way of things. This is ancient Chinese wisdom."

Halter explained that for thousands of years, the Chinese have examined the way energy flows through a space. What they discovered was a predictable pattern between different physical locations in your home and different aspects of your life. A certain area of your home relates directly to your love relationships, and others to your health, career, family, abundance, and children. If an area is missing, no energy flows to that aspect and will require a cure. On the other hand, the parts of the home that receive a lot of attention have a direct correlation with prosperity in that aspect (where attention goes, energy flows)!

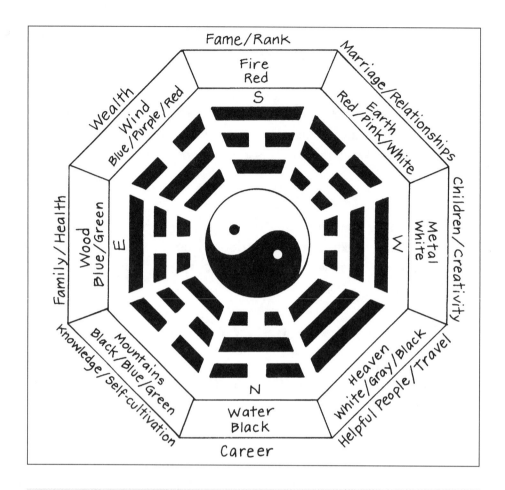

FIGURE 4-4: The Bagua
To use the bagua, place the career side along the entrance side of your space (which can be as general as your yard or as focused as your desk). That is your starting point.

The Map

The bagua's energy map shows how energy flows through our physical world. To bring harmony and balance into your life, use this map to match the energy in your home to the different energetic patterns represented by the different sectors of the bagua. To do this, you'll first need to map the bagua onto your home, starting with your front doorway, so you know which areas of your home relate to which sectors.

The use of the bagua for your home, or even for each room, is something that is often misunderstood in feng shui. But in Black Hat Sect feng shui, the front door is *always* the mouth of chi (where the energy enters the home). Looking back at the bagua, you'll notice that in this school of feng shui you will always enter the home in one of three different sectors. Standing outside looking toward the door, it will be in either knowledge/spirituality to the left, career/life path in the center, or helpful people/travel to the right.

Picture your home as a big square or rectangle or even a tic-tac-toe board that divides your home into nine equal sections. Now align the bagua with your front door. If your front door is in the center of your home (like many center-hall colonials) then you'd be entering in the career sector of your home and the other sectors would follow suit accordingly. It's really this simple!

Reading the Map

Now that you understand how to position the bagua, think about the deeper energies of each sector. Chapter 1 only touched on these things, so here is a closer look at each area and how you can take it from your front door through your life.

Career

The career corner can represent your career/job, but also your life path or your soul's purpose. Career can be represented by the water element, a meandering shape, or the color black.

QUESTIONS?

What are some "career" questions?
Are you passionate about what you do for a living? Do you feel your work is balanced with other areas of your life? Do you feel a connection to your soul's purpose?

If this area is lacking in your home's bagua, enhancements or cures to this sector would be anything relating to water, such as a fountain, aquarium, picture of water, or the color black. It doesn't need to be a lot—just remember it is your intention as you place the object that gets that energy moving for you.

Knowledge

Wisdom and spirituality are the fundamental keys to knowledge. The image of the mountain and the colors of blue, green, or black are representative of the knowledge corner.

QUESTIONS?

What are some "knowledge" questions?
How much time do you spend alone? Do you welcome it? Do you meditate? Is your spirituality an important part of your life? Do you want it to be?

Enhancements and cures begin with asking yourself what spirituality means to you, then adding that element to this sector. If you want to learn how to meditate, your knowledge center would be a wonderful area of your home or room to use. Surround yourself with things that help you to relax. Consider using a beautiful aromatherapy candle in the color blue (the most auspicious color for this sector), incense for your rosary, Buddha, or any other object that represents spirituality/self-knowledge to you. Creating this "sacred space" will be very helpful in tuning out the world and tuning in to your higher self.

Ancestors or Family Heritage

Your ancestry, or family heritage, is represented by the wood element, the colors green and blue, the image of thunder and a vertical rectangle shape (like a column or tree trunk).

Enhancements or cures to use in the family sector include family photos, the element of wood, the color green (most auspicious), plants, trees, and heirlooms. Based upon your intention, you can use anything else that reminds you of your family in a positive way—even if it's to gently remind you to let go of the past.

QUESTIONS?

What role does "heritage" play in your life?
How are your relationships with your family? Are you holding on to things from the past that could keep you from moving forward? Are you holding on to family heirlooms because they bring you joy or out of a sense of guilt?

Wealth

Cold, hard cash is nice, but wealth equals abundance in all things. In the bagua of your home, it's represented by the image of wind and the colors purple, red, green, and blue. Purple is the most auspicious color.

QUESTIONS?

How do you measure "wealth"?
With respect to this area of the bagua, ask yourself: In which areas of your life do you feel abundant? Do you have control of your money or does it control you?

To enhance or cure any missing piece of this sector in your wealth corner, use anything that represents wealth to you. Think about what abundance really means to you and what form of it is lacking in your life. Many people associate wealth with having a lot of money, but true abundance takes many forms—and it's amazing how right when we begin to realize this, the green stuff begins to start flowing back into our lives.

Fame

Fame, here, is not notoriety, but rather visibility or noteworthy presence. This recognition is represented by the element of fire, the shape of a triangle or pyramid, and the color red.

If your answers are negative in any way, you can enhance or cure the corresponding area by adding anything that represents fire and the color red. Simple items include red candles, pyramid-shaped objects, or representations of the sun. You can also incorporate awards or recognitions you have received for a job well done, or things that are self-esteem builders—perhaps something you've made that was a real challenge or accomplishment for you. Get the idea?

QUESTIONS?

Are you "famous"?
To determine your own fame, ask yourself: Do you feel you have something valuable to share with the world? How would others describe you? Do you feel visible?

Relationship

The relationship corner represents love and commitment. Relationships, or their place in your life, are demonstrated by the image of earth and the colors pink, white, and red, with pink being the most auspicious.

QUESTIONS?

How do you feel about your "relationships"?
Meditative questions to ask yourself about relationships include: Are you in an intimate relationship? If so, do you feel fulfilled? Is there romance in your life—and is the spark still there or do you need to ignite one? Are you having trouble finding your life partner?

If you are not experiencing perfect love, you can enhance or cure this corner by adding anything that reminds you of the love that does exist in your relationship, or is representative of the love you are trying to create. Display a picture of you and your partner depicting happy times, or if you haven't found your partner, find a picture of a loving couple symbolizing what you want in your life. If you are using objects, don't forget to pair items together—use two pink candles or two pink rose quartz stones, two lovebirds or pictures of two people together. All are terrific items to use in your relationship corner as a means of attracting what you want.

Children or Creativity

This corner is represented by the metal element, or round or white items. Don't be too literal! The children or creativity sector can represent either children in your life or your inner child.

QUESTIONS?

How will you know your feelings about "children" or "creativity"? Do you take yourself too seriously? Do you make time to play and relax? How do you express your creativity? Are you having trouble getting pregnant? What are your relationships with children like?

If there are issues or obstacles in the way, you can enhance or cure the area by thinking about what you rally want to create. Maybe it's a new life, or a baby. Are you clear about your intentions, and have you given up any fears that may be holding you back? Sometimes clearing out a space for a new arrival can shift that energy. Or maybe you need something to remind you to relax—in which case, you might want to add a whimsical piece of art or a picture of yourself when you were a child having fun and being silly! Of course, you can also add anything in the metal element (maybe the picture frame), the color white, or something in a round shape.

Helpful People

The helpful people corner is also related to travel and is represented by the image of heaven and the colors gray, white, and black (with gray being the most auspicious). The sector is representative of friends, mentors, angels—basically anyone who has helped propel you on your life course.

QUESTIONS?

How important are "helpful people" to you? Do you have a support group around you? How often do you extend yourself beyond your family? Are the friends in your life nurturing your soul? Do you want to travel more?

To enhance or cure this corner, use pictures of friends, mentors, or teachers, or use things related to travel, such as art you've bought on a trip. Putting these kinds of items in this sector can help reflect more of that energy into this space. Heavenly objects work well here, so get out those angels and celestial symbols!

Health

Health is at the center of the home's bagua—and it's where all the energies of the other sectors combine and balance. Represented by the earth element, the health sector symbolizes your ability to nurture and support yourself. The shape is square, and the color associated with health is yellow.

QUESTIONS?

Do you need to address the importance of your own "health"? Do you get sick often or take longer than most to heal? Are you supporting your physical body with the proper nutrition and exercise? How do you *really* feel?

If all is not really well and whole, you can enhance or cure this area of your bagua by keeping this space as clear as possible. This is important, since it's a reflection of the state of your health. If you've been sick lately, you may want to place a picture of yourself in this area of when you were feeling vibrant and alive to remind your body, mind, and soul to try and return to that healthy state. Earthenware objects and the color yellow can also be used as good, healthy symbols in this sector.

Step Inside This House

Much like the front door projects an image of you to the rest of the world, your entrance (foyer for some, lobby for those of you blessed with a larger entranceway) reflects the image of who you are *into* your house. It picks up on the energy of the front door and brings that image right on inside.

The entrance is still part of the mouth of chi, so it's important to keep the airways open in the entranceway so that good chi can "breathe" throughout your home. If you have a large entrance to your home, you won't have to do much to enhance this area from a feng shui standpoint. But if your entrance is narrow, you would greatly benefit from a metal wind chime hung from the ceiling. The door, when opened, will immediately start circulating the chi, sending it out from your entrance to all areas of your home. If there's a window near your entrance, make sure you slow down the chi with some billowy curtains, mini-blinds, or a plant in front of the window, especially if you've got a wind chime helping to spread good chi. You don't want it to go running out the window, right?

For hallways, the most common problem is that they are too narrow, which can be translated in feng shui to symbolize a narrow mind. Open up the space with hall mirrors and a round crystal to reflect light and double the space. The crystal will also help get the chi flowing in many directions.

Staircases are very important in feng shui because they represent the "arteries" that carry energy throughout your home. If your door opens to a staircase that leads down a level, your positive chi will run down the steps; if it opens right to a staircase (as is often the case in apartments), you'll get too much negative chi at once. Place a small mirror on the outside of your front door to shield yourself from the rush of negative chi.

ALERT

Many feng shui practitioners agree that a good ratio for windows to doors is three to one. Too many windows can cause disruption and argument in a home, and too few can be stifling. Skylights count as windows.

If you have a staircase that appears challenging in any way, you can lessen the challenge by adding some visual elements like family pictures, décor with a particular theme, or something that shows movement and progression. Using accents will provide the mental message of "you can do it!" to anyone who feels up to the challenge of climbing your stairs.

You have a duty to create a pleasant journey for anyone brave enough to ascend!

SSENTIALS

In terms of staircases and their design, feng shui practitioners generally hate spiral staircases because they look so much like corkscrews. If you have one of these, place a small potted plant on one of the levels to slow down the chi a bit.

Closing the Door on This Chapter

Your front door, entrance, and stairs attract and lead opportunity throughout your home and into your life in the forms of new people and ideas. Creating a comfortable, easy-to-navigate path to your soul will bring new opportunities to you effortlessly, as if they were delivered to you via a package delivery service ringing the doorbell of your life.

Answer the door—let good chi enter your home and spread its happy vibes everywhere it may travel. Be mindful of all you have created, and thankful for the beauty that is waiting for you each time you open up to the world.

CHAPTER 5

Adding Life to Your Living Room

The living room is a place where memories are made, but it's also where good memories are preserved. Call it "the museum of you." From family pictures on the mantel to that fabulous ottoman you reupholstered yourself, your living room symbolizes the harmony you have in every relationship in your life, from family to community.

First Impressions

In many homes, the living room is the first room everyone sees upon entering through the front door. Ideally, it is visible from many areas of your home, as is it considered the "hub" of energy in feng shui. The "heart" of your home—a place that holds your memories and spreads joy into the rest of your living space throughout the house—the living room should be clearly visible or easily accessible from other rooms. The same can be true of your den, family room, or great room, especially if your home's layout doesn't feature a "formal" living room. Keep in mind that wherever these rooms are located in your home's blueprint, they have an inherent family energy and should be decorated or enhanced accordingly.

Surprisingly, the formal living room, in all its splendor, is often the one room in the home reserved for special occasions and visits from friends, family, and "company." Don't be one of those people like your Aunt Ida, who enshrines her living room furniture in sheets of protective plastic and constantly reminds you not to touch the "good" furniture. Good feng shui also means living life in flow with the Universe, and life is way too short to spend hundreds of dollars decorating a living room that can't be lived in!

Room for Living

Your "room for living" should reflect who you are, and who you would like to see yourself become. It's a place for dreaming and introspection and connection with the self as much as it is for connection with others.

If you have lots of hard corners in your living room, try adding triangular-shaped shelves in the corners; then add decorative items in various shapes and textures. This will soften the edges of the room, lessening the effects of harshly converging chi.

Incorporate your family traditions into your living room, too—even if it means you watch football every Sunday in your living room or have a Friday-night movie "date" with your significant other. The important thing is to create a warm, welcoming, and "safe" place for you and other members of your family to come together to share your hopes, dreams, and ideas in a receptive, caring environment. That's what your living room is really all about.

Bring in Healthy Chi

Use wisdom and power to enhance this meaningful room. First, you need to look at the direction the room is in. The best energies for a living room in feng shui come from the south, southeast, or southwest. These directions inspire creativity, lively conversation, and the positive exchange of ideas. West is also a good location for entertaining, so focus on that area of the room when having a party or get-together in your living room.

FIGURE 5-1: Cozy Conversation
A sectional couch draws guests together for pleasant conversation in the living room. Note the geometric shapes of the lamp and candle accent pieces. In the far right, a water fountain greets guests at the door.

Position furniture so that it supports the main purpose of the room, which is to build a strong sense of family cohesiveness and community. That means you should have your sofa and chairs positioned so that they face the center of the room. Allow family and guests to choose their own best direction to sit, but be sure that no one is placed with their back to an entrance or window; angle the piece so that your guest's back is protected by a corner or wall. You don't want your guests to feel open and vulnerable. Remember that your guests all need to be able to see an entrance to the room from where they are sitting, and you will be fine.

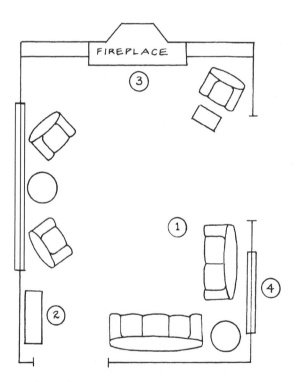

FIGURE 5-2: Living Chi
Chi needs to move freely through the living room, but you also want to maintain some intimacy. 1. Position the furniture so that the pieces face each other to facilitate conversation. 2. A small desk or bookshelf will compliment your knowledge corner. 3. Note that the furniture should not directly face, or confront, your fireplace. 4. A large mirror over the loveseat eliminates your guests' vulnerability from having their backs to open spaces.

With end tables, coffee tables, and the like, be sure to soften sharp angles or "poison arrows" by angling the softer pieces of furniture in a way that cushions or supports the sharper energy coming from such arrows. Watch for incomplete shapes in the form of furniture that is not well balanced. Use smaller pieces to complete square or rectangular shapes not accomplished by larger pieces grouped together.

Decorative Elements

The décor of the room should be warm colors, soft fabrics (such as velvet), and comfort-producing accessories such as plenty of soft pillows, blankets, or throws. Add an animal element such as a faux fur rug to add interest—or, better yet, let the real pets roam your living room so the chi is really moving throughout the house as animals move from one room to another!

FIGURE 5-3: Fame and Fire
The desk here is located between the wealth and fame corners. The small lamp represents fire, as do the red panes in the stained glass window. Fire and the color red serve a dual purpose here, representing fame as well as encouraging a little extra wealth!

FIGURE 5-4: Balancing Art
The mixture of circles (the round clock, mirror, and vase) and lines (the art deco and bamboo frames), as well as the mixture of metal, wood, and fire elements, brings a yin-yang balance to this mantel.

Fireplaces add the fire element to the living room nicely, but keep in mind that the furniture should not face the fireplace if you want to promote harmonious relationships. Facing the fire can bring problems in the form of fiery confrontation.

Speaking of fire elements, make sure there is enough light in the hallways leading to your living room. Doing so is much like making sure the arteries to your heart are clear and open: It will help direct the healthy chi to the heart of your home.

Accent with colorful art work to boost chi in the room, or you can use pastels to soften the room even more. The more colorful accent pieces work great for lively parties and entertaining, while soft pastels enhance the room's more peaceful meditative qualities. Choose whichever best suits your needs—the main idea is to have art and accessories that are pleasing for you and your guests to look at while you are engaged in meaningful conversation.

FIGURE 5-5: A Touch of Velvet
Strong wood cabinets can anchor a corner and make the area a position of strength in a room. An antique velvet chair with a handcrafted pillow accents this corner and gives the hard wood a soft balance.

Ideally, the well-balanced living room will contain an invigorating mix of colors, shapes, and textures—a healthy dose of yin and yang opposites. The room should be connected to all other rooms in your home, since it is considered the hub of activity in the house. It's the room everyone congregates in before and after meals in the kitchen or dining room, and therefore deserves all the balance and attention you can muster in order to serve up the best in creature comforts to your family and your guests.

Engage people's interest by appealing to their senses as well. Add smell-enhancing aromatherapy items such as scented candles, oils, or potpourri; soft music or a water fountain to appeal to the sense of sound; and lighting in a variety of types to appeal to the sense of sight. Touch is covered by the soft fabrics in the room, and taste is represented by any food or beverage you choose to serve.

Bringing the Bagua Alive

Imagine the sheer joy of waking up on a weekend with nothing to do except plop onto your sofa, kick up your feet, and read a good book, all the while sipping coffee, tea, or hot chocolate.

That's the feeling you want to experience in your living room day after day. You can start by keeping a journal of all the things you really like to do in your living room. That will tell you most clearly what kind of space you need to create in your "room for living."

Do you like to relax and read most of all? If so, you'll need to create a small library of good books in your living room, and place a soft, comfortable chair in the knowledge corner to increase the positive learning effects of your reading.

SSENTIALS

If you are uncertain about which changes to make, contact a qualified feng shui consultant. A great consultant can really get the chi moving—and can inspire your own creativity tenfold!

Maybe your living room is a place for rejuvenation of your health and spirit, in which case you might want to focus more on the health area or center of your living room. Here, you can place a small fountain and arrange your furniture in an octagonal shape to draw in all kinds of healthy, positive chi.

Think about what you are doing in your living room and why. Remember that good feng shui dictates that you practice mindfulness in every room of your house. Your living room, like any other room in your living space, needs to support your life goals while maintaining its own purpose, which is to create a strong sense of community. Working with this energy in mind, you can create a living room that both strengthens your personality and makes visitors feel as though they are welcome guests in your world.

The "No-Work Zone"

Above all else, be especially mindful of inadvertently mixing business with relaxation by letting your work find its way into your living room. It's amazing how quickly books, files, and even computers can grow legs and creep into your living room, disturbing the peace and disrupting your family life by adding an aura of chaos and mixed boundaries.

Like clutter, work can pile up quickly in your living room, so be sure to declare it off-limits in this important room for family gathering.

If you have been feeling a distance between yourself and your family members, work could be the culprit—check around the total living room area to be sure that there are no stray work papers, cell phones, or sticky notes to get between you and some quality family time.

Create Intentional Boundaries

How do you really accomplish a "no-work zone" in your living room? By arranging your furniture in such a way that it promotes peace, harmony, relaxation, and communion with those closest to you.

Move the sofa and guest chairs in more of a square or octagonal position to create a strong sense of community and sharing—and to keep outside influences from entering that sacred space. It's much harder to bring your work into the living room when the furniture is arranged in this manner, and, from a feng shui standpoint, this is the position that solidifies healthy communication between family members. With solid communication in the family, there will be less of a need to sneak work into this space, and more of a need to stay balanced in your personal and professional lives.

Break It Down

In the living room, the bagua can be as alive as it would be in any other room or area of your home. Place the bagua at the main entrance to your living room with the career side aligned with the entrance wall. In which section of the bagua does the doorway fall? More than likely, it will be in the following areas of the bagua: children, family, or knowledge. In any of these three areas, you'll want to include items that celebrate or relate to each of these main "bagua entrances."

E-WISDOM

Place pictures of your family in one special area of your family room—perhaps on a mantel above your fireplace or, better yet, on top of a piano or table by a window. Group the photos together for family cohesiveness.

You can also incorporate items that correspond to each area of the bagua in its specific corner or area of the room—this will strengthen or emphasize each, depending on your intention. If you want a stronger, more cohesive family life, you can focus more intently on the family corner of the bagua in your living room, giving more attention to groupings of family photos on your mantel (especially if it's in the family section of the bagua). If your mantel is not located in the family area, you can create a small space for a group of family photos on a table or shelf in that corner.

If you've had difficulties with a specific member of your family but want to make things better, try hanging a small crystal from the photo of that person, or burn a small stick of peace-making lavender incense near that person's photo. Intentions are powerful, so expect things to happen just by focusing your attention in that direction!

In the bagua as it relates to your living room, you'll also want to pay particular attention to your wealth corner. Your living room is the life-giving heart of your home, so if you're concerned about the wealth of your family, this is a good room in which to activate some positive chi with respect to finances and abundance in general. To do this, hang a crystal or place a Zen fountain in the wealth corner of the living room.

If you don't have space for a fountain, or if it's not appealing to you to have such a water element in the living room, you can also hang a lucky bamboo flute, since wealth in feng shui is also symbolized by wind, and the flute is a wind instrument. A flute created in bamboo is doubly lucky, as the Chinese see bamboo as one of the luckiest plants around.

Since the dining room, which is often but not always adjacent to the living room, symbolizes the helpful people in your life, I would focus your attention more on the travel aspect that also corresponds to this corner of the bagua. Here, you might include a photo of a favorite place your family has visited (such as Yosemite, the Grand Canyon, or Cape Cod), or perhaps include something pertaining to Heaven (angels, a religious icon, or an altar). For some, a picture of an archer shooting an arrow at a row of stars might symbolize goals and reaching for the stars. You will find what works best for you.

E-WISDOM

Let intention drive your choices. It may seem unusual to have a stereo in your relationship corner, but if music or dancing is important to you and your partner, then a music source is symbolically matching your endeavors.

The children and creativity corner can have pictures of your children, gifts from your children, even gifts from other children who are close or special to you. Remember that creativity is equally important here. You needn't have children to focus on the creativity this area can celebrate or bring to your life. In fact, many people who paint, quilt, or crochet hang their creations in this area of their living rooms as a way of sharing their talents with family, friends, and guests.

Using the bagua and your pure intentions, you can do wonders in the meaningful placement of furniture and accessories in your living room.

Pulling in the Elements

In addition to bringing the bagua to life in your living room, you should also focus on balance when revamping the room according to feng shui principles. Too much of one kind of element can greatly affect the balance in the room, which in turn can create blockages and stagnant chi. What you really want most of all is to balance the elements in a way that instantly creates a feeling of calm in the room. Remember, the living room is a room for peaceful relaxation as much as it is a room for warm gatherings with family and friends.

Here are some suggestions for boosting the chi with each of the five elements:

- **Fire.** To increase the representation of the fire element in your living room, use lots of the color red, light candles, or use your fireplace often. You can also boost the fire element in the room by adding spiky plants such as a cactus or ficus.
- **Wood.** You can add more of the wood element to your living room by incorporating more green as an accent color; including taller, treelike plants; or adding more wood, wicker, or bamboo in the form of furniture and accent pieces.
- **Earth.** Grounding your living room space with more earth elements can really enhance an ethereal space such as a living room with a vaulted ceiling, skylights, and the like. Another way to boost the earth energy in the room is to add soft linen, cotton, or even silk pillows, draperies, or slipcovers, or add a blanket with warm earth tones to your sofa. If you want even more earthiness, consider a clay pot or ceramic sculpture.
- **Metal.** Reflective metal lighting fixtures work well to increase the metal element within a living room, but you can also include items that are white or spherical. Again, think creatively as well as efficiently: Metal picture frames or sculptures can incorporate several elements.
- **Water.** The easiest way to boost the water element's energy in your living room is to add an aquarium. In feng shui, nine is an auspicious number, so it is highly recommended that you have nine fish in your aquarium at all times. If one dies, replace it immediately. If aquariums

are not appealing to you, you can use a Zen water fountain, hang a mirror, or use black and blue colors to represent the water element in the living room.

Balancing the elements is very easy to do in each room in your home, beginning with the living room. Just remember that you have options. Take a literal approach and add each element by choosing an item that concretely depicts or symbolizes it, or be more associative. Represent each of the five elements with the colors or shapes that correspond to them.

When you are creating balance in a room, you are creating harmony in your life—and that extends to the life of your family, too.

"Manifestation Central"

Not only is your living room a place for rest, relaxation, and community, it's also a space for creative visualization and manifestation. Here, you can dream your dreams—but you can also set them into action and bring them to fruition by adding specific elements to draw them into being.

E-WISDOM

If you want the help of your ancestors in a particular aspect of your life, place photos or objects that once belonged to them in that corner of a room. For instance, if you want their help in business, put their portrait in your wealth corner. Don't forget to say a daily prayer of thanks to your ancestor!

You can do your best to manifest the people or things you want to add to your life—as long as your intention is focused on the highest good for all involved. Keep your intentions honest, pure, and of benefit to all, and you cannot go wrong.

Whether you want a new relationship (in which case, you should put pairs of things in the relationship corner of your living room) or a new job (in which case, you should activate the chi in the career section of your living room by hanging a crystal), know that you can affect change and make things happen simply by focusing your intention on a specific area of the bagua. Again, it's your manifestation tool!

Life Support for Living Rooms

While living rooms can be the easiest rooms in your home in which to apply the principles of feng shui, they can also present some problems that can be turned into opportunities if handled the feng shui way.

Here are some typical problems that may have you reaching out for "life support" for your living room in the form of a feng shui cure:

- **An unusually shaped room.** Maybe your living room isn't the perfect rectangular or square shape it ought to be to be in perfect balance with nature. But nature isn't perfect, either, so create the illusion of any "missing" corners of the room by hanging mirrors in the area they would be located in. For living rooms with an extra corner, you can hide the additional area with large potted plants or pieces of furniture. If you choose furniture for such an area, be sure to curve it so that it faces the other pieces of furniture in the room so that no one is ever left out of a conversation.

Pictures and photos reflect the things that are most important to you. Carefully choosing which pictures will hang in which areas of your home will have positive outcomes. For example, if you'd like to have better health, a picture of a lovely, healthy plant in your health corner will do wonders. Even better is a real healthy plant!

- **Bad mirror placement.** Sometimes, a mirror can be hung at a disadvantage in a living room (or anywhere else, for that matter). Don't place a mirror in a position where it will reflect the front door; this can send the good energies running or absorb and reflect negative ones into the room. Use mirrors to enhance space, not simply to reflect it.
- **Bad views.** Does you living room have a window that overlooks an undesirable view? Maybe you live next door to a hospital or a waste

dump. If you do, you can still practice good feng shui by blocking the negative view with a large plant. You can also use plants to round off sharp corners.

- **Clutter everywhere.** Okay, the only cure for this is for you to roll up your sleeves and pitch the clutter. Get rid of things you no longer need, and put away the things that are useful to you but that block the energy of the room because they don't belong there. The living room is for living, not for burying yourself in the debris of your life!

ESSENTIALS Use plants to soften harsh corners in your home. Be sure you care for them well, and that they have sufficient light.

- **Stuck sofas.** Position your sofa in a way that inspires free exchange of ideas and communication. Under a beam is a bad location, because it can cause headaches and make the person sitting on the sofa feel oppressed and vulnerable. Too close to a TV can also disturb relaxation periods, since the electricity can interfere with rest. Try to imagine your sofa as a soft oasis, an escape from the pressures of the world. Keep it from getting its positive energies stuck in bad positions.
- **Bad beams.** Beams create barriers and block energy everywhere, so they are not the best option in feng shui. You don't want to block your good fortune in life, so hide the overhead beams with a false ceiling or soft draperies. If you can, install a light or a ceiling fan on the main beam to keep chi flowing and to redirect the energy in the room.
- **Sunken ships—and lost living rooms.** Architects absolutely love sunken living rooms because they are a creative alternative to the norm—but in feng shui, sunken living rooms are something akin to the *Titanic*. Here, you are symbolically showing the world that you don't mind being stepped on, which means you will always be stuck in a subordinate job and never be paid what you're really worth. Try to cure the space by placing a coffee table with a mirrored top in the center of the area—reflecting and elevating your energy back to a level of strength and power.

- **Second thoughts.** If the space is used for a secondary purpose, other than as a center of community and family togetherness, be sure to find a way to section the secondary purpose off at times when the room is not used for that purpose. For instance, you might need to use the living room as an office at times, but you should either section your desk area off with a screen or some plants or buy a desk that has cupboards that totally enclose the work space so that it is not visible when you are using the living room in its intended or primary purpose. (P.S.—The same is true of that other secondary activity: TV addiction. If you must watch TV in your living room, be sure to keep this and all other electrical equipment sectioned off neatly in its own compartment. This will minimize any negative energy from the electrical current.)
- **Noncentral living room.** What if your living room is not the hub of your home? Maybe you have an unusual layout in your home, one that places your living room in the basement or another noncentral area. If this is the case in your home, you can install a ceiling fan to dissipate the energy from your living room into other areas of your home, or you can use sound (stereo, fountain, or wind chime) to attract others to your living room location.

Creating a living room space that lives, breathes, and grows with the entire family is sometimes challenging work from a feng shui standpoint, but it is ultimately quite rewarding. In this magical room of your house, you can fantasize about the people, places, and things you would most like to manifest into your life, and then you can set about the visualization work that brings them to reality.

You can dream it, and you can do it!

CHAPTER 6

Dynamic Dining Rooms

Unless you live in an apartment, the dining room is usually the most formal room of your home. It's where all the high-level entertaining and family discussion usually takes place—simply put, it's where a lot of the chi in your family gets moving!

Welcome Helpful People

In most traditionally designed homes, the dining room often falls in the helpful people corner of your bagua. This is no accident—often, it's the people who help you most in your life (family, friends, business associates) who are invited to your dining room for celebrations of all kinds. Whether you entertain with lavish parties several times a year or invite a few friends over for an intimate dinner once in a blue moon, you'll want your dining room to reflect the fact that you appreciate the helpful people in all areas of your life.

Mirrors reflecting the dining room table are another way to symbolize abundance. If the food is magnified, it will symbolize plenty of healthy abundance for all who are seated around your dining room table.

SSENTIALS

An object and its reflection symbolize abundance. If the food on your table is doubled by its reflection, it will symbolize plenty; an orchid will symbolize wealth; even the reflection of people seated in your living room multiplies the positive, loving energy of friends.

Think about it for a moment: Your dining room is dynamic. Many of your important life decisions and changes happen at a family discussion around the dining room table. People have decided whether to buy a home (and finalized the paperwork) in the dining room. They have filled out college applications, announced engagements and pregnancies, and talked about the future sitting at the table. For most families, many wonderful holidays and celebrations have taken place there as well. Memories are served with each and every dinner!

In feng shui, the dining room is a room full of symbolism that affects every important aspect of your life. Here, you can place items that remind you of or celebrate the people who have helped you in life, but you can also place photos or paintings of interesting places to travel—whether you have already been there or just hope to go—since the helpful people corner of the bagua also corresponds to travel.

Of course, if you have a dining room that is located in another area of the bagua, you can simply look at its corresponding life endeavor (such as career or self-knowledge) and incorporate symbolic items in the room. Remember that your intention is personal, so you can choose any items you'd like as long as they are symbolic for you.

E-WISDOM

Just because the helpful people corner is in the area of the bagua where most dining rooms fall does not mean you should focus only on those who can help you. You can also use it as a reminder of the many ways in which you can serve or help others.

Sometimes, your own helpful intentions can lead to intuitively perfect feng shui. In the Black Hat Sect of feng shui, feeling is everything—and your intuition is usually right on target. How's that for serendipity?

Inviting Atmosphere to the Table

Once inside the dining room, how do you use feng shui to create a warm, spacious, and welcoming atmosphere?

Start with the entrance to your dining room. Is it near the kitchen and the living room? It's good to have the dining room close to the kitchen, since going back and forth for food will not take you far from your guests' enchanting company. The closer your dining room is to the living room, the more comfortable your guests will feel mingling with others—especially if you've grouped people from different areas of your life, mixing family, friends, and coworkers. Like healthy chi, your guests will want to flow in and out of rooms rather than be kept prisoner in one small room of your home!

ESSENTIALS

If your dining room doesn't have windows, your chandelier or a small ceiling fan will help circulate the chi in your dining room. Best if your chandelier has a round crystal ball hanging from it!

Be mindful of maintaining a properly flowing chi. It is best if you have at least one window in your dining room to help fresh chi come in, but if you have two windows, you might want to use draperies, mini-blinds, or even beaded curtains to slow down rushing chi. Otherwise, your guests might come and go like the wind!

In terms of décor and furnishings, remember that the dining room is like a fine restaurant within your home. You'll want it to appear fancy and worth the visit, but also very clean. Assuming you have no clutter in your dining room, consider the different elements of décor and ways you can enhance the ambiance with mindful use of feng shui. (If you do have clutter, see Chapter 2.)

Lights

When it comes to lighting, less is most often more. You might want to install a dimmer switch so you can have more light in the daytime and soft, romantic light in the evening. Of course, candles add the fire element to your evenings of entertaining, and they provide a calming, warm, and inviting energy. Don't forget to share the warmth. Take the opportunity to have "romantic" candlelight dinners in the dining room with your children or your friends. Remember that any night you spend with people who are important to you is a night worth celebrating!

Draperies

Windows are critical elements in controlling flowing chi. For window treatments, you definitely want soft and flowing. Your draperies shouldn't cover the window completely, but serve to slow down the chi and soften the windows. If you have are concerned about too much sunlight or not enough privacy, install fabric or mini-blinds so that you can let the chi back in when you want it.

QUESTIONS?

What is the best way to cure a room with too many windows?
If there are too many windows in your dining room, hang a drapery or pull a shade while entertaining. Too many windows can be very distracting for guests, who will become more focused on passersby than on your meaningful conversation!

Floors

Wood floors are ideal in a dining room because they really ground the energy in the room, and depending on the levels of energy you have, this may be an absolute necessity! Enhance your wood with a colorful area rug, since color enhances appetite and is considered good for digestion.

Try to avoid wall-to-wall carpeting because it absorbs a lot of energy and can bog down the room. Not only will the carpeting give the room a heavy feeling, it will make your guests feel full well before their stomachs are at capacity. If you do have wall-to-wall carpet in your dining room, try placing a multicolored area rug under the table to add interest and dilute the heaviness.

Art and Artifacts

Choose interesting, stimulating, and conversation-worthy art and accessories with which to adorn your dining room. A large print of a watercolor that features a young woman getting her palms read by a fortune-teller will add a little folklore to your helping people corner, while a painting or item that represents your favorite destination is mindful of the travel aspect. You can include paintings that speak to you—and that you don't mind talking about—in your dining room.

E-WISDOM

Create a calm, relaxing atmosphere for yourself and your guests. If you have an overstimulating dining room, it can disrupt the digestion of everyone at the table. Moderation in all things, including décor!

Handmade work by local artisans can really add an earthier feel to the room. Incorporate some functional art you've collected, such as hand-made serving dishes, hand blown wineglasses, or one-of-a-kind silverware. This is your shining opportunity to share such loveliness with others, so pull it all out for a lively evening of entertaining!

FIGURE 6-1: The Little Things
Note the picture behind the fern; the owner is representing her fondness of Paris in the travel corner of this room.

Dining the Feng Shui Way

Whether you eat to live or live to eat, you'll find the experience so much more enjoyable in a dining room that conforms to the principles of feng shui. When the energy flow is favorable, the flow of conversation improves, too, and you, your family, and your guests will have an appetizing and stimulating meal without even realizing how much the arrangement and décor of your dining room is contributing to your sense of satisfaction. But a dining room that does not have good chi is one in which guests eat quickly and depart early and neither the taste of the food nor the table talk lingers.

Be Mindful of Your Elements

In some homes, the tables are too large and the chairs too numerous for the space allotted. Guests sit elbow-to-elbow at a long, rectangular table that also is closer to the front door than to the kitchen. The poor host or hostess can barely squeeze into and out of the space to get to the kitchen. Guests begin to feel sorry for their hosts and start looking at their watches. Few stick around long after coffee and dessert.

Try placing the dining room table closer to the kitchen, and consider a round table. After all, it worked for King Arthur. Round tables make people feel more at ease, and no one has to take the "head" position, which can feel intimidating in someone else's home. Also, rounded, smooth lines and curves encourage smoother energy flow. Leave enough room for guests to easily get into and out of their chairs, as well as to turn to speak to other guests. The table should be of wood or metal, which offer good support, rather than more distant, less inviting marble or glass.

When arranging furniture in the dining room, be sure that chairs don't restrict anyone from moving easily through doorways. There should be ample space for guests to walk to and around the table.

Avoid having clocks in your dining room if you don't want your family and guests to feel rushed. Lighter colors are easier on your digestion, but some red can help inspire conversation. Abstract art is better placed in another room, unless you want your guests distracted by puzzling over what it represents. Disturbing or nightmarish images also are inappropriate for a dining room, and erotic art belongs in a bedroom. Still lifes of food or happy family gatherings—especially family photos of good times—are much more appropriate.

Applying the rules of feng shui, you can make your dining room a feast for the eye and a warm and relaxing place to nourish and entertain those you care about most.

Table Tips

The table should be the main area of focus in your dining room. Comfort is first and foremost, since comfort aids in the digestive process (and keeps your guests interested in the conversation rather than their sore backs!).

The shape of the dining room table greatly affects and influences chi in the room. It can be yin shaped (rectangle, oval, or round) or yang shaped (square)—or even octagonal, bringing in energy from all directions.

- **Square.** For serious events such as business dinners, you'll want to use a square table top, preferably in a heavier, more grounding surface such as marble. A solid wood table can be grounding for business deals conducted over the dinner table as well.
- **Round.** Romantic dinners require a small round table for maximum feng shui benefit. Glass tops are good for relationships needing introspection and quiet reflection, while a round tablecloth in a color like red or pink can be an intimate way to begin a romantic dinner for two.
- **Oval.** Family meals are energized most by oval-shaped tables, and a good solid wood like oak can help symbolically strengthen the bond of the family. The more rustic the table, the better off you'll be. After all, you want your family life to be as strong as a solid, heavy tree, and a rustic table will symbolize such strength best of all.
- **Rectangle.** Formal buffet-style dinners are best served on a rectangular table, since the yin energy of such a table creates a relaxing mood that encourages guests to graze and stay a while. The darker the wood, the more yin balance you have added, but do stay away from white or black tabletops (unless you and your guests are all actively trying to lose weight) since neither is very conducive to eating.

Who Sits Where?

Good feng shui dictates that your most important guest should sit facing the main entrance to the room—never with his or her back to the entrance, as this is the vulnerable position. You never want your most honored guest to feel vulnerable in your presence! Use the energy of direction to determine who should sit in which position—and then use placeholders with name cards so that each person knows they were intentionally placed at your table.

If you have a quiet, shy, or introverted person, position him or her in a southeast chair that faces northwest. The yang energy of this direction will encourage your guest to open up and join in the conversation.

East facing west is the traditional Chinese position of the eldest son, so it has an aura of ambition and power attached to it. It's also the romance position, with a little power and drama combined. An auspicious chair to find oneself in.

E-WISDOM

An even number of chairs around the table is best in feng shui, since it represents balanced energies and inclusiveness.

Younger children fare better in chairs that are located in the northeast corner of the table, and benefit from facing the encouraging energy of the southwest. This location is best for those who need a little encouragement or motivation in life.

Those who sit in the northern chair while facing south balance yin stillness with yang passion and excitement, making it a wonderful place for an attractive older person to sit.

Leaders should sit in chairs that are positioned northwest but that face southeast. In ancient (and often modern) China, this is where the father of the home traditionally sits. A strong position of power and leadership!

The mother in Chinese homes traditionally sits in the southwest corner of the table, facing northeast. This gentle energy is smooth going for family chi.

ESSENTIALS

Remember that an even number of chairs is important—and seat the honored guest in a position that faces the doorway. Curved chairs are ideal in feng shui because this shape represents the "dragon embracing the tiger."

The ingénue, or attractive young woman, fares best when seated opposite the eldest son position, or sitting west but facing east. Here, attraction is tempered by the playful, almost teasing, energy of the east. This is a great place to seat anyone who is looking to meet someone new—at your dining room table, of course.

Your most intriguing guest should probably sit south facing north, since this is the position of mystery and quiet ways. Traditionally associated with the middle daughter in Chinese families, this chair's position will bring out the most expressive and interesting conversation in the whole room. Save this chair for a person who is lively, fun, and interesting—and who will likely lead the conversation along as smoothly as a babbling brook over rocks.

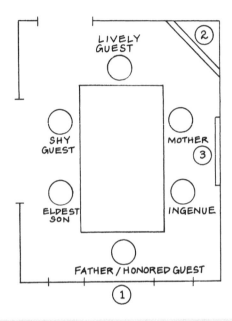

FIGURE 6-2: To Table
1. The father is seated in the least vulnerable position. 2. A corner cupboard softens the hard lines of the room and the rectangular table. 3. A mirror opposite the open arch will make the room seem more spacious, and will also reflect back to those with their backs to the arch.

Keep in mind that many times, people don't need to be strategically placed at your table. As an experiment, have a dinner party where there are no placeholders and everyone chooses his or her own chair. Note where each type of personality chooses to sit—it probably won't be too far off from the suggestions included in this chapter!

Remember Your Intention

Now that you know who should sit where, it's time to take a look at what kind of party energy you want overall—yin or yang? A yin party is ideal for quiet get-togethers, informal lunches, or everyday family meals where you want the rest of the world to stay away for a little while. Yang parties are best for formal occasions where you want lots of creative energies to blend.

Are there special tips for creating a yin or a yang party? You bet.

The Yin Dinner Party

Low-key lunches, dinners, or family get-togethers are yin parties. For these, you'll want to decorate your table using yin elements:

* Wooden utensils (and chopsticks, if serving chow mein–type dishes).
* Wicker, bamboo, or cork placemats to ground the energy even more.
* Napkins, tablecloth, and linens in pinks, blues, or greens. (Natural fibers work best.)
* Wood chairs covered in soft cushions in pale colors.
* Wooden or earthen tableware (dishes, serving plates, etc.).
* A live plant as a centerpiece, symbolizing good health.
* Foods that contain water (salads and fruits).

To further enhance a quiet yin get-together, use soft music such as bamboo flute, soft piano, or even nature sounds. Keep the lights dimmed, and turn off electrical disturbances such as a TV or static-filled radio. Keep sharp objects stored neatly away when not in use.

The Yang Dinner Party

Yang parties are those fantastic soirees that we all look forward to having once in a while. Lively, well-traveled guests provide intellectually stimulating conversation at yang parties. You will usually serve wine and cheese, and you have plenty of exciting artwork around to keep everyone's interest and energy high. However, a sparsely furnished room enhances all this excitement—leaving the evening wide open to great possibilities.

For your invigorating yang party, you'll want to decorate your table using yang elements:

- Square placemats (especially if your table is round)
- Reflective surfaces such as sparkling crystal and sterling silverware (Of course, a mirror under your food will make it appear twice as plentiful, too.)
- Napkins, tablecloth, and linens in bright colors (Splashes of red to bring in the yang fire element.)
- Sturdy metal chairs with brightly colored seat cushions (Red or orange will sure light a fire under your guests to keep things lively and energetic.)
- Fine china to exude an aura of wealth and prosperity.
- A centerpiece with roses and candles to ignite passion and romance.
- Yang foods such as spicy Cajun dinners, whole grain breads, smoked salmon, or peppered steak. (A nice, hearty red wine such as a Cabernet Sauvignon or even burgundy can finish out the yang energy in your food offerings.)

Yang dinner parties require exciting and creatively inspiring music such as modern jazz, classical music, or even some rock and roll. With a yang party, the idea is to live it up as much as possible!

Typical Problems—and Their Cures

In feng shui, every problem area is a place full of opportunity. You simply need to identify the problem, then cure it with a feng shui solution that reverses the negative energy the problem caused.

The Furniture

One of the most typical problems in the dining room is a table with sharp, pointed edges. Here, the solution is simple: use soft linens to cover the table, or position the table diagonally in the room to lessen the effect of the poison arrows.

Another problem that often occurs is furniture that is not a comfortable fit—for your guests or the table. If your chairs don't fit smoothly under the table in your dining room, it may be time to purchase some new ones. And while rustic antique chairs may seem to add ambience, they can detract from the positive flow of chi in the room if they are not in good shape.

Table size can be a problem for those who like to eat at the dining room table even when there isn't anyone else to join in the meal. For times when you are dining alone, you can cure the problem of seating imbalance by creating the illusion that others are dining with you. Drape the table linens over half the table, and group some photos together at the opposite end of the table. Add a living plant as an additional "guest" at the table.

Stay on top of the clutter—remove it the second you see it. Your dining room is, in fact, very much like the altar of your home. It is a place of reverence, not disrespect. Honor the dining room and you'll be honoring your family as well.

When entertaining, don't use tall centerpieces, wobbly tables or chairs, powerfully fragrant candles (they'll interfere with the smell of wonderful cooking), or irritating music. Beams over tables are considered very inauspicious and should also be avoided in the dining room.

Tabletops should be smooth and easy to clean. If you have an old wooden tabletop with lots of grooves in it, food particles can get stuck in your table for an eternity—creating lots of stuck energy. If it's not easy to clean, cover the table with something that is.

The Room

If you live in a smaller home or apartment, your dining room may not be as easily identifiable as it might be in a larger home with a separate dining room. In such smaller spaces, you can create a dining room with its own energy by separating the table area off with a screen, area rug, or even a group of indoor plants. This way, you'll create a dining space that has energies all its own.

You can also create a separate space for special-occasion dining outside by joining some trellises and draping them with soft, pastel fabric coverings. This is an especially good thing to try for a romantic outdoor dinner for two. Just be sure to use a small, cozy table for two, and bring your dinner items out on a small cart or tray.

Always use soft lighting in your dining room, as well as soft colors such as greens and yellows. This softness will help keep the energy in the dining room flowing and positive, especially if you have guests who are prone to incite arguments.

The issue of mirrors can be equally good or bad for a dining room. While mirrors are good for enhancing the feeling of wealth and abundance in the dining room, stay away from mirrors that are large and heavy. You don't want to overpower people with an exaggerated image of your abundance.

Mirrors can be especially disruptive to dinner parties if they reflect activity outside of the room—or worse, outside of the house. You don't want your guests looking at everything but the meal in front of them. Before you know it, they'll be looking at their watches, too.

Clutter in the dining area is bad feng shui because it blocks your potential for wealth and prosperity. The dining room and the kitchen are both symbolic of the wealth in your family, and clutter is stagnant chi comprised of unfinished business and decisions that have yet to be made. With that much inertia, how could you ever go places in the world? Don't let your dining room table become a dumping ground for all your past and current projects. It is a place of honor in your home, and if you don't honor the space, how can you expect to receive any beneficial energy from it?

If you only use the dining room for special occasions once or twice a year maximum, you might want to reconsider this practice. Just as you should "spread the wealth" by alternating use of the burners on your stovetop, so should you alternate the use of the kitchen and the dining room for meals. This will activate the chi in both rooms, filling it with the loving rays of your family's energy and greatly increasing your family's prosperity in the meantime!

A butler's door in your dining room can be a good way to shut out the distraction of cooking sounds in the nearby kitchen. It can also be a good mover of chi, since it swings open and closed frequently.

Finally, if your dining room seems engulfed in walls without windows nearby, you can activate the otherwise stagnant chi in the room by hanging a crystal from the chandelier or by hanging a wind chime in the entrance to your dining room.

Blessings and Clearings

When you host a dinner party of any size or style, you are inviting new and different energies straight to your table. While this is a wonderful and generous thing to do, you should also observe some of the more ceremonial principles of feng shui.

When sending out invitations to your guests, send them in red envelopes along with your blessings. You might even invest in a small set of Chinese rubber stamps, and seal each envelope with a Chinese symbol that is meaningful to both you and the people you're inviting. Detach yourself from the outcome of whether they will be able to attend your soiree, and focus instead on your good intentions of seeking their presence, and of this opportunity to provide nourishment for their minds and bodies. What a wonderful gift it is to entertain our friends and family!

If guests ask to bring you a gift, suggest that they wrap it in red for good luck. Bottles of wine can be wrapped in soft red cloth, and food gifts can be tied with red ribbons.

Remember to offer a blessing to your guests when they are seated at your dining room table, about to dig into some of your delectable treats. Offer thanks for the togetherness you share and for the food whose life-giving energies are going to fortify you.

After each dinner party, do a space clearing to reclaim your space from the exciting chi that graced your home for a short while.

The Chi of Food

Finally, for every dining experience in your home, you need to give some thought to the main object of attention in the dining room: food! After all, that's what everyone is gathering in your dining room for in the first place (aside from your wonderful company, of course!).

Food represents the energy that activates the chi within your body. A good meal sustains you, certainly, but it also inspires and heals you. In Eastern medicine, food is considered a healing element for many illnesses and is therefore an important part of treatment. So it is for your guests, who have come to your dining room for nourishment and for replenishment of their souls as well as their bodies.

ESSENTIALS

Keep your options open—you can apply the bagua for individual rooms as well as to your entire home. There's bagua and bagua-within-bagua—for maximum effect and enhancement, use the bagua both ways.

When you eat a piece of food, you are also consuming its chi. The environment in which you consume this chi is key, because food can be affected by negative chi. That's why it's important to create a calm, comfortable environment in which your guests consume new energy—you want them to be able to leave your table healthier and more whole than they were before they came to your house for dinner. Bet you never thought of a simple dinner party in this way before, huh?

A relaxed environment is best for digestion. When you or your guests feel rushed, there will be a feeling of stress and tension, not conducive elements to proper digestion, to be sure. The Chinese believe that where there is good digestion, there can be good conversation, and that's what ultimately makes your dinner party a resounding success.

Don't forget that along with good chi in and around your dining room, there should also be an element of fun in your feng shui. Taken too seriously and intensely, any major changes to your dining room for the sake of feng shui may create a situation in which there is less of your own unique personality, and less fun for you and your guests. Apply what is meaningful to you and concentrate on removing blocked or heavy chi. Then let your personality shine through—you are in the spotlight on the home stage of your dining room!

CHAPTER 7

The Well-Balanced Kitchen

I f the entrance of your home is the mouth of chi, then your kitchen is definitely the stomach—and, just as the fortune cookie says, your stomach never lies. Like meals, some kitchens are nourishing and inviting, while others are too heavy and cause indigestion.

Health and Balance

Good feng shui in the kitchen depends on many things, but most of the importance rests on harmony, balance, and mindfulness—both in design and practice. After all, the kitchen is the informal, yet critical, center of your home, where everyone gathers to eat, talk, and plan for the future. It's where meals and dreams are often shared. The kitchen is the core source of your family's wealth, health, and prosperity, so it should be treated with the utmost reverence.

E-WISDOM

Your stomach tells the truth.

—Chinese fortune cookie

The ancient Chinese recognized this wisdom centuries ago, long before there was Williams-Sonoma, microwaves, or dishwashers. Westerners, slow as they are, at first considered feng shui in the kitchen to be a bit too "new agey." However, once its health and safety benefits were recognized, people began to adopt feng shui principles in the design and regular use of their kitchens. In fact, kitchen feng shui has come so far as an East-meets-West concept that it is regularly offered as a popular program through the National Kitchen & Bath Association. It's gone from being "ancient history" to a "hot trend"—in just a few thousand years!

The Feng-tional Kitchen

Although the following concept applies to all rooms, it bears repeating: You don't just start designing or redesigning your kitchen without clearing the clutter first. There's a modern feng shui saying that goes like this: "When you burp, you are full. Is your kitchen burping?"

Your kitchen will "burp" (or seem like it needs to) if the drawers and cupboards are full of things you no longer use or need. As an experiment, one person actually went through each cabinet and her pantry and put all the food she wasn't using into a huge pile. By the end of the day, there was enough food to feed a family of four for two weeks—and that was just food the woman didn't like!

Clean out your cupboards, donate food you don't want to homeless shelters, and pitch the things you don't need anymore. You'll be surprised how much lighter this will make you feel, and how much it will help your prosperity when you give up the need to hoard.

Clear Channels

Keep your kitchen clean because it represents prosperity in the form of good health and wealth. Dirty dishes, stoves, and refrigerators can block your abundance in these important aspects of your life, and they can also cause digestive problems in your body. Dirt can "clog" the arteries of your soul, making you feel unhealthy physically *and* financially.

Food should be stored away when not being used for cooking. You should use metal or wood canisters to store bread, flour, and sugar, especially if your storage canisters will be located between the stove and the refrigerator. This will balance your elements of fire (stove) and water (fridge) with a little wood and metal in between.

To cultivate good chi, you must harmonize the five elements in your kitchen: wood, fire, earth, metal, and water.

Speaking of refrigerators (or do you have a food museum?), you can also apply the principles of good feng shui to the inside of your cold food storage. Use the bagua to determine which foods best correspond with each element—or simply go by the usefulness factor. If you sort food by its usefulness to you and your family, you will always keep the things you need within close reach, and you will begin to practice the kind of mindfulness that helps you instinctively remove the things you don't need or use.

Practicing mindfulness will make a huge difference in lightening your mind and your body. You will store only the foods you know you'll use, effectively eliminating the kind of refrigerator clutter that makes people pack on extra pounds out of boredom.

Implementing Design

Once you are starting with a clean kitchen slate, you are ready to chalk up the day's special: designing a functional kitchen that allows plenty of good chi to flow through it. A "feng-tional" kitchen will invigorate and nourish all the inhabitants of your home.

QUESTIONS?

What makes a kitchen "feng-tional"?
A good "feng-tional" kitchen allows the maximum amount of good chi, neither stagnant nor rushing, to pass through it.

Chi that moves too quickly through the house can represent quickly draining finances. Rushing chi needs to be slowed down using a variety of cures such as butler doors, potted plants, or screens. Barriers like doors, which can open and close, are good chi slowers, as are mobiles and plant carts.

Stagnant chi is much more problematic in the kitchen and bathrooms than any other areas of your house because it can symbolically affect your health and finances. Stuck energy can manifest in your bank account as an inability to increase wealth, and in your stomach as difficulty digesting food properly. Get chi moving in these rooms by adding a small ceiling fan, hanging a crystal, or placing a small fountain in a corner of the room.

A kitchen that faces your front door is thought to be in a less-auspicious location unless you are in the food preparation or catering business. It's a little too head-on to the chi, and you don't want the chi to hit you square in the forehead as you cook! The ideal direction for the cooking area of your kitchen to face is north.

E-WISDOM

The stove is symbolic of wealth and prosperity in feng shui. You cannot grow and prosper without a way to cook your food. The more burners the better, and placing a mirror or reflective object that doubles their appearance helps, too.

The stove or oven (yang fire elements) should be located at least two feet away from the refrigerator or kitchen sink (yin water elements). When you have two opposite elements in close proximity, they will cancel each other's energy out. The oven should not face the kitchen door, either, since this will let too much "heat" out into your home.

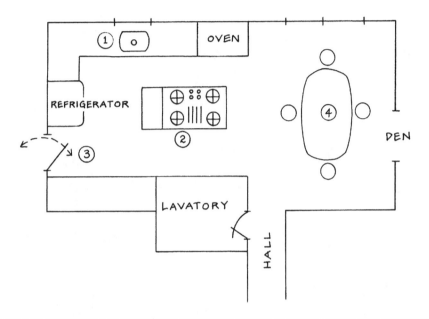

FIGURE 7-1: Feng-tional?
1. The stove and sink are not too close. 2. The person cooking can see all the doorways from one position. 3. A swinging door to the dining room prevents the chi from rushing straight through the kitchen. 4. The table set off to one side slows your guests down, too, and creates a more intimate setting for family meals.

A stove should face inward and contain reflective metal elements if this positioning puts you with your back to a door. If the stove has you with your back to a side door or back door, consider items like metal canisters or a metal utensil holder so you are not vulnerable and can see anyone approaching from behind you. A small mirror would work well here, too.

Alternate use of the burners on your stove to keep your prosperity well balanced. Many cooks favor the two burners toward the front of the stove simply because they are closer, but it is best in feng shui to spread the energy around to maintain balance.

A final note about your stove: It should not face a bathroom or bedroom door. A stove too close to a bedroom wall can pose a fire threat to you and your family. It should also never be positioned in the middle of your house, since this is a fire hazard. The ideal location for a stove is in the open and not under low ceilings or tucked into tight corners.

Additional Considerations

For aesthetic reasons more than feng shui, your cooktop should not be placed in front of a window (particularly if it has a screen) since this reduces the airiness and openness of the design. Also, the front of your cooktop shouldn't face an entrance to your kitchen, since this would make it difficult for you to effectively greet all who enter your kitchen in hopes of fellowship and a good meal.

FIGURE 7-2: Clear, Not Cold
Note that although the kitchen is predominantly white (which denotes cleanliness), it is not *only* white (which would give off a stark, clinical feeling).

Another area worthy of attention in your kitchen is that of furniture. Do you have too much stuff in too small a space? Such a situation can block your chi. Open the room up by moving out pieces you don't absolutely need! Overall, your kitchen should be light, open, airy, and as spacious as possible. It will make your guests feel welcome while increasing your own sense of health and well-being.

FIGURE 7-3: Kitchen Comfort
The lines of the grasses (wood) complement and balance the round, metal elements of the table and vase. The circles of the table and lamp also keep chi flowing smoothly.

Cooking up Good Chi: The Fundamentals

The kitchen is the hearth and heart of your home, and it's especially important for that room to have good chi. Following is a helpful checklist:

- [ ] **Eliminate clutter.** Throw away what you can't use; donate or recycle what will serve others.
- [ ] **Keep your kitchen clean,** since it represents prosperity in the form of good health and wealth.

☐ **Allow the maximum amount of good chi to pass freely** through your kitchen, invigorating and nourishing all of the inhabitants of your home.

☐ **Maintain ventilation** to circulate chi and clear the room.

☐ **Light and color are very important.** Overhead, full-spectrum lighting is best.

☐ **Earth colors,** like forest green, which is associated with growth, balanced with bright white, work best in kitchens.

☐ **Cook up good chi using the freshest ingredients.** Buy only what you know you will use. Balance meat with fresh vegetables, and appeal to all senses throughout each dining experience.

☐ **In Chinese thinking, you literally are what you eat,** so try to balance yin and yang foods.

☐ **Include ancestors in the family dining experience,** through photos, recipes, or a place at the table, and give thanks to the Universe for every meal so that you will continue to be so blessed.

As you continue to use feng shui, certain practices will become habit. Occasionally review the list, however, to remind yourself of your intentions, and refocus your energies where needed.

Open the Air

Ventilation is another area worth consideration in the "feng-tional" kitchen. Cooking delectable dishes can have the unpleasant "aftertaste" of thick, smoke-filled air that lingers long after the meal has been digested. Install a ceiling fan if you don't have over-the-stove ventilation; an overhead fan will keep the air (and chi) circulating throughout the kitchen and its surrounding areas.

If you live in a place where you cannot install a ceiling fan, consider opening windows and hanging a wind chime in the window over your sink. This will also work well as a cure for stagnant cooking-related air.

Removing grease and debris from your cooktop regularly can also help cut down on the smoke-filled air that can fill your kitchen, block good chi, and choke your prospects for wealth.

For both feng shui and safety reasons, be sure to check your kitchen for proper airflow on a regular basis.

Optimize Light and Color

Light and color are very important to the development of a healthy and "feng-tional" kitchen. If you have few windows in your kitchen, light is even more important to generate lots of positive chi. You should always have plenty of overhead lighting in your cooking and eating areas, and it is best to use full-spectrum lighting that is closest to outdoor lighting. Never use fluorescent lighting in your kitchen, since it is oppressive. Ceiling fans with lights in them work well, because they allow you to alternate light and motion, or use them full-strength together.

Remember that in Asian culture, white represents death and mourning. If your kitchen is mostly white, bring in other elements, brighter colors, and items that symbolize health and life.

In terms of color, earth colors like forest green balanced with bright white work best in kitchens. Green is associated with life and growth, so it is an ideal kitchen color. Country blues, beiges, and warm tones are okay as a second choice, provided there's lots of good lighting. Stark, white kitchens should be avoided—not only do they look "clinical" in Western culture, but in Asian culture, white represents death and mourning. If your kitchen is mostly white, you can balance it well with brightly colored pictures of healthy fruits and vegetables. This will bring vibrant energy to your kitchen!

Kitchen Feng Shui Is Elementary

To cultivate good chi, you must harmonize the five elements in your kitchen: wood, fire, earth, metal, and water. Since water represents prosperity and wealth, be sure that your kitchen faucets are not leaky. Leaky faucets are sure to "drain" your finances!

In addition to the sink, your refrigerator represents water in your kitchen, so make sure it's in good running order as well. The "fire" element of the stove is balanced by the "water" of your refrigerator and sink, so you're covered there. Remember to balance the other three elements, too.

A Healthy Kitchen

Wood is the most powerful element in cultivating good health from your kitchen. In your décor, you can use wood elements such as paneling, plants, wooden paper towel holders and kitchen accessories, and any décor item that serves up a picture of wood elements (including trees or paper and blue or green tones).

Do not overuse symbols of prosperity in the hopes of attracting more money. An overzealous nature can create negative chi and counteract your intention.

Prosperity can also benefit from the addition of wood elements like bowls of fruit, pots of fresh herbs or vegetables, a collection of wooden utensils, or vases with flowers. (You may prefer silk flowers, since fresh flowers can represent death due to their rapid deterioration.) The options here are multiple; you'll want more than one of each wood element to attract prosperity, since like attracts like in the abundance game.

Reflective Alternatives

Metal objects, because of their reflective properties, are useful for enhancing smaller nooks and hidden corners of your kitchen. Metal canisters work well in a small pantry or breakfast nook. However, metal knives should never be stored out in the open, whether hung on walls or in any kind of glass enclosure. When knives are left out in plain view like this, practitioners say that there will be many arguments and much pain in the household. Store your knives and other sharp objects in clay earthenware, a wooden knife block, or safely tucked away in a drawer.

Speaking of sharp objects, one of the most common kitchen injuries occurs when you bump into one of the many sharp edges in your kitchen—whether you hit a drawer, the corner of a countertop, or the sharp edge of a cupboard door. In feng shui, sharp edges are known as poison arrows. To minimize them in your kitchen, apply corner covers (available wherever childproofing items are sold—most grocery and drug stores have them) or reposition things so that you do not have to put your body in danger to get to them. Waist-high cupboards are preferable to overhead ones to reduce the risk of injury or accident.

E-WISDOM

Be sure to open your heart and trust the process. Be clear about your intentions; trust your instincts to know what is right for you. When you walk into a room and do not feel comfortable in that space; most likely it is because the chi is stagnant or rushing through, which means it will require a cure.

Proper use and balance of the five elements of feng shui is critical to the success of each room, but especially in the kitchen. Take a look around your kitchen to see how many elements you've already balanced instinctively—you'll be surprised by how much feng shui there is just because something seemed to "feel right."

Main Ingredients

You may have a small kitchen, but don't let that limit you. Consider using a mixture of elements to open your space and keep the feng shui moving. When you use metal objects (for their reflective energies) and balance them out with wood, you'll end up with a nice chi going in your tiny space.

In the right environment, you may be inspired to cook more often—something you probably didn't do before. Good use of feng shui principles in your kitchen should inspire you to "nest" and even try new things. The positive, creative yang energy will be grounded and balanced when it is complemented by fresh yin cabinetry.

Optimize Nutritious Chi

So, how else can you cook up some deliciously good chi in your kitchen? Here are some things you can do to maximize the amount of nutritious chi for your family:

- **Purchase the freshest ingredients.** Heavily processed food has stagnant chi, while fresh foods offer vitality and life-giving energy.
- **Buy only what you will use.** This applies to food, but it especially applies to kitchen appliances and equipment. Don't buy a bread maker, high-speed blender, juicer, or other specialized gadget unless you plan to be doing lots of homemade cooking. Waste is bad feng shui, because it represents wasted wealth.
- **Balance your meat and vegetables.** Limit your meat intake, and be sure your meals include fresh vegetables. Meat alone is too yang and can upset your stomach, as well as contribute to heart disease. Meat represents life taken away, while vegetables offer restoration. Chalk up a point for vegetarianism!
- **Do a quick meditation before you start to prepare food.** Take a deep purifying breath, relax, and focus on the task at hand. You are creating nourishing food that will help your body (and your family's bodies) to grow. You are a giver of life, so take a moment to give thanks to the Universe for providing the great food you are about to cook and serve. You know, your own personal chi can be absorbed by the meal you are creating, so make sure you are cooking with good intention. Don't cook if you are in a bad mood; you should always be relaxed and focused.
- **Set the mood.** Before you start to cook, you may want to put on your favorite feng shui CD (Chinese bamboo flute, very soft and simple yin to complement the creative yang of cooking). Pour yourself a small glass of wine (or the beverage of your choice), light a candle or two, and go to it. Before you know it, there's a nice dinner to go with the

music and candles. Don't wait for special occasions—every day you can eat dinner with your entire family is a special occasion. You should do whatever you can to create comfort in your kitchen—you'll keep excess weight off if you create comfort rather than eat it!

While you are cooking, do a quick feng shui assessment. Is everything cleaned up the way it should be? Are you amassing clutter as you cook? If so, clear it away as soon as you can. Yes, that means that you will begin cleanup as soon as you begin cooking! Store your trash out of sight, either under the sink, in a pantry, or in another room. Rinse dishes, especially if you know that you won't get around to cleaning them right away. Keep extra composting bags handy to put food scraps in before, during, and after your meal. You won't want to put these in the trash, since they will start to decompose and smell quickly. Bad smells equal bad chi!

Create a Sensory Experience

What makes for a total feng shui kitchen experience? Nice use of all elements, coupled with a balance of items that appeals to all of the senses. Taste is enhanced, of course, by the wonderful foods you cook; smell can be positively affected by the same or by adding a simmering potpourri. Use soft chair covers or a silky tablecloth to appeal to touch. Good use of color and light in your kitchen, as well as in your food, is visually appealing.

SSENTIALS

Remember, also, that a clean, clutter-free kitchen positively impacts the sense of sight.

For the all-important sense of sound, invest in some classical or jazz CDs for your dining pleasure, or you can run a smooth Zen fountain in the background. Although you may have a fountain somewhere else in your house (such as in the wealth corner of your living room), you may be able to hear it clearly in the kitchen while you are eating.

The Yin-Yang of Eating

In Chinese thinking, you literally are what you eat. If you eat lots of hot and spicy foods, you are eating more yang than yin. If you eat lots of foods that are grown underground, from the earth, you are eating more yin foods. Neither is bad for you, but you should always strive for some kind of balance with your own personal, internal chi.

Mindful Meals

If you are feeling a little on the lethargic side, try eating more yang foods to counteract that feeling. If you're a little agitated, a yin food—one that grows outside in the sun and fresh air, like tea—can also work to calm you down. The feng shui art of balance applies to your insides as well as your surroundings!

While you can't arrange your food neatly within the bagua of your stomach, you *can* control what goes in and why. This takes you back to the practice of mindfulness, of thinking about what you do and putting purpose behind every action. You are literally practicing good feng shui inside your own body if you listen to its cues; if you are mindful without being "stomach-ful."

Instinctive Balance

Mixing yin and yang food energies will not only nourish your body, it will also balance and purify the spirit and soul. Rarely will you see someone in China consume very spicy foods without some palate-settling chrysanthemum tea. This is also true of Chinese-Americans, many of whom seek this balance instinctively. No wonder so many Americans suffer from indigestion.

ALERT

Meandering energy can create distraction for the cook—distraction that can cause disharmony and even safety problems in the kitchen. Rushing chi in a kitchen can make its inhabitants restless and unfocused, leading to kitchen injuries and mishaps.

At Chinese restaurants, the yin-yang food balance is most evident in the sweet and sour chicken and pork dinners. When you get carryout, you'll notice, too, that there is always tea in there to counteract hot oils and mustards. This is mindful eating at its most convenient!

Homemade Remedies

So, what if your kitchen isn't the ideal feng shui masterpiece? Then what do you do—buy another house? Not necessarily. Except in the case where a kitchen is actually designed into the center of a home (this definitely calls for a major move or remodeling job), all you may need to do is cook up a homemade remedy, a cure.

QUESTIONS?

Why is it bad feng shui to have the head of your bed near your stove?
Having your head against the wall shared with your stove is, in feng shui, like sleeping with your head to the fire. It's an inauspicious, not to mention unhealthy, location.

A common feng shui problem in the kitchen is if the kitchen door faces a bedroom door and the bedroom door (and stove) can be seen from the foot of your bed. Not a good idea, since in Chinese culture, this particular position represents the "taking of the dead." In other words, if you died in your sleep, you'd likely be carried out this way! Move your bed so that it is at an angle, away from the stove and doors.

If your stove puts you with your back to an entrance, hang a mirror above it so that you are not in a vulnerable position. You may also want to position the mirror so that it reflects the burners on your stove—that is said to increase your wealth by magnification!

Finally, consider the traffic pattern in your kitchen. If you have a kitchen island in the center of your kitchen, this can be the best design because it is the most open. The only time this is not true is where there isn't sufficient seating near the island. For example, what will happen if, in the center of a large, open kitchen, there is a kitchen island that faces two wide-open walls going into two other rooms? The kitchen, the nourishing center of a home, does not invite people to stay still for very long; instead, it encourages pacing and constant motion. The broader effects of that can be reflected in guests and family members who similarly wander into and out of your life.

Remember Your Roots

One final area of feng shui that is often lost in modern translation is the reverence and inclusion of ancestors in the family dining experience. In ancient China, such reverence was prominent. Families often had altars dedicated to their ancestors in their homes, and thanked their ancestors for their part in the family's wealth and happiness of today.

In modern times, people may not have an ancestral altar in or near their kitchens, but they can still find nice ways of including ancestral energy in family mealtimes by doing simple things:

- Group old family photos and hang or place them in the helpful people corner of your kitchen, using the bagua with the bottom center positioned at the entrance of your kitchen.
- Place a recipe box filled with old family cooking secrets in your family corner, again using the bagua.
- Use kitchen implements that have been handed down. Inherited cooking utensils and kitchenware will bring you great comfort as you cook for your friends and family.

Certain ancestors or family members warrant special consideration. If you've recently lost an important relative, you might consider keeping a place at the table open for that person's spirit. You needn't use a place setting, but rather could include a small potted plant at that end of the table to signify life that goes on. A hopeful transition in honor of a loved one can be a very healing experience.

Our Daily Bread . . . Giving Thanks

Practicing mindfulness in the kitchen also means being aware of the source of your wealth and prosperity. Give thanks to the Universe for each and every meal, and you will be continually blessed with more than enough wealth—and the "fruits" of your labors in the form of food.

Even if you're not particularly religious, you can offer your brief thanks in the form of an acknowledgment of the blessings of the earth. Native Americans (and some African tribes) apologized to animals they had to kill for meals—they would explain to the animals that they needed to feed their families and that they were grateful to the animals for providing food and sustenance. In the modern world, you can give thanks, too.

Recipes for Kitchen Success

There are many ingredients to a successful "feng-tional" kitchen. To make sure your kitchen is the best it can be from a feng shui standpoint, here are the minimal essentials:

- **Wood floors and lots of wooden cooking utensils or storage bins.** Wood energy is fantastic in the kitchen, especially for floors. Ceramic tile is very yang and can make you feel tired and overwhelmed in your kitchen.
- **Proper placement of critical appliances.** Be mindful of where you place any new addition, even if it's just a coffeemaker. Every new piece affects the energy in your kitchen differently and must be balanced properly to maximize its positive effects.
- **Good housekeeping.** Keep your kitchen and all of its surrounding areas clean and clutter-free.
- **Regular disposal of useless items.** Always toss broken or chipped dishes and plates. Imperfections like these attract stagnant or negative chi. Keeping anything broken or useless in the kitchen shows a lack of respect for yourself and your food.

- **Good balance of elements and energy.** Open, airy opportunities for good chi, combined with a good use of the five elements. Use a mutable element between two opposites; for instance, place a pot of fresh herbs (earth) between a stove (fire) and refrigerator (water) that are too close to one another.
- **Fresh fruit and flowers.** Keeping bowls of fresh fruit and flowers can attract positive chi into your kitchen and food. Just be sure to throw out anything that starts to deteriorate.
- **Mindfulness and purpose.** Always take inventory of what you use and how you use it in your kitchen. This same mindfulness applies to the kitchen itself: How do you really use this room, and how can you best arrange things to enhance and support that use?

Above all else, your "feng-tional" kitchen should be a place you enjoy spending time in, a place where you and your family can feel healthy, alive, and whole. Spending a lot of time evaluating your kitchen and using feng shui principles to enhance its potential can be a joyful and enlightening experience for the whole family!

CHAPTER 8

Positive Flow in the Bathroom

If the front door of the house is the mouth of chi and the kitchen is the stomach, the bathroom is without doubt the internal plumbing of chi. This plumbing ties in to your personal chi as well, and you can suffer from an ill-positioned bathroom unless you pay attention to the finer details.

A Neglected Necessity

In feng shui, water equals wealth, and in the feng shui bathroom, too much water can literally drain a family of its financial and spiritual resources. But rest assured, if you have the kind of luxurious bathroom that might be featured on a Sunday home show, you could probably shell out just a few more dollars for some feng shui cures.

The Forgotten Room

The reality is that whether the bathroom is large or small, opulent or humble, few people take the time to decorate it, never mind use feng shui. The idea is not to spend too much time there, especially if you have more than one child and only one bathroom! Spending money to decorate the bathroom is almost always an afterthought, something to do only after you've spent lots of time, energy, and money sprucing up every other room in your home.

E-WISDOM

A clean body is a tranquil mind.

—Chinese saying

But there is that one cold splash-in-the-face of reality in feng shui: Your bathroom can be a major source of money loss if you don't pay attention to it. It can also affect your health in ways you would prefer not to think about, especially if your bathroom is located in the center of your home's bagua, which is the health area. Traditional Chinese homes were built with enclosed courtyards in the center of them, and this was a place of spiritual contemplation and meditation. So, the ancient Chinese would have found it terribly distasteful to perform other bodily functions in this sacred space.

Although the ancient Chinese didn't have modern facilities in their homes, the basic philosophies of feng shui that pertain to sacred space— as well as water and its significance—still apply. You should, at the very least, practice mindfulness in the design and décor of your bathroom, or you will run into problems with health and financial well-being. Hang that on your towel rack!

Location, Location, Location

The best direction for your bathroom to face is north, because that direction's corresponding element in feng shui is water, and water is a good thing in the bathroom since it is for washing and cleansing. If your bathroom faces a different direction, such as south (which represents fame, reputation, and recognition—more qualities you'd rather not be flushing away), you can place a mirror on the wall opposite the north side of the room to reflect northern energy into the room.

ESSENTIALS

Mirrors are always good for opening up small, cramped bathrooms into seemingly larger and more appealing ones. Just be mindful of where you place them, so not only light but also good chi are reflected in the correct direction.

The ideal location for a bathroom is away from the wealth and health sectors of the home bagua. If it's in the wealth corner, you'll need to use more cures to keep your finances from going down the drain. The health corner is in the center of the home, and fortunately, not many homes are designed with bathrooms in this particular location. Still, if yours is one that happens to defy the odds, you can hang a crystal in the doorway of the bathroom to activate healthy chi all around you while you are indisposed. This will especially help if you have digestive or intestinal problems.

Other less-auspicious locations for bathrooms include bathrooms facing kitchens, bedrooms, or meditation rooms/altars, and bathrooms located on the second floor just above the main entrance door downstairs. If your bathroom is in any of these positions, read the list of possible cures you can use to open the chi and correct the space.

Also give consideration to the position of the bathtub or shower. Just as with a desk in your home or office, you never want your back facing a doorway—it's a position of vulnerability, and someone could sneak up on you. The same is true if your doorway opens to face the tub or shower head-on. If your bathtub or shower puts you in either of these less-than-ideal situations, try positioning a small mirror inside the shower area (the wall-mounted variety that can be extended work great for this).

You could also try to section the area off with a screen or with soft draperies to give you a little more privacy.

What are some possible cures for a poorly placed bathroom?
If your bathroom puts you in a vulnerable position, hang a small bamboo chime near the door. The sound and movement of the chime will keep the chi flowing and will also alert you to nearby motion. The bamboo represents wood, which balances water's energy.

R$_x$ for Health and Well-Being

Be mindful of lighting when creating a healthy bathroom. Too much bright light can be disturbing and offensive; too little can be depressing. Ideally, your bathroom will have plenty of natural light in the form of windows or skylights. Of course, you can use candle lighting for baths . . . or a dimmer switch to allow for when you want more light in the room and when you want less. Since light kills many germs, especially in the bath-room, try to keep as much light in the room as comfortably possible.

If the bathroom opens directly into a central room, like your kitchen, it will seem more private if you at least keep the door closed. This will, in turn, keep you and your guests healthier. Better health saves you from going to the doctor, which also allows you to keep more of your wealth. See how it's all tied in?

Some health-affecting issues can be insidious, as in the case of the bathroom facing a kitchen. Your dinner guests need to use your bathroom, only they are too embarrassed to go in the one close to the kitchen, so they hold it until they go home. This can lead to bladder infections and other retention-related illnesses.

The Bathroom As a Metaphor

More than anything else, the bathroom is used for cleansing. Either you are cleansing the outside of your body in a bath or shower, or you are cleansing the inside of your body by expelling waste. So, it follows that your bathroom itself should be as clean as possible. Your bathroom, simply put, is a metaphor for how you care about yourself in terms of cleanliness, which is even more about how you present yourself to the outside world.

Keep It Clean

Begin by clearing the countertop of any item you don't need, even if it looks good there. In feng shui, we ultimately want things that are visually appealing yet useful to us in some way, even if their only purpose is to balance elements or slow down rushing chi.

Color is also important to the cleanliness issue because too much color in the bathroom can make it appear full and unsanitary. The best color choices for bathrooms are white and soft, warm tones in the honey-beige family. If you want to use your bathroom as more of a peaceful escape, you should lean toward the warm earth tones like yellow and brown to minimize any negative energy, or even use a faux marble finish to add an aura of softness and luxury simultaneously.

Mindful Décor

If you have a clean, pristine white bathroom interior, you should decorate with hues of blue and green, since these colors will help you relax and your drainpipes to flow freely. Color psychologists agree that the color blue can actually reduce stress levels by lowering blood pressure, while green provides rest from eyestrain and has a calming effect similar to a soft, green field.

Some feng shui consultants will tell you that red is a good bathroom color for those who have difficulty waking up in the morning, but think about this powerful color carefully, since the bathroom is often the last room you are in before retiring to your bedroom at night. Red is a fire color, and while it can wake you in the morning, it can also keep you up for a restless night. Plus, the water elements in the bathroom will "put out" the fire element of red and its other incarnations in shape and object, making it less effective anyway.

> Earth overpowers water, so using earth tones (and earthlike elements like faux marble) will keep the water from draining out—and keep your wealth in your family!

What about tiles on the walls? These can be okay in terms of their reflective qualities (water), especially if you have a small bathroom that needs to be symbolically enlarged. My bathroom has pink and blue glass tiles, which are not only lovely but also reduce stress, making our upstairs bathroom a great place for an unwinding luxury bath any night of the week. But mirrored tiles are not a good idea in the bathroom, since these create a wealth-constricting effect that keeps the money contained rather than flowing.

However you decide to adorn your walls, do keep them clean. Hair can accumulate on walls, courtesy of the blow dryer, and on floors, courtesy of the brush. Cleanliness is key to good feng shui in every room of the house, but especially in the bathroom.

Behind the Medicine Chest

Feng shui consultants love mirrors for their reflective and space-enhancing magic—just keep them useful and away from one another in larger bathrooms, since dueling mirrors can block energy. Mirrors that break up the image can split the energy they give off, so it's generally best to have a nice round mirror that is one brilliant piece.

> Be as mindful in the things you keep in your bathroom as you are in other rooms of your home.

If you don't have a round mirror, you can soften the hard edges of a square one by framing it or by having the glass cut in the corners to keep chi flowing and avoid poison arrows of sharp surfaces. Willow twigs in a clay jar next to the mirror will also help.

In feng shui, bathroom mirrors work best if they are simply flush with the wall, or function solely as mirrors. So, the protruding and multifunctional medicine chest can be less than ideal. It can still work in the feng shui bathroom as long as it is kept clean and clutter-free. The problem with many medicine chests is that they tend to become the storage bin for things that "might" get used someday (misplaced energy) or, worse yet, for things that are useless (stagnant chi). Hoarding things, even small items like makeup and tweezers, can block your prosperity by keeping new things from coming into your life.

Seating Arrangements

One of the things you'll hear every feng shui teacher say in a beginning class is that the toilet lid should always be closed to keep your wealth from going down the drain. This is a commonly held belief across all schools of feng shui: The toilet lid, if left up, will allow chi to drain away and take your money with it. So, women have it right with their preference for the lid and seat down.

If the toilet can be seen from the entrance to the bathroom, you might consider using a small screen and keeping the door to the bathroom closed when not using it. If you can do it in a less-than-obvious way, conceal any water pipes that can otherwise be easily seen by you or your guests. You don't want to "see" your wealth slipping away, right?

Water should not be seen flowing away in the form of a dripping sink faucet, tub, or shower stall. In Chinese tradition, wasting water is wasting money.

If your toilet happens to be located in that tricky southeast corner of your home, you can close the lid and keep a nice big stone on the toilet cover as a way of using an earth element to "ground" your finances. For a toilet that is in the north corner, which pertains to business and career, you might place an earthen clay wind chime near it to keep the chi moving and to balance the water energy with an earth element. Such cures will keep your business success from going down the drain.

If you want extra protection and chi activation, hang a small mirror on the outside of your bathroom door facing outward. The Chinese prefer a window in each bathroom for ventilation purposes, but if you don't have any windows in a bathroom, you can use mirrors in their place around the room and above the toilet.

One last word about toilets: If they are backed up, you will likely be backed up. Since the bathroom is in part an extension of your bodily "flow," you'll want it to be in the best working order possible at all times. You don't want it to overflow, keep running, or become blocked.

Scenes from a Stress Junkie's Bathroom

Bathrooms can suffer from the same "blocked chi" feeling as cluttered kitchens, offices, or garages, and they can be a major source of turmoil, especially for the stress junkies out there. You can probably tell a stress junkie when you see one: He or she is always "on," always living on the edge of several simultaneous deadlines. Here are some other telltale signs:

- **The bathroom décor is sloppy and haphazard.** Nothing seems to match—or even coordinate well—in the stress addict's bathroom. Pictures, towels, and accessories aren't even close to the same color family or in the same style. A Martha Stewart nightmare!

- **Abundance of unrelated items in the bathroom.** Stress junkies try to pack so much into their days, that there is little time set aside for a relaxing bath. So, they stack piles of unread magazines or books near the toilet or tub. This way, they reason, they can read while bathing or, well, you know. These are the same folks who will jump into a "relaxing" bath with a twenty-ounce soda filled with sugar and caffeine, and wonder why it's so hard to unwind at night!

- **Clutter everywhere.** The stress addict is 100 times more likely to have dirty towels piled on the back of the door or on the floor, with dirty clothes thrown in, too. On the countertops, you'll find scads of near-empty toiletries and razors that should've been pitched years ago. Don't even look in the cupboards—you can imagine. The stress addict is too busy to keep up with clutter—the cleanup will happen someday. Except, with stress addicts, someday never seems to come.

- **Dust and dirt abound.** Remember, the whole purpose of the bathroom is cleanliness. The stress addict more than likely has dried flowers with cobwebs in the bathroom, soap dishes so full of residue you could probably carve out another bar, or dust and stains or spots that were never wiped up.

If you are a stress addict or know one, the best thing you can do is apply feng shui to the bathroom, then create an oasis for total relaxation (see "Creating a Spa Oasis" below). Not only will you notice a marked difference in the flow of positive energy in and beyond the bathroom, but you'll also notice that greater wealth abounds. Be sure to do a space clearing ceremony after you clear all the clutter—you'll want to start the feng shui process with a clean slate!

Creating a Spa Oasis

Aside from being a place of cleanliness, your bathroom can be a sanctuary for relaxation and renewal. But how do you create a spalike atmosphere and still follow the principles of good feng shui?

Just as you did with the kitchen, you need to appeal to all senses, mixing your "personal indulgences" with the five elements in a balanced, yin-yang way that makes for a winning combination of nature and nurture.

The Peaceful Retreat

Creating a "no stress" zone in your bathroom can be done in a weekend—but if the thought of a complete overhaul creates more stress than it would seem to relieve, do it in small bits and pieces, one piece at a time. Each time you add something new, it will feel like a new experience—one step closer to the new, totally balanced you!

Before you start to create a bathroom that offers peaceful retreat and restful relaxation, be sure to clear the clutter and clean the bathroom.

You should also do a space clearing before every spa experience to maximize the health and well-being of your time alone.

Keeping the space clean and visually appealing will appeal to your sense of sight, as will good lighting and soft, curved shapes in your bathroom versus dark, angular areas.

Air the room out regularly by opening a window whenever you can, or by circulating the ceiling fan after each use of the bathroom. Fresh air is important to your health and also to the cleanliness of the bathroom. Opening the window also brings in a nice breeze while you are having your luxury bath—and simple, natural pleasures like this are truly wonderful and soothing.

Soothe the Senses

Set the mood with some quiet, meditative music. Consider anything by Yanni, a *Meditations on the Wind* CD, Chinese bamboo flute music (which brings in the wealth-luck symbol of bamboo for a nice feng shui complement), or Ray Lynch's *Deep Breakfast*. Whatever your musical preference, you should choose something that is reflective, soft, and uniquely you to appeal to your personal sense of sound.

Enhance smell in the bath by adding mineral sea salts, bath-oil beads, bubble bath, or potpourri. Here are some other "scent-illating" suggestions:

- **Apply the basics of good aromatherapy.** If you are feeling depressed or anxious, use bergamot or geranium scent. Lavender is good for insomnia, and peppermint and orange help boost energy. For particularly rough days, use chamomile, lemon balm, or ylang-ylang. Violet scent helps meditation. Milk baths can also be soothing. Essential oils are available at most health food stores and can be used sparingly in a warm bathtub to enhance scent. Remember, it doesn't take more than a few drops!
- **Cleanse your body and your soul.** Mineral sea salts are the absolute best for a total cleansing, both inside and out. You can use Epsom salts as a

substitute if you aren't near a health food store. Dissolve the salts (about a pound of them) in warm bathwater; then sit back and relax for half an hour. You will be amazed at how good this will make you feel. There's a reason people have used sea salts for thousands of years!

- **Use scented candles to enhance the senses of both smell and sight.** Candles offer wonderful aromas while being visually appealing—use colors that are significant to you. Be sure to use only pure and natural scents (with essential oils), as these are the strongest elements.

- **Inhale your scents, but don't forget to exhale them, too.** Zen wisdom says that each breath draws in new energy, while each exhale cleanses the body of toxins. Remember this balance when you are meditating in your luxury bath—it's the best place for you to practice the meditative art of good breathing.

The sense of touch can be enhanced in the spa experience when you use oil beads (which soften the skin) or loofah scrubs (which loosen and remove dead skin). Removing dead skin is crucial to good feng shui care of the body, since dead things create stagnant chi. Try a fruit (like apricot) scrub once every two days or so to exfoliate; it really helps your skin feel fresh, smooth, and young if you make it part of a regular routine.

QUESTIONS?

How can you pamper yourself if you don't have a tub?
If you still want to reap the benefits of the sea salt scrub, moisten your body in the shower, then scrub with the salt, just as you would with a loofah. Rinse off with cool water, and you will feel awake and alive again!

You can also massage the muscles on your face, neck, arms, legs, and feet while you are enjoying your spa bath. This will stimulate circulation, making your body tingle with rejuvenation. When you leave the "sacred space" of your tub, pat yourself dry with soft, fluffy towels in relaxing hues of blue and green. Don't forget moisturizer as a soothing finishing touch!

To complete your total feng shui spa experience, you need to appeal to your sense of taste. Make yourself a fruit smoothie or a nice big glass of water with a lemon or lime twist. You'll want to replace the precious water that escaped your body via your pores. Fruit drinks are especially good; not only do they provide critical vitamins and minerals, but they also restore the inner balance of your water element with fruit that is from the earth (earth element).

E-WISDOM

Speaking of Zen experiences, try practicing the art of meditation while immersed in the water element known as your tub. Your bathtub can be a place for cleansing, but it can also be a place for pondering the Universe.

A final note on the feng shui spa for those who have children: If you have highly energetic children (as many do), you can encourage them to take luxury baths complete with soft scents; dimmed lights (candles would be dangerous for smaller children); and soft, pleasing music. Be sure to watch your children at all times. After a special luxury bath, your children should be fully relaxed and ready for a good night's sleep. They're also better behaved the next day!

Pulling It All Together

As you feng shui your bathroom, the two most important considerations are the position of the toilet and the appearance of cleanliness in the room. Always begin your process in this room with a clutter removal and space clearing to "clean" the stagnant air and get the chi moving again in the room. The clearing will greatly improve the way you feel when you are in the room, and it will also keep your finances and general well-being in perfect flow with the Universe.

When you are finished applying feng shui to your bathroom sanctuary, give thanks for your peaceful oasis, and for a place to cleanse your body and soul on a daily basis.

Are You Draining Your Resources?

For such a small room, the bathroom requires understanding and implementation of many elements to maintain balance and healthy chi. Test your knowledge of bathroom feng shui with a quick quiz:

1. Why might it be bad feng shui to have double sinks, showers, and toilets?
2. If you're building a new home, why should you avoid placing the bathroom in the center of the bagua?
3. Why is it best if your bathroom faces north?
4. Why should you avoid having lots of bright, vivid colors in your bathroom?
5. Why is cleanliness so important in your bathroom?
6. Why should the toilet seat be left down and leaky faucets be fixed as soon as possible?
7. What position is best for bathroom mirrors?
8. Why should you keep your medicine chests and cabinets free of clutter?
9. Why shouldn't your bathroom door face the kitchen?
10. What can you do to make your bathroom a haven of relaxation?

Answers

1. Too much water can drain your financial and spiritual resources. The chi is likely to be held in rather than allowed to flow freely in and out.
2. Because that's the health corner of your home. It's best to avoid having the bathroom in the wealth and health corners of the bagua to keep from draining finances and from feeling drained physically!
3. Because that direction's corresponding element in feng shui is water.
4. Too much color makes a bathroom appear unsanitary, and bright colors are exciting. You want your bathroom to be a place of peace and relaxation.

Answers, *continued*

5. A clean bathroom says something about your personal cleanliness and also is appropriate for a space in which you and your loved ones go to cleanse yourselves inside and out.

6. A toilet lid that stays up allows your wealth to go down the drain! The same with leaky faucets.

7. They work best if flush with the wall, rather than protruding and multifunctional.

8. To enhance the free flow of chi. Like other rooms of your house, clutter in bathrooms impedes positive energy flow.

9. Because guests are embarrassed about going into a bathroom that is so close to an area in which you are working with food and entertaining. They are therefore less likely to use it even when they need it, making their stay shorter and less comfortable for them.

10. Try bath oils and salts, aromatic candles and soaps, fluffy towels, quiet colors, and soft music. Scents, textures, and even flavors of delicious drinks can create a spalike atmosphere.

Results

- 1–3 correct answers: It's a good thing that you are reading this book! You will find the information herein essential in improving your bathroom's feng shui.

- 4–6 correct answers: Your bathroom is a fairly comfortable and healthy space, with just a few more adjustments needed to make it ideal.

- 7–10 correct answers: Your bathroom rules! Family and guests probably regard it as an oasis of health and relaxation. It projects an image of you as clean, financially sound, and centered.

CHAPTER 9

Bed Peace: The Feng Shui of Sleep

W hen you were small, you couldn't sleep because there were monsters under your bed. Now, they're in the clutter under your bed, atop your dresser, and in your closet. They are not the scary bed creatures from your childhood, but they prevent the flow of healing energy that can help you achieve a rewarding love, life, and a good night's sleep.

Placement of Your Bedroom

Unless you are building your home from scratch, you obviously did not have anything to do with where your bedroom was placed. Chances are that when you bought or rented your home, you didn't think about feng shui or even know about it. The questions of which direction it faces in and where it is in relation to other rooms or doors or bathrooms did not concern you. If, after you learn a bit more about ideal placement, these aspects do begin to concern you, don't lose sleep over it! There is usually a remedy that will allow you to get a good night's sleep.

Sleep Tight

Contrary to what many people think, a small room is best because the energy is contained, so long as the room is not filled with clutter. The best location for your room is far away from the front door of your home, where so much energy flows through.

E-WISDOM

A bedroom is for sleeping. That is its main purpose.
—Feng shui wisdom

If insomnia is a problem for you, "west is best" for the direction in which you should face, because that's where the sun sets. However, if you find it easy to fall asleep but difficult to wake up, try facing east. The direction of the sun, rising or setting, will help you determine what works best for you. Room color can help offset too much or too little sunlight, as well.

Tossing and Turning

If you slip into dreamland almost as soon as your head hits the pillow, you probably can move on to another section of this book. But if you're not finding a smooth transition from wakefulness to dreamland, it could be because your bedroom feng shui is closer to a nightmare than a dream. The following checklist might help.

1. The foot of your bed should not be facing the door—the so-called death position. Nor should your bed be parallel with the doorway. It should be positioned so that you can see the doorway, however.

2. Eliminate mirrors. There are some exceptions to this rule, but, in general, mirrors displace the energy in your room and impede astral travel—your soul's overnight adventures.

3. Get rid of the clutter! Having remnants of your day, your work, and other aspects of your wakeful life scattered about your floor, hiding under your bed, and covering the surfaces of your dresser and any other furnishings impedes chi and your sleep.

4. Try not to sleep directly under the bathroom on a floor above you. Being close to plumbing tends to drain chi.

5. Have calm, soothing colors on your walls, floor, and furnishings.

6. Keep electronics out of the bedroom as much as possible to avoid the constant flow of energetic electrical current while you're trying to catch some *ZZZ*s.

7. Put only soft, comfortable sheets and blankets on your bed, and avoid using dead animal skins. No bearskin rugs on the floor! Dead animals in a room are very bad for chi.

8. Keep your work area in another room, or cover it up when you sleep. Work and sleep just don't mix—and you don't want one of those frustrating dreams in which you're at work, only to wake up from your restless sleep and actually have to go there!

Rest Easy

Safety and privacy in your bedroom are important to restful sleep, too. A bedroom that is too open to the rest of the house may be disquieting. If you must sleep in a space that otherwise lacks privacy, such as a living room, you should try to define the sleeping area clearly and protect it with a piece of furniture such as a bookcase or, perhaps, a tall screen.

Remember, too, that your bedroom should offer a contrast to your hectic, daily life.

Mirror, Mirror . . .

Your bedroom should reflect your personal style, but mirrors should not reflect you—or you and your spouse or lover—in your bedroom. Mirrors displace the energy in your room, affecting your sleep, and even could draw a third party into your romantic relationship. Mirrors over the bed are especially bad for that reason!

Also, not only might you be startled by your own movements in a mirror if you should get up in the middle of the night, but it's thought that each night, as we sleep, our souls travel through space and time. As they begin their journey, they, too, may be jarred by reflections in a mirror, including those of anything that is less than aesthetically pleasing in the room.

 **SSENTIALS**

The advantages of mirrors in interior decorating—opening up space and making a room appear larger and brighter—are serious disadvantages in the bedroom for those same reasons.

A mirror opposite the door of your bedroom is a bad idea, too, because it will reflect energy back toward the entrance, interrupting the energy flow of your room. Exceptions to the no-mirrors rule are:

- If you cannot avoid having your back to the door, then a mirror on the opposite wall allows you to see anyone coming into your room. But use only one mirror, preferably circular, which facilitates a blending of energies.
- If your bed is directly under ceiling beams or a sloping ceiling, which disrupts or suppresses energy flow, then a mirror facing upward can help.
- If you use a mirror to reflect scenery from outside into your bedroom.

If you cannot simply remove the mirrors in your bedroom, you might consider covering them, such as with drapery or fabric art. If you do so, though, remember to use fabric of a muted shade because bright colors are stimulating and can disturb your sleep.

Bedtime or Bedlam?

Where should your bed be? Let's first talk about where it should *not* be. Your bed should not be facing a doorway, with the foot of the bed toward the door. This is viewed as the death position in many cultures and is highly unlucky. Your bed should also not be aligned with the door because you should be able to see anyone coming through the doorway. Also, this parallel position will create a disruption in energy flow that could disturb your sleep.

E-WISDOM

> Placing your bed against a window is not a good idea either, since the chi will flow too quickly out of the room.

Another inauspicious location for a bed is under a beam, sloping ceiling, ceiling fan, bright light, or overhanging shelf or cupboard. All of these things disturb or suppress energy flow. Don't put your mattress on the floor, either, because that causes disturbed sleep and will literally hold you down from achieving your dreams. In your bedroom, you should seek to elevate yourself!

More caveats:

- If possible, you should not sleep on a bed that was owned by someone else because beds absorb a person's energy, and chances are, you do not know whether the energy of the previous owner was good.
- Don't sleep in a metal-framed bed. Not only is metal cold, it will also enhance the electromagnetic energy of electrical appliances in your home, which could prevent a restful night's sleep. Speaking of currents, unplug as many of your electrical appliances in your room at night as you can to cut off the constant flow of electricity through the wiring.
- Don't sleep in a room directly below a toilet on the floor above, and if there is no door between your bedroom and bathroom, use something to separate the rooms. Bathrooms are believed to be "draining," literally, of your energy.

- If you are a couple who values your relationship, it's recommended that you not sleep in a king-sized bed, which is too large and can have the same effect as sleeping separately.

You should have a solid headboard (but not one shaped like a headstone). Use a canopy to separate your bed from what's over it if your bed is under a sloping ceiling, structural beam, or toilet on the floor above. Place the bed diagonally opposite the doorway to your bedroom, in a corner, so that you will see the door without directly facing it. Being able to see the doorway provides added security, which facilitates sleep. The idea is to be out of alignment with the energy flowing through the doorway while still keeping the doorway in sight.

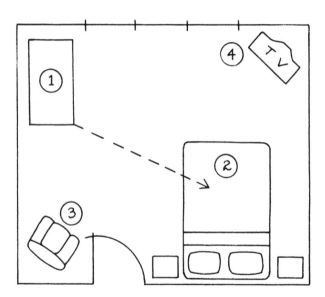

FIGURE 9-1: Feng Shui Nightmare
In this arrangement, 1. The dresser (or bureau) is shooting poison arrows at the bed. 2. The bed itself is in a very vulnerable position, as the people in it cannot see much of anything, least of all the door. 3. The chair behind the door is probably not used for its intended purpose, but rather gathers discarded clothing, contributing to clutter and stagnant chi. 4. The television is placed at a soft angle, which is okay, but it allows the television to give off electrical energy, which can disturb sleep.

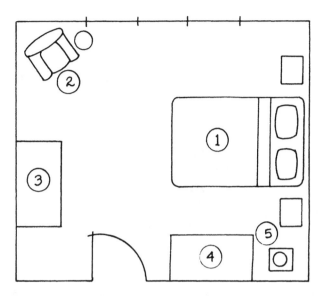

FIGURE 9-2: Feng Shui Dream
1. The bed's new location is much more auspicious, nestled between the children and relationship corners. It also has a view of the door. 2. With the chair in the corner near a window, one may be more inclined to sit and read in it. 3. Shelves, or an armoire, along that same wall (your knowledge/health areas) can hold your books, family photographs, and even your television (closing it off when it's not in use). 4. The dresser is now in the helpful people corner—helping you stay organized and clutter-free. 5. A mobile, or small piece of sculpture, in the corner next to the dresser will keep the chi from getting trapped next to the bed.

The Clutter Monster under the Bed

Many people have a tendency to allow their bedrooms to become filled with stuff. They rationalize that any guests who visit them will be highly unlikely to see their bedrooms, so why not throw all of those old boxes and magazines underneath the bed? It's that kind of thinking that can keep you up at night!

For the best possible energy flow and a good night's sleep, you really do want a room that is free of clutter. For instance, clothing that retains energy from your daily life should be put away. The space under your bed should be just that—space: no storage boxes or fuzzy bedroom slippers, no snack food or dishes. No clutter of any kind. Also, except for the reasons noted earlier, there should be no mirrors in your bedroom, and few, if any, knickknacks. No electrical appliances, including television sets, radios, stereos, computers, hair curling sets, or hair dryers. No exercise equipment, and absolutely no work desk!

ESSENTIALS

If you must have a workspace (like a desk or computer) in your bedroom, just be sure to cover the work area at night. Hide your computer, for instance.

Try to reduce the amount of *things* you have, from the menagerie of glass animals to the jungle of real or artificial plants. In fact, living plants in your room at night are a bad idea, anyway. Nighttime is when plants give off carbon dioxide and take in oxygen, just the reverse of the process during the daytime.

Too many pictures on the walls, piles of books and magazines on the chairs and floor, and similar clutter will block the flow of natural energy and prevent you from achieving the best possible night's sleep. Even very large bedrooms should be sparsely furnished. Don't feel compelled to fill every inch of space, unless you truly enjoy insomnia.

Eliminating clutter doesn't mean you have to eliminate the things you enjoy. Without banishing books from your bedroom, for example, find a way to accommodate them and enhance the energy flow that induces sleep. Just place a pyramid-shaped bookcase in the wisdom corner of your bedroom. The books will be much more neatly arranged, and the shelf's pyramid shape works nicely because it is an ancient symbol of higher knowledge.

Watch Your Tone

First and foremost, your bedroom is a place to rest your body, mind, and spirit. Be mindful of your decorative elements and their sensory impact. Calm colors, soothing fabrics, and subdued lighting will help you release the stresses of your day and prepare you for the sleep your body needs.

FIGURE 9-3: Mindful Space
Make corners cozy by adding lots of round design elements, including a mirror to bring the rest of the room in. The subdued color of the wall is soothing and complements the wood flooring.

Color Me Sleepy

Colors can do a lot to enhance your bedroom, but they can cause disturbance, too. Be especially color conscious if you have difficulty sleeping. For instance, bright red is a great color for a fire engine, but not for your bedroom. Just as it startles and wakes up drivers and pedestrians, who rightly associate the color with emergencies and adrenaline, it will keep you awake at night.

Instead of using bright or glossy white, try off-white, like eggshell or cream. Soft yellow, for instance, is considered an excellent color for a bedroom and is very conducive to a good night's rest. Gentle, warm colors, like some shades of pink, are exceptionally soothing. Who can stay awake for long while gazing at a soft nutmeg or soft, but rich, apricot?

Very strong colors, including deep purple, red, and orange, are too strong for a relaxing bedroom. Green and blue are cool colors, better off in the bathroom or elsewhere in the home, and probably should be saved for accent, rather than serving as the dominant color scheme. Light green is preferable to dark, and dark blue, like the color of deep bodies of water, should be avoided.

Vivid colors of any hue will interfere with a restful night's sleep. Similarly, avoid the day-brightness of solid white; use it sparingly.

The same is true for patterns. Busy wallpaper and/or carpet will keep you buzzing all night long. Also avoid the skins of dead animals in your bed-room, including sheep or leopard skin. Solid, soft colors, fabrics, and textures, preferably of natural materials, are your allies in winning a nice, long rest.

Night Lighting

It's generally recommended that overhead lighting not be used in a bedroom because of the intensity of light that will shine over your bed. Remember, too, that light is energy and therefore must be taken into account when the switch is on.

It is generally best to keep computers and other electrical devices out of the bedroom if you want peaceful sleep. Electricity is forced energy, and can interfere with good sleep.

Even when the lights are off, however, electrical current continues along its merry way, affecting the energy flow in your bedroom and, ultimately, your ability to sleep. Rather than an overhead light—and that includes single or dual reading lamps that some bedrooms feature—try standing lamps or table lamps, off to the side, not shining over your bed.

Room for Romance

Not all of your time in bed is spent sleeping, of course. And if you're very fortunate, you have a wonderful, loving partner with whom to explore the other possibilities. If you would like such a partner but do not presently have one, don't despair—feng shui can help you in the romance department, too. All it takes is a little planning in your furniture purchases and arrangement, as well as your bedroom décor, and you can attract the relationship you most desire.

Starting Over

If you have recently ended a long-term relationship, and you can afford to do it, consider buying a new mattress. A bed, like other furnishings, absorbs the energy of the people who sleep in it, and you don't want any "old business" casting a shadow over your new relationship.

Throw away the holdover, sentimental pieces from your past relationship(s)—the theater or concert stubs and programs, old pictures, small gifts, souvenirs of trips together, et cetera—but if you can't part with them altogether, at least keep them out of your relationship area.

E-WISDOM

The end of a relationship is the perfect time for a clearing. Clear your space, certainly, but also consider freshening up or changing other elements of your bedroom. Your intentions will be personal, but they should also aim to change and improve the energy flow.

You want to attract a new person and a new way of relating to that person. After all, if your old habits were effective, you wouldn't be looking for someone new!

Art Inspires Life

In your bedroom, your artwork should depict happy, loving couples, not wistful-looking men or women sitting all alone. Nor is it a good idea to have pictures of lonely looking, wave-battered cliffs, or isolated islands or rocks surrounded by a cold, blue sea and ominous, gray skies.

You should have pairs of objects in your relationship bagua, located in the right-hand corner of the room as you are looking into the room from the doorway. For instance, a picture of a loving couple (or pair of birds), a pair of red candles, or two heart-shaped boxes. Some consultants suggest throwing sexy red lingerie into the corner and, in this particular area of the bedroom, hanging a round mirror to keep the energy moving.

E-WISDOM

> Erotic art is appropriate in the bedroom, but refrain from displaying it in public areas of your house.

Be sure to keep your relationship corner clean—no dirty laundry, cobwebs, or dust bunnies. Red is the color of passion, and so some red in your relationship corner is desirable, even though you don't want that to be the color of your whole room. Symbols of romance and togetherness, such as hearts or a pair of doves or lovebirds, are ideal in that corner, especially since these birds mate for life.

Incorporating elements of feng shui works not only for attracting a new relationship, but also for enhancing one you have. Just keep your intention clear and positive, and don't place dried or wilted plants or flower arrangements in your relationship corner, since they represent death and decomposition (and you don't want these things to happen to your relationship!).

Build It Anyway

Beyond your relationship corner, your entire bedroom should be set up for two, even if one is still your loneliest number. You should have two nightstands, one on either side of the bed, for instance, and a double or queen-sized bed, rather than a twin bed, which screams, "I'm still single!"

Make your bedroom appear welcoming to a special someone who might want to spend some time there with you. It should offer an obvious place for this person to put his or her clothing and other personal items without feeling too awkward about it. The room should, in other words, look like you were expecting company rather than building a private fortress or retreat.

Some lighter, brighter, more whimsical furnishings or decorative pieces are helpful, too, because a loving relationship includes lightheartedness and fun. Avoid having a television, computer, VCR, and DVD, as well as workspace, in your bedroom, because these will distract and detract from your relationship as well as disrupt the energy flow of your room. The only way around this in feng shui is to keep these electrical items tucked away in a small entertainment cabinet with cupboard doors that close when the item is not being used (i.e., when you are sleeping). To get the best sleep possible, be sure to turn all of these things off when you feel yourself nodding off to dreamland.

Back to Décor

In keeping with the general advice about bedroom colors, take inventory of yours. Blues connote isolation, for instance. Warm earth colors, on the other hand, encourage closeness. In addition to having pairs of furnishings, you will want to achieve balance throughout the bedroom. Women whose rooms are ultrafeminine should consider adding some neutral or more masculine décor, and vice versa, to allow for a mix of yin and yang, which is ideal in relationships.

Mirrors over the bed invite trouble into a relationship, possibly even attracting a third party.

Balance larger, heavier furnishings with some smaller, lighter ones. Arrangement of the bed and other furniture should be conducive to good energy flow, and mirrors, except maybe for a small one in your relationship corner, should be avoided—especially over the bed.

Assess whether all areas of your room are open to the touch of another person, or are you still, in some way, holding back by guarding some precious items that you think of as being for you, alone? Ideally, the person you hope to attract into your life, and your bedroom, will eventually add some touches of his or her own, but the attitude and energy established by you before that point are critical.

Sexy Feng Shui

All right, so you never thought of your furniture arrangement as being especially sexy. But it can be—or, at least, *you* can be—once you have made the necessary adjustments to your bedroom. Sexual energy will be flowing like crazy then, and your only problem will be finding the time for all those men or women who will want to get to know you a little better.

Bed Position

Do not sleep with your feet facing the door. The death, or coffin, position, as it is known, is symbolically highly unlucky. If you pay attention to chakra points, you will also know that the ones in your feet will be drained as you sleep if your feet are facing the door.

E-WISDOM

Instead of placing your bed against a wall, keep the space free on both sides of the bed for ideal energy flow. As noted elsewhere in this chapter, the space should be free under the bed, as well.

You want the bed to point toward a wall in such a way that you still are in view of the doorway (preventing vulnerability), but not directly in line with it. This is also known as the emperor's position (regardless of whether you're in a king-sized bed!). Keeping all of your energy intact can only improve your love life, right? Bedrooms are good places for amazing feats—not deflating feet.

What's Your Frequency?

No, not "how often do you 'do it,'" but, in what year were you born and how are your home and bedroom situated? If they are resting in a direction that puts you in a frequency that conflicts with the one for the year in which you were born, or if your home is on a slope in which left and right sides are uneven, negatively affecting yin and yang, you might have some trouble dating and mating.

When yin and yang lack harmony, they destroy each other. If something is yin, therefore, it must face in that direction. I'd advise seeking out a feng shui expert who may use intuition or take compass readings (using a luo pan or geomancer's compass) to determine possible disturbances in energy flow, if you suspect this is a problem.

In general, though, it's best to have your bedroom in the back of the house and to pay close attention to what you place in your relationship corner, the far right corner as you face the room from the doorway. Think red, hearts, candles, pairs of objects, pictures of happy couples, sexy lingerie, perfume, love poetry, and erotica. That's the corner that will help you turn the corner in your love life, so treat it well!

A Sensual Experience

Mood music, aromatic candles, soft lighting, soft colors, and soft fabrics all contribute to a sexier bedroom, as well. The art of seduction lies in elements that are soothing and sensual, not loud and brassy.

It also helps to relocate the family reunion from the bedroom to another room in the house. That is, remove pictures of your mom and dad, your kids and siblings from your bedroom walls. Who can feel sexy and uninhibited with these eyes on them? You might as well douse yourself with cold water and throw on some flannel!

QUESTIONS?

How can using feng shui improve romance?
If you want to have more love in your life, consider buying a pair of lovebirds and positioning them in the upper right-hand corner of your living room. What is more mindful than putting a pair of birds that mate for life in your relationship corner?

Sleeping Like a Feng-Shui Baby

Assuming that you have been wildly successful in your efforts to establish a loving relationship with a partner, and that you now are blessed with children, you will need to address feng shui in their bedrooms, too. When it comes to arranging and decorating infants' and young children's rooms, many of the "adult room" feng shui principles still apply. However, children are not adults, so, naturally, there are some big differences. There's more about feng shui and children in Chapter 10.

Keep It Simple

It is not uncommon for parents—especially first-time parents—to over-decorate. Preparing for baby's arrival is fun and exciting, but try not to overdo it or concern yourself too much with interior design trends. For infants and small children, simplicity and muted colors, especially pastels and warm, gentle earth tones, plus soft textures in bedding and furnishings, are best for encouraging a restful state.

Vibrant colors, wall hangings, designs, and toys will all keep the child awake and active and may even overstimulate him or her, leading to crankiness.

Try to avoid hanging too many mobiles or other exciting toys from the ceiling. Keep it simple—one or two gentle ones would do it. The rest of the house can wake up the child with brighter colors, a variety of textures, and bright sunlight, but the bedroom should, like yours, be quiet, peaceful, and calm in all ways. It's best to have interesting things, such as textures and toys, on the floor, where children can explore them when they are awake. Low furnishings with soft, rounded edges are best.

Position and Placement

As with your room, the foot of the bed should not face the door to the room or be placed under a window. And it's best if the door to the child's room does not open directly onto the stair landing or face a bathroom. Try to avoid placing the child's bed under sloping ceilings, skylights, structural beams, and anything, such as a bookshelf, that might overhang the bed. Not only will items over the bed interrupt the chi, but they pose a safety hazard, as well.

Feng Shui Grows Up

The single biggest problem in most kids' and teenagers' rooms is clutter. Toys need containers. Children's rooms should be kept free of clutter, just like their parents' rooms, to permit better energy flow. Make cleanup fun with imaginative toy boxes, clothing hooks, and other kinds of organizers that are cheerful and whimsical so kids want to keep things neat, or at least are a little less averse to the idea!

Furnishings that are sized appropriately for children, and that can be augmented or replaced as they grow, will help them feel comfortable and welcome in their own home. Make sure that they can see their door from their bed to heighten their sense of security. Furniture should have rounded edges and curving lines, to avoid a feeling of rigidity as they grow.

E-WISDOM

Although bunk beds are practical, they are not good feng shui. The claustrophobic feeling of the lower bed, and the closeness to the ceiling of the upper bed, will stifle both occupants.

Remember to allow plenty of space for playing. Abstract art is beyond the comprehension of younger children, so provide art that is simple and that stimulates imagination. Storybook characters, or scenes of nature or the stars, will spark their creativity. Wall paintings can be a beautiful and comforting way of capturing a child's imagination or making him or her feel secure. Guardian angels or even protective animals such as friendly looking dogs help make children feel watched over. Encourage them to hang up their own art, too!

Whenever possible, your children should have their own rooms because they need privacy and the space to express themselves in their own living space, especially if they are more than a few years apart.

ESSENTIALS

Cupboards and bookshelves should be tall, reflecting the growing child. Vertical stripes on drapes, linens, or other decor also enhance the feeling of growth.

Personalize It

Beyond the basic guidelines, nurture and accommodate your children's personalities in other specific ways.

- *Less-energetic children,* for instance, do better in larger, brighter rooms in which they can move around a bit, with some vibrant splashes of color on the walls, the bedding, or the furnishings to stimulate them.
- *Physically active children,* however, fare better in smaller bedrooms with quieter colors, where they cannot move around quite as freely. Especially helpful for these "Type-A" kids are construction toys, books, educational toys, and creative activities. Quiet games they can play in their rooms will allow their minds and imaginations to come into play as well.
- *Shy or anxious children* are better off in rooms that feel secure, without rough edges or harsh lighting, and with soft fabrics, warm colors, and soft window treatments. The bed should be placed well away from the windows and the door, for better energy flow and a feeling of security.

A small collection of stuffed animals (be mindful of clutter) and some soft music as part of the bedtime ritual provide security for all types of children. Remember to turn off the music as soon as you know they are comfortably asleep, since you don't want the electrical "noise" to interfere with their dreams! As added protection against nightmares, hang Native American dream catchers in their rooms to ward off any scary apparitions.

The Teen Challenge

Speaking of scary, teenagers are a different feng shui beast altogether. Specifically, your teens may favor black in their rooms—the outward manifestation of their inward growth and introspection (remember how deep that time seemed?). These are years of metamorphosis, and so the self-absorption expressed by the color black should be accommodated in some way, if not on the walls, then perhaps in some of the furnishings.

You may choose to accommodate your teen's preference by using black bedding, some black desk furniture, and some posters that are primarily black. Aromatic candles and incense contribute to self-awareness—if you are willing to allow your child to use them. Relative freedom to arrange or rearrange his or her living space is important to a teenager, who is on the verge of adulthood, even if the teenager's preferences do not conform to the rules of feng shui!

ALERT

Remember—with children of *any* age—to monitor and/or establish nonnegotiable ground rules regarding candles, incense, or any open flame. Setting a clear example yourself will help them establish safe habits that will last a long, healthy lifetime.

Ever-Growing Spirit

In general, children's rooms will need to change and grow as they do. Rearranged furnishings, different furnishings, and different décor will all be desirable as they grow and their needs change.

Children should be given the deciding vote in how their room will look. Although you probably will want to keep the walls, floors, and ceilings fairly calm to facilitate healthy sleep, allow your children some freedom in accessorizing through their bed linens, toys and toy containers, posters, and even some of their furnishings.

A little bit of autonomy will go a long way toward teaching children how to make decisions (a good skill for adulthood). They will also acquire a sense of taste all their own—equally important. The axiom about giving children both roots and wings is exemplified in how parents allow them to use their own, private living space—an excellent dress rehearsal for their lives once they leave the nest. And you can always paint over their walls after they leave!

Making sure your entire family gets a good night's rest isn't rocket science. All it takes is the same care, planning, and mindful attention to detail that you're using in all of the other areas of your home. The practice of feng shui in the bedroom is really the practice of creating the most restful, pleasing place to rejuvenate your body and soul. Make it a peaceful oasis!

CHAPTER 10

Feng Shui with Kids

Your children are miracles—but their rooms can be disaster areas. Whether or not you mean for it to happen, the toy-and-clothing pileup can quickly engulf your little miracle's room. Just as clutter impedes your life, it will make it harder for the real miracles in children's lives to happen.

Just Suppose . . .

You're exploring the role feng shui can play in your life. You're interested in putting its principles into practice. In your contemplative and mindful state, you walk past your child's room and are brought crashing down by a wall of chi. Are your kids' rooms a complete and total mess? Is there so much blocked chi in the room that it will take three hours to get them settled in for the night? Does the playroom look like an explosion went off in Toyland?

ESSENTIALS

Take a good, hard look at the kind of example you're setting for your kids, and make regular assessments of the chi in all of the rooms they "hang" in.

Many parents think the same thing about their own kids. Maybe they don't go softly to sleep at night. Maybe many parents have the same kind of nights—sitting at the top of the stairs, pulling their hair out, wondering, "Where did I go wrong? I read all the Dr. Spock books! This can't be happening to me!"

The Monster in the Closet

The two main problems (or opportunities, if you want to look at this in the Zen manner) with kids' rooms are clothing and clutter. Actually, these two are part of the same problem: an overabundance of all the things parents think children should have in order to have a fantastic childhood.

How do you know you have a problem with clutter in the kids' rooms? One sure sign is the telltale mountain of clothes that is piled on top of the dresser, and your child stands before it, unable to decide what to wear. When your child says, "I don't have anything to wear," what he or she really means is, "I have too many things to wear and can't make a decision." Having too many options is very cumbersome, especially to smaller children who just aren't equipped to deal with those kinds of choices yet.

Children really need only a few good outfits to wear—enough clothes for seven to ten days, maximum. Everything else will take up valuable space in the closets, until it begins to overflow and create monster piles everywhere else.

E-WISDOM

First and foremost, as with any other room in feng shui, your kids' rooms need to be clutter-free. Clutter (even too many clothes) can really disrupt the minds (and bodies) of your children, inhibiting their growth by holding down their energy.

Feng shui dictates that all things, including children's clothes, should be acquired and used as they are needed, and never hoarded. Hoarding leads to blocked or buried chi; if you have too much stuff, inevitably some of it will never be used. Uselessness is not conducive to good chi, is it?

Kids' Cleanup Checklist

Okay, so *kids* and *cleanup* seem like mutually exclusive terms. But cleaner, neater kids' play areas and bedrooms *can* be achieved by using some of the same psychology we would use on a pack-rat roommate or spouse.

1. Approach your child in a friendly, congenial manner and ask if he or she would like some help in putting things away. Sometimes, children—especially younger children—are reluctant to work alone because the task seems so overwhelming. But if you pitch in, even a little bit, the child's enthusiasm often grows. Be sure that you're not doing all the work, though. The lion's share should still be your child's!

2. If you don't think your child uses or plays with some items anymore, don't just start putting them away or, worse, throwing them away or threatening to do so. Like anyone else, kids are fiercely protective of their things. Respect your child's need for some privacy and ownership.

3. Try to get your child to see the logic in getting rid of unused items by asking some simple questions: "Is this still serving you? Does it bring you joy or have special meaning? If so, we can find a special

place for it. If not, maybe we can donate it so that someone else can use it." Children often respond to the image of other, less fortunate, children who might derive some pleasure from the items that they, themselves, no longer use.

4. Take the lead by becoming a positive example. When you clear your own clutter or "toys," you may inspire your children to do the same. Of course, items for donation must have all their parts and be in good, working condition. You don't want to give your children the notion that it's all right to pass on unusable junk to charity.

5. Create opportunities for storage solutions by placing a "collection container" in the child's playroom and/or bedroom. If there is a designated place for clutter collection, the clutter will become part of a more organized thought process—the first step in elimination! Colorful toy boxes with safety lids that can't shut on the child if he or she should try to hide inside them are ideal. Hampers work, too.

You'll want to be positive, not punitive. Try to make cleanup less like punishment and more like fun. For example, start a race, with some small prize such as an extra bedtime story for the person who puts away the most items the fastest.

It is important that you not interfere too much with your child's process of getting rid of unused items, especially if the child seems reluctant. Inspire your child by setting a good example of a person who is free of the binding nature of "too many things." You don't want to be the "Do as I say, not as I do" parent, but a positive role model.

Once upon a Time

Storytime can be one of the best times to bond with your little miracles, but it can also be an enlightening experience for them if their books are stored in the best location for learning.

Of course, the knowledge corner of the bagua is the ideal location for a small bookshelf full of tall tales and wonderful stories—but if that's where the bed is, then use this location to read stories that teach your kids something.

Storage

In terms of storage, books for fun and creativity can be grouped and shelved right along with books for learning and growth. Where you can, try to use classic stories as a launchpad for mini-lessons on feng shui. For instance, you could talk about the three little pigs' trying to find a home with good chi, while trying to escape the bad chi of the big, bad wolf.

E-WISDOM

The knowledge corner can also be a good place to position your child's desk, since it is there that your child will be likely to read lots of good learning materials (including the dreaded homework!).

Be creative and have fun—that is the surest way to capture the interest and attention of your little wonders. Soon, you'll have them right there with you, putting down the toilet lids and hanging crystals all over the house. Make feng shui a positive activity full of learning opportunities, and you'll have happy, well-adjusted, and perfectly balanced kids!

Mindful Balance

One way to make sure the kids stay well balanced is to practice mindfulness and purpose in their rooms. Begin with making sure the bedroom is used for its rightful purpose, and that the activities of learning, sleeping, and healing are maximized.

Take all of the toys out of the bedroom and keep the books in their knowledge corner. You may notice right away that they instantly become more interested in learning. Take advantage of their enthusiasm and set up a little table to play "school."

Videos and Electronics

Can you imagine Glinda the Good Witch in *The Wizard of Oz* asking Dorothy whether she had good chi or bad? Wouldn't it be great if Dorothy and her friends had been on a feng shui journey, seeking the best flow of chi in the land?

If at all possible, designate a specific area of your home as an office/computer room, and keep the computers, TVs, and video games out of the bedroom. For example, consider an eight-year-old who would not relax enough to go to sleep at night. In the child's room, there were forty-eight movies stacked up next to a small combined TV/VCR unit. A Nintendo was connected to the TV, as well! This electronic playground, coupled with scads of books, toys, and clothes piled everywhere, was the real reason the child couldn't unwind at bedtime. Really, who could with all that interference with chi?

QUESTIONS?

Is it okay to have electronics in a child's room?
In feng shui, electronics and electrical items are best kept away from the bedroom—their constant current can greatly interfere with sleep, and that's not a situation you want with growing kids.

Ideally, kids' bedrooms are for sleeping and studying, and not for watching all-night TV when they should be in a peaceful dreamland that helps them grow and thrive. Remember, it is your spiritual duty as parents to teach your children how to create the spaces that will most benefit their growth, and rooms that serve their earthly purposes will always be the most auspicious gifts you can give them!

Getting Direction

Ideally, the best location for children's rooms is wherever there is sunlight. As flowers need sunlight to grow, so do children. Take a look at the yin and the yang of it all, first.

The Chinese believe that the birth order of a child is what helps determine the child's potential for success in life—and that the room should ideally have more yang influence than yin. In other words, the room should be full of life and potential, with mentally and visually enriching items.

Yang Opportunities

Consider the following yang additions to a child's room:

- Posters or colorful pictures on the walls
- Bright or colorful painted walls
- CD player or radio with plenty of learning-oriented tapes, stories, and songs

Be careful of things like poison arrows (sharp lines), most often seen in the form of pointed shelves, study tables, or bedposts. Minimize harsh edges by draping soft cloth around them (as you might with a canopy bed), or deflect them by placing round or curved furniture (such as an inflatable or soft, rounded chair) nearby.

Things to avoid in a child's room: open doors, thick or heavy furniture, clutter under the beds (or anywhere else), headboards that are directly below windows, and electrical equipment that stays on constantly.

Speaking of poison arrows . . . avoid sharp objects that depict any kind of war theme, including toys or pictures on the wall. To be able to sleep in peace, your children must also live in a peaceful room—that means no Ninja Turtles with swords, no Power Puff Girls punching anyone out, and definitely no play guns hanging on the walls. Keep these kinds of toys stored away to keep their negative energy from interfering with your children's study or sleeping time.

Braving the Elements

When it comes to kids' rooms, don't forget the five elements of feng shui. Balance them in your children's rooms just as you would anywhere else in your home—except here you'll want to be a little more mindful of safety issues.

For instance, if you have a curious three- or four-year-old, you might not want to put a Zen fountain in your child's room for fear of having a carpet full of rocks and water. But if you have a preteen who has trouble concentrating on homework, a Zen fountain may be just the thing to help settle his or her nerves and maintain focus. The water element is good for reflection.

E-WISDOM

Our children are the souls of our future. Nourish their minds and hearts with wisdom, love, and tenderness.

—African saying

Children can have specific elements associated with their Chinese birth sign, too (see the chart in Appendix C). Determine which element your child's year of birth corresponds to, then balance out that element with its opposite for maximum yin-yang effect.

Get Oriented

Now, on to location. You shouldn't locate the child's room in the center of the house or the back of the kitchen. Such locations are considered to be unfavorable in feng shui. A square or rectangular room works best for children. If two kids need to share a room, make sure they both have adequate and equal space, or there will be lots of arguments. Each child will also need to have something in the room that is uniquely his or hers in order to have a healthy spiritual attachment to the room.

According to Chinese thinking, the best locations for your child's bed or study table are:

- North for the middle son
- Northeast for the youngest son

- East for the eldest son
- Southeast for the eldest daughter
- South for the middle daughter
- West for the youngest daughter (or *mei-mei,* which is Chinese for "little sister")

Since the sunlight tends to come in through the east and southeast corners of your home, these are the best locations for your children's bedrooms. The west is also good, especially for hyperactive children, because the sun comes into this area of your home later in the day.

Face the Sun

East is favorable because it is associated with the dawning of the new day and the beginning of new growth and development. This energy is really very invigorating and encouraging to children, who need the promise of a new day in which to grow.

The chi energy in the southeast is a bit more calming than the east, although it, too, promotes lively activity. If you want smoother kids who are neither hyperactive nor totally lethargic, look to the southeast for placement of the bedroom. Western energy is quite settled and most auspicious for children who need lots of rest and a bedroom that is more of a peaceful retreat.

E-WISDOM

As a parent, you are your children's guide through life. It is your responsibility to help shape them, and to get them moving in the right direction in life. In essence, you are the director of their chi, since you help shape their lives.

If you cannot have your child's room in any of these sections of your home, you can tone down the bossy chi of a northern room by hanging a mirror that sends the dominant energy of the room back to yours— putting you back in control of the house, which, as parents, you should be. A simple feng shui cure will help you keep your rightful place as "the law" of the house.

Bagua for Kids

The bagua and its nine areas can be used in a child's room to create harmony, peace, and well-being, but you needn't get too worked up about making sure every single corner of the bagua is represented fully and completely in your child's room.

ESSENTIALS

Luckily, only a few areas of the bagua need specific concentration. For example, it's highly unlikely that your two-year-old is looking for a love relationship beyond Mommy or Daddy, so you needn't go to too much trouble in the marriage corner.

Start instilling a respect for ancestors early on by including old photos of yourself as a baby or of other family members in the family section of the room's bagua. Such mindful efforts are especially auspicious if you include pictures or former belongings of a namesake.

The health area of the room is in the center, so be sure it's open and clear for the best chances of your child staying healthy year-round. When your child has an illness, you might consider hanging a healing crystal in the center of the room. It may work as many wonders as a good antihistamine, without the drowsiness!

The knowledge corner, of course, is covered in the room's bagua by books or a study desk. If you use a nightlight (symbolic of fire, which corresponds to fame nicely) or even a mirror (if your child really wants to seem "bigger and stronger"), you will enhance the fame/reputation area, too.

E-WISDOM

If your child is afraid of the dark, use a natural flame nightlight on a high shelf in the room. Candles have calming energy and are safe as long as you are nearby to keep a watchful eye. Otherwise, purchase a plug-in nightlight that is red or that contains a picture of a fire element.

The main thing in using the bagua to enhance your child's room is to stay focused on the purpose of each corner—and think of creative ways to incorporate elements of each bagua in as many corners of the room as you can.

The Ideal Feng Shui Kids' Room

In the perfect feng shui kids' room, the lighting is reflected up to the ceiling and bounces off of it much like strong tree energy that lets the sun in and out of the room.

Toys, books, and clothing are stored neatly in boxes, which are stacked in a closet and not hidden under the bed, since stuff under the bed can lead to sleep disturbances. Make sure you keep the storage boxes within safe reach for kids, and make them partners in keeping the toys where they belong by scheduling a nightly toy cleanup. Staying on top of the clutter on a daily basis will eliminate it for sure.

ESSENTIALS

Make feng shui a game with your children: Offer a reward to the child who can remove the most clutter. Enlist the help of your children throughout your process, and teach them a respect for chi or "life energy."

Feng Shui Furnishings

The bed is placed in the room with the head facing north; if there are two beds, the beds are both facing the same direction to avoid trauma and sibling squabbles. The beds are covered in soft, comfy cushions with a few pillows or stuffed animals tossed in for added critter comfort.

The furniture in the room is rounded or curved, with few, if any, sharp, pointy edges (poison arrows). If the children face east when they sit at activity tables or desks, their chi is heightened by the warm energy of the sun. Furniture in bright colors is very stimulating to the minds of children.

Floors are best left in the grounding energy of natural wood, and can be softened by an area rug. If you want to add some interest to the room, you can do this with a brightly colored rug as opposed to a calming pastel.

Color Creatively

In the ideal feng shui kids' room, paint walls in harmonious, calming shades of blue and soft yellow. Consider hanging pictures of higher aspiration symbols (like mountains), or slow down the chi a bit with some fabric sculpture. Positive imagery should support and encourage your child to grow in a healthy manner.

Stimulate creativity by using bold color in unusual ways—perhaps hang a colorful picture of playing animals on a calm wall. Balance the calming yin colors (soft greens, pale blue or yellow) with invigorating yang ones (bright orange, red, or primary blue)—with the exception of the hyperactive child's room. Here, you'll want to balance out your child's extreme yang with extreme yin—lots of soft, pale colors that help keep the mind from racing. In terms of the wall and overall décor of the room, a lot is going to depend on the age of your child, along with the child's personality and interests.

QUESTIONS?

What colors help calm or soothe an overactive child?
If your child is hyperactive (or extreme yang), paint the walls a calming shade of yellow, which is also good for study and quiet, introspective yin activities. Avoid reds and bright primary colors in the bedroom, as they keep the child active and disrupt sleep.

Speaking of interest, mobiles can make a terrific addition to any feng shui process in a child's room, since they really get the chi moving in all directions. The best part is that a mobile doesn't necessarily have to be for infants alone—there are plenty of interesting ones for older kids, too!

For the younger set, the feng shui toy of choice is anything made of the wood element, since wood is strong and durable. But it's also earthy and nice to touch. Keep toys in plastic containers kept out of sight during sleep or study times.

The most important thing you can do in your child's room is create a sense of belonging and balance. You want to encourage activity and creativity, but you also want your child to get rest for growth, too. This yin-yang combination is a bit trickier to manage for children's rooms, but it is definitely not impossible! Keep moderating the energy as often as you can, and be sure to do regular space clearings in your kids' rooms to keep the "monsters" away!

Rec Rooms . . . Not "Wreck" Rooms

In your house, do you have a rec room, or a "wreck room," disorganized and full of clutter? When you first assess the room, you will realize something you haven't before: In trying so hard to create an exciting life for your kids, what you were really doing was filling their lives with too much blocked energy. In essence, the amount of *stuff* that has accumulated may be holding them back from their true potential.

Your rec room should not become a dumping ground for all the toys in the house. Nor should it be completely spare. A good balance in this room will include a small variety of stimulating toys, books, games, and videos to help your children expand their minds.

E-WISDOM

Remain mindful of the room's purpose, which is to entertain and stimulate your kids, not push them to overactivity and exhaustion, and you will have peace in your home.

If you have too much clutter in your rec room, why not donate some of it to a doctor's office for their waiting room, or to a battered women's shelter (where kids often stay as well)? Put the extra items to a healthier use in another space, and keep your own space for your kids' play area as open and inviting as possible.

Hittin' the Books

In China, education has a very high value in the lives of young children and their families. The Chinese believe that education is the only chance for their kids to escape poverty and move forward in their lives.

To create a study area that offers your kids the best opportunities for advancement in life, start with the furniture. Position the desk as you would in your own home office—with the child angled toward and facing the doorway, rather than with his or her back to it. If you can't position the desk any other way and the child's back is to the door, hang a mirror so that the child isn't made to feel vulnerable. If he or she is worried about who is coming up behind them, he or she may not be able to concentrate very well.

SSENTIALS

Play "Follow the Feng Shui Leader": Set the example so that your kids know that feng shui can improve all of your lives. If you tell the kids they can't have a TV in their room, don't sit up late at night watching yours until you fall asleep.

The chair needs to be free and clear, without sharp points that can cause negative energy. Even posters, pictures, or book covers with angry or hostile scenes can cause study disturbances. Position a few pictures that symbolize higher aspirations, such as mountain scenes. Or hang a crystal over the desk to keep chi circulating and ideas flowing.

Don't place your child's desk so that it faces a window, since a window and all the outside activity will diminish your child's attention span. If you want greater concentration on studies, you can also place a Buddha on the desk for focus and meaning. If your child is a preteen who gives you "attitude" when you try to place a Buddha, you can always substitute a modern-day equivalent sage—why not try a Yoda figurine? Hey, if it keeps them focused, that's the point, right?

Ideally, your child should be able to study in one room and sleep in another. This is not always practical, so when study time has to be conducted in the bedroom, be sure to bring closure when it's time to close the books and go to bed. Have your child place books in a book bag for school the next day and clear off the desk every night before turning out the lights. This will bring closure to the day's work and make you both feel ready and able to tackle the next day's offerings.

E-WISDOM

Do or do not, there is no try.

—Yoda, *Return of the Jedi*

Sleepy Time

How do you best get your children settled in for a quiet night's rest? Create a sensory experience that is conducive to good sleep (Chapter 9 will give you additional information, as well).

1. For starters, make sure there is no clutter under the bed. Dim the lights and create a routine around relaxation. Set the mood with a soft nightlight and some meditative music.
2. Enhance your child's sleep patterns by remembering to turn off the music or any other electrical device after the child is asleep. This will minimize any possible interference with your child's sleep and allow the child to reach the deep state of sleep that is necessary for growth and rejuvenation.
3. If your child has lots of sleep disturbances, look for clues in his or her surroundings. Are the walls painted bright colors? Is there too much going on in the room? Are there too many pictures that depict action versus rest?

Think about what the room is saying to you, all the while asking yourself if this room is really promoting peace. If it's not, you'll need to make some changes. One of the easiest changes you can make using feng shui principles is to paint the walls a soft, meditative color such as lavender or yellow, which are considered highly conducive to sleep.

Double-check the direction the bed faces. If your child has a difficult time sleeping, move the bed so that its head faces either north or west—both directions are quite conducive to a good night's sleep. Northeast is not a good direction, especially for children, because its harsh energy can antagonize kids and cause more tantrums.

E-WISDOM

Achieve good sleep by taking lots of things into consideration and maximizing them for the intended purpose, which is sweet dreams!

Finally, don't forget to use other areas of your home to invite peaceful sleep to your children's rooms. For instance, you can practice some yoga or Zen breathing exercises in the living room before bedtime, followed by a trip to the bathroom for a warm, relaxing luxury bath.

Room to Grow

In feng shui, it's often the empty spaces that tell the best stories about the future. In your kids' rooms, the open spaces tell the story of your children's future: If the clutter is gone and there is open space that allows the chi to flow in a positive way, your children will have the best opportunities for a healthy and lucky life.

But leaving room to grow in your child's room can serve another important purpose: It can leave you room to add another child if or when you feel ready.

As you look over the rooms of your current and future children when setting sail to the "Land of Good Feng Shui," be mindful of the little miracles that you can create for them just by opening up their space and balancing the chi—and remember that you're teaching them how to create their own miracles in life, too.

CHAPTER 11

Taking It All Outside

E very year, people spend billions of dollars on vacation travel just to "get away from it all"—to go to that magical place where summers last forever and the beauty of nature has the effect of actually slowing down time. But, if you do it right, you can find peace, comfort, and rejuvenation in your own backyard.

Gentle Nature

Whether your garden is a plethora of green and reflective water, as in Monet's *Waterlilies;* a meditation garden with an altar; or an outdoor oasis filled with colorful flora and fauna, know that your garden can and will support you in all of your life's endeavors. Aside from being aesthetically pleasing, gardens are essential to your well-being. Here, you are literally planting your seeds of the future!

In feng shui, a healthy garden means, quite simply, a healthy life. Untidy gardens with rampant flowers and weeds or foliage can drain the healthy chi that surrounds your house, not to mention your own personal chi on the day when you finally do find the time to tend the garden!

FIGURE 11-1: Send It Back!
Soften poison arrows in the form of sharp corners by adding elements that redirect their intersecting energies. Here, a metal "garden fairy" points the energy back down along the wall from the point where the two walls meet.

Always begin your garden work with a space clearing, which in this case means getting out your garden tools and removing any weeds or debris in your yard or garden area. Trimming the hedges that line your walkway can clear the path to good chi outside, and a clean sweep is also good for activating the chi in the earth.

Remember, your garden's main purpose in feng shui is to soften the negative energy caused by the sharp edges directed at your house.

Good balance and healthy chi in your garden is easy to achieve using the principles of yin and yang, the bagua, and the five elements. Add water and a good dose of intention, and you're all set to begin creating the garden escape of your dreams!

An Elemental Garden

Before you can fully understand and apply the five elements of feng shui to your garden and the outside of your home, you need to take another look at the principles of yin and yang. Think about it and take the time to look around; you'll be amazed at how many things in your garden are yin-yang. The garden is definitely one place where opposites attract!

Equal and Opposite

Achieve a yin-yang balance in your garden by combining unusual shapes, orientations, structures, or arrangements that contain different energies. For instance, flat land needs to be combined with undulating land (or rolling hills); stone (including pebbles, gravel, brick, or marble) should be combined with free-flowing water.

Combine nonliving objects (like angel statues or perhaps a bird bath) with living objects such as plants, animals, and birds. Animals in pairs enhance the power of two, which greatly helps your relationships. Aside from that important benefit, however, animals help to keep chi active both inside and outside your house.

Other areas of yin-yang balance in and around the garden include combinations of grassy spots with paved ones (as in lawn with driveway or walkway) and flowering plants (morning glories) with foliage plants (pachysandra).

E-WISDOM

The yin and the yang of it is this: In your garden, you must nurture and support that which supports and nurtures you.
—Feng shui saying

Withstand the Elements

Knowing how the five elements relate to each other in the creative and destructive cycles is critical to creating a harmonious, total garden experience. As a quick reminder, in the creative cycle, fire creates earth, earth creates metal, metal creates water, water creates wood, and wood creates fire. In the destructive cycle, fire melts metal, metal cuts wood, wood moves earth, earth muddies water, and water puts out fire. Got it? Good.

- **Wood** is organically represented by trees and plants but can be materially represented by adding a wooden deck, gazebo, patio furniture, or fencing. On the bagua, wood is connected to the area of ancestors and helpful people, so wood elements ideally may remind you of your family "roots," or may actually be gifts from family either through inheritance or just plain giving.
- **Fire** can be represented in your garden by lighting (even torch lighting), candles, outdoor grills or clay firepots, crystals, sun symbols, and triangular shapes (including triangular-shaped plants such as pine trees, hostas, and astilbe). The bagua's fame section is home to the element of fire.
- **Metal** exists in many places surrounding your home, from the yard sprinkler to wind chimes and gazing balls. The shape associated with metal is round, so anything round in your garden counts toward use of the metal element. Wind chimes, of course, also activate the chi

outside your house and have the protective bonus of letting you know when an intruder or a storm is near. Since metal is associated with the children and creativity section of the bagua, a metal swing set would also be appropriate in your backyard area.

- **Earth** exists all over your garden in obvious places (such as flower beds and grass), but it can also be represented by stone sculptures or terra cotta planters, wind chimes, or garden stepping-stones. Gravel, brick, and clay are also earth elements; use them to balance energy in your garden. The bagua position of the earth element falls in the marriage and relationship corner.

ESSENTIALS

Be sure to include a place to sit so that you can always take time to stop and smell your roses. A park bench located in a special place (such as in the marriage corner of the bagua, near a small gazing pond) can add a meditative or calming aspect to that area of your life.

- **Water** should be in as many places as possible in your garden, since it is the element that creates wood, which creates fire, which creates earth. Most often, water in the garden comes in the form of ponds, rivers, lakes, waterfalls, and birdbaths. A small wood-and-metal park bench overlooking a tiny pond in your backyard could be the perfect spot for meditation and quiet "reflection." Do whatever feels right to you in terms of water placement; whether it be a pond or simply a reflective surface such as a mirror or a piece of glass, place it with intention. Whichever you choose, use it to reflect on your career, too, since this is the area of the bagua containing water as its element.

In addition to remembering the cycles and how the elements interact with each other, be mindful of the element associated with your birth year. How you choose to use and symbolize the elements in your garden (or anywhere) does not have to follow set rules, as long as your intention is in keeping with your goals.

Color Photograph Reference

1. Your front entrance represents how the world sees you. In this well-balanced example, all of the elements (earth, fire, water, wood, and metal) are represented either in shape, color, or composition.

2. In the fame area of this garden, the triangle-shaped plants, red Japanese maple, and hanging ornaments represent the element of fire and the color red, which both radiate fame.

3. The relationship area of the garden needs tending as much as any other area of your home. Here, a bench for two is complemented by pink flowers, a pair of trees, and a pair of birdhouses. A great place to cozy up to a loved one!

4. Poison arrows in the form of sharp corners can be softened by adding elements that redirect the intersecting energies. Here, a metal "garden fairy" points the energy back down along the wall from the point where the two walls meet.

5. Feng shui practitioner Kris Halter made this stained glass window piece to add color to her dining room, incorporating all of the elements of feng shui. For instance, the red triangles represent the fire element.

6. Ferns help ground the energy force of electromagnetic fields, but they can also keep chi from getting blocked behind doors. Note the picture of Paris behind the fern; the owner is representing her fondness for the city in her travel corner.

7. Round mirrors are especially favored in feng shui because they don't have any sharp angles. Mirrors are also powerful reflectors of chi. The orchid is symbolic of wealth, which is doubled by the reflection in the mirror.

8. Hallways can have rushing chi, but you can slow this down by adding color, elements, or large pieces of fine art to anchor the hallway and become a focal point in a place that visitors to your home would otherwise rush past.

9. This living room is a terrific example of the mixture of yin and yang. Here, there is light and dark, round and sharp—and all five elements are fully represented for perfect balance. Animal-print pillows heighten the chi in the room.

10. Strong wood cabinets can anchor a corner and make the area a position of strength in a room. An antique velvet chair with a handcrafted pillow accents the corner and gives the hard wood a soft balance.

11. The potted plant here slows chi by the window, adds movement, and adds a decorative element to an otherwise wasted corner. The desk is located between the wealth and fame corners. The small lamp represents fire, as do the red panes in the stained glass window. Fire and red serve a double purpose here, representing fame, as well as encouraging a little extra wealth!

12. On the mantel, which is located in the ancestor area of the room's bagua, the owner has included a goddess theme to add power and meaning to the pictures of her parents and grandparents. The dark-haired statue once belonged to her grandfather, who purchased it because it reminded him of his daughter (the owner's mother). There is a strong female energy here. The mixture of circles (the clock, mirror, and vase) and lines (the art deco and bamboo frames), as well as the mixture of metal, wood, and fire elements bring a yin-yang balance.

13. This cozy room is in the wealth corner of the owner's home, and since this owner defines prosperity in spiritual terms, she has made it into a meditation room.

14. The bamboo sticks symbolize wealth, but they also protect the room from the "poison arrow" of the sharp corner. The picture of the shaman on the left enhances the idea of spiritual wealth, as does the winged angel on the right.

15. Make corners cozy by adding round design elements, including a convex mirror to bring in the rest of the room. Note how nicely the water shade of blue on the walls complements the wood floor.

16. Reflective metallic surfaces and salt/pepper shakers decrease the feeling of vulnerability on the stovetop, and are balanced by the tan and wood elements of the counter. The two pink flowers above the sink area (which is also the relationship corner of this kitchen) depict the "pairs" needed for a loving relationship. Note that although the kitchen is predominantly white (which denotes cleanliness), it is not exclusively white (which would give off a stark, clinical feeling).

17. Seating is very important in the feng shui kitchen. Here, a breakfast nook in the relationship area of the kitchen is intimate and cozy, with cushioned seating for two. The lines of the grasses (wood) complement and balance the round, metal elements of the table and vase. The circles of the table and lamp also keep chi flowing smoothly.

18. Clean, crisp and clutter-free, this bathroom is very refreshing. The darker vase with willows really balances out the space.

19. Bedrooms are for romance, sleeping, and healing—nothing else. There is no television in this bedroom, nor is there much in the way of electrical equipment. In fact, the clock next to the bed is battery-operated to minimize interference with sleep. The billowy white scarves soften the metal edges of the bed, and panels on the windows slow down chi. In the relationship corner just above the head of the bed, there is a photo of a couple embracing.

20. In this home office, the mirror over the workspace and the reflective surface of the Chanel poster work well to decrease vulnerability. The person sitting at the computer can see everything behind her. Note that the bookshelves are neat and clutter-free, keeping the worker's mind clutter-free as well.

Photographs by David Shoenfelt.

Colorful Intentions

The significance of the bagua in the garden doesn't stop with the elements. It also includes the use of color in your peaceful retreat, and color, placed strategically and with best intentions, can have a healing, almost magical power.

Mindful Planning

How should you go about planting the seeds to sprout your best possible future? Look at the bagua and its nine areas of intention to determine which colors will be likely to harvest your best opportunities in life.

- **Career—Black.** Although this used to present a bit of a challenge to the novice gardener, today there are more choices than ever in this color category. Choose from chocolate cosmos, black-faced pansies, black irises, black Johnny jump-ups, black daylilies, and even black roses.
- **Knowledge—Blue.** Use blue flowers such as ageratum, morning glories, nigella, bluebells, bachelor buttons, petunias, forget-me-nots, and hydrangea.
- **Family—Green.** Restful shades of green in foliage like hostas, ferns, and shamrocks or in herbs like parsley and dill will represent your family corner.
- **Wealth—Purple.** Plant larkspur, geraniums, pansies, asters, purple cone-flowers, heliotrope, lavender, or violets to enhance your prosperity. You can also have African violets inside your house.
- **Fame—Red.** Achieve good representation of fame and recognition by using the color red in your garden. Draw fame to yourself—or at least enhance your reputation—by using this color in the fame area of your garden in the form of dahlias, sweet William, cockscomb, petunias, zinnias, snap-dragons, impatiens, California poppy, roses, and red trumpet vine.
- **Relationships—Pink.** Pink is a soft, caring, and tender color that takes the edge off challenging relationships and keeps the tenderness in long-term ones. In the relationship corner of your bagua, you can plant pink

roses, snapdragons, zinnias, dianthus, impatiens, geraniums, azaleas, and anemones, to name but a few. A rose by any other color simply won't do in the "love" corner!

FIGURE 11-2: Like a Rock
Manifest what you want most in easy, direct ways with garden stones marked with your intentions. This garden's owner wants more love to give and share.

- **Children and creativity—White.** Healthy shades of white will benefit the children and creative ideas corner of your garden. Moonflowers are wonderful in this area, as are petunias, alyssum, impatiens, pansies, lobelia, cleome, foxglove, irises, veronicas, peonies, Shasta daisies, and chrysanthemums.
- **Helpful people and travel—Gray.** Since it balances the yin-yang energy of black and white, harvest the helpers in your life by using the harmonic effects of gray. Or use it as a celebration of your own service to others. Plant lamb's ears, junipers, gray heucheras, silver-foliaged laven-der, artemisia, and woolly thyme. If your intentions are to have it as your travel corner, plant exotic flowers from other lands!

- **Health—Yellow, brown, and orange.** Finally, enhance your own health or that of your family by planting the earthy shades in the center of your garden. Marigolds, zinnias, Mexican sunflowers, pansies, daylilies, cassia, butterfly weed, and chrysanthemum work nicely in the health section of your garden's bagua.

Because the plants you choose and where you place them, is dependent on many factors, not the least of which is your green thumb, the ultimate decisions on how you choose to apply the principles of feng shui in your garden are entirely up to you.

Nobody's Perfect

Nature, of course, is full of imperfection—so don't rush out and get one item of every element and every color to put in your garden. As with anything else in the Black Hat Sect of feng shui, you must ultimately go with what feels right to you. Which colors speak the most to you right now, at this point in your life? You may be attracted to a particular color, shape, or element because of a current life situation. You can always make changes later on, after one situation has passed and you are working through another!

E-WISDOM

Plants and flowers carry special significance and meaning. For instance, the chrysanthemum symbolizes endurance and long life, juniper represents tolerance, hydrangeas signify achievement, and pine trees depict longevity. Every tree and every flower tells a story about how you see yourself!

Your preferences can also reflect the current energy of your house. If your house feels comfortable, your garden will likely exude the same characteristic—after all, it's all about you and where you are at this stage of your life.

FIGURE 11-3: Gardens
Feng shui is often the art of creating balance where there previously was none. The best way to do that, of course, is by balancing the elements. For example, soften a high, straight fence with a curved or flowing border. The birdbath represents water and wealth, and the birds bring motion, life, and sound.

The Shape of Things to Grow

Ideally, your garden and yard form a perfect square. But many yards aren't like this, so what's a feng shui gardener to do?

If your yard happens to be triangular, you can plant some trees or bushes to cut off the sharp angles of the yard. This will also make your yard appear square. The area behind the trees or bushes can be a perfect spot for a meditation area, or even a rock or vegetable garden.

Land Formations

Ancient Chinese thinking speaks to the lay of the land itself. The Chinese believe it is best to have a mountain in the backyard and flowing water in the front. In traditional feng shui, the luckiest homes are those embraced by the four "celestial" animals: white tiger (west), green dragon (east), crimson phoenix (south), and black turtle (north). Combined, these animals offer the homeowner support, protection, wealth, and abundance in all things.

You should be able to see all four animals from inside your house, looking out. The higher dragon hills are usually to the left, lower tiger hills to the right. When the front of the house has a slight hill, this is said to be an auspicious crimson phoenix position. Turtle hills are always behind the house.

River of Prosperity

To incorporate the positive chi of water in the front yard, keep in mind that small ponds or even antique water troughs can do the job. You shouldn't have to build a moat! The Chinese believe that having water near the house is always a good thing, or *wang shan, wang shui* (which means "prosperous mountain, prosperous water," or "good for people, good for money"). The thinking is that what is good for the mountain is good for people, and what is good for water is good for money. Since water is a precious resource that is critical to all life, having some in your front yard will show the Universe that you intend to always have enough resources at your disposal.

QUESTIONS?

How can you add the water element to your yard or garden? Birdbaths are a wonderful way to add the water element to your garden and activate the position chi of nature. Remember that the activity of birds dipping in the bath will spread lots of chi!

Less Is More

One of the nice things about visiting China is seeing the beautiful simplicity of its gardens. For the Chinese, less is always more. Chinese gardens accent simplicity and usually include one tree or bush, or focus on one type of flower at a time. There are not layers and layers full of impeccably landscaped floral arrangements!

Here are some tips to keep your garden crisp and clean—the feng shui way:

- Alternate a succession of budding trees or flowers in bloom throughout your landscape. Plant evergreens in each corner of your garden's bagua to ground your success and cultivate your life's potential.
- Contain the chi in your garden by creating boundaries or borders with bushes and shrubbery. A fence would work, too. Creating boundaries helps keep the chi contained in your immediate surroundings, not dissipating into thin air.
- Create a compost area in a place that feels right to you. Most people drop compost over the ledge of their backyard if there's a drop-off, but you can also incorporate a composting center, so to speak, in you wealth corner. Think about it: You are taking what has grown from the earth and provided for you, and returning it to the earth for another growth cycle. This is nature's prosperity center!
- Invite a sense of mystery and intrigue in your garden to keep it interesting. Add or change elements often, especially things like outdoor art or sculpture. Incorporate colorful objects of different shapes to maximize a sense of interest, wonder, and excitement in your garden.
- Finally, treat your yard with love and respect. Your landscape is a living thing that "talks" to you, your family, and just about everyone else who stops by for a visit.

Remember to clear garden clutter regularly—prune, weed, clear, rake, and water on a weekly basis. Overgrown gardens contain oppressive energy.

Your garden and its surroundings communicate a message to others and create a particular feeling in others, too. How many times do you hear, "Wow, is it nice and peaceful here!" That's what others should be saying to you about your garden.

Building on a Good Idea

Gardens can be self-contained spaces offering a plethora of organic pleasures, but they can also be home to small structures like greenhouses, sheds, or cottages.

Greenhouses come naturally equipped with their own light, so that's not an issue. But size and location are definitely important. A greenhouse should be in proportion to the landscape; it should never be so large as to overwhelm it, nor too small to perform its intended duty. Of course, a greenhouse should always be located near a water source.

E-WISDOM

Make your garden a peaceful, meditative retreat. Put in a small pond with a park bench next to it, or a gazebo with built-in seats. Garden stones and lighting balance out the elements, making your retreat a perfect yin-yang spot.

Sheds are perfect places to store outdoor furniture in the wintertime, or lawn accessories and tools in the summer. Just keep your shed in a good location several feet from your house—if it's too close, you'll worry about the yard work you haven't gotten to yet, but if it's too far away, well . . . out of sight, out of mind.

A small cottage or studio in your yard can be a wonderful escape from the rest of the world, a place for reading, journaling, meditating, or just plain relaxing. As with the shed, find a good location that's not too close by (you'll feel guilty when you're not able to relax) or too far away (it will always seem like you are struggling to break free from your regular routine). I used a studio at my previous home as a home office, and it was the perfect way to keep work and home life separate.

The choice of which kind of structure to include in your backyard is entirely yours, just be sure to position any poison arrows (sharp edges of the structure) away from your house so that you don't send any negative chi back toward your home. That would defeat the purpose of a peacefully intended freestanding structure.

Cultivating Energy

Once you create a peaceful oasis in your garden, you'll want to connect your own personal energy to the space. The best way to do this is by incorporating what in feng shui are called the eight enhancements: light, color, sound, movement, life, straight lines, stillness, and mechanical devices.

Anyone who's ever embarked on an ambitious garden project, or who's read an edition of *The Farmer's Almanac,* knows that there is a time to plant and a time to grow, but there is also a place to plant for real garden success. Certain plants (and most flowers) do better when there is more light, while others (usually bushes and thicker foliage) do just fine when not in direct sunlight. Take the time to plot out the areas of your garden that receive more light so that you can plant your flora in a place where it will absorb the energy of the sun.

Let's not forget the kids! They, too, can have an outdoor structure like a tree house or a playhouse, which will raise the levels of the fun "fire" element in your yard.

Keep in mind that light is one of the best ways to use the principles of yin-yang, too. Sunlit areas should be next to shady ones, and brightly lit corners should be near areas left in darkness. Balancing light in the garden is tricky business but can be achieved with planning and forethought.

Color and Sound

We've already discussed color in-depth, but remember that adding color emphasis to a particular area of your garden's bagua will focus more energy on that area of your life. If you want more fame and recognition, for example, use lots of red!

Nature is full of wonderful sounds, from trickling water to singing birds. The wind has a sound, if you are quiet enough to listen. To attract more positive nature sounds, plant bamboo in your garden. It makes a very subtle sound as you brush past it.

Movement, Life, and Stillness

Bird feeders work well to increase movement of chi by birds and small animals. Squirrels can be good movers of chi! Animals can also be a positive source of chi activation in your yard or garden. Fish tanks work, too, but are not as practical outside unless you live in a warmer climate.

Wind chimes move chi indoors, certainly, but they are especially good for enhancing a garden space. Antique water pumps will also enhance the sense of flow and movement.

You may use your garden primarily for solitude and reflection. In Zen, quiet stillness is an essential ingredient for peaceful meditation. Sculptures, stones, and other permanent fixtures can be good focal points for meditation in your garden.

Straight Lines

In other areas of feng shui practice, straight lines are not considered good for chi, since they allow the chi to flow too quickly. As you have learned, curved lines are best. The exception to that concept is in gardens, where there are already too many curves. It's a yin-yang thing, but you can definitely employ a few straight lines to an otherwise meandering garden.

Improvise!

Creating the ultimate feng shui garden can be a wonderful experience, one rife with possibilities if you have lots of space to do all of the things you'd like. But what if your space is confined to smaller spaces, as in the case with apartments and condominiums?

Relax. Just because you don't have oodles of space to plant every pachysandra or morning glory you'd like, you can still apply feng shui principles to keep a garden that flourishes on a smaller scale.

Way up in the Sky

For rooftop or balcony gardens, which many city dwellers tend from their high-rise apartments, apply the traditional Chinese garden rule of simplicity. Less will always be more in this space, and you'll want to keep all your possibilities open to the future by keeping your rooftop or balcony as open and simple as possible. After all, the higher rooms in your dwelling always symbolize your greater aspirations in life, and you don't want to dampen your dreams with too many living things requiring water!

Be sure to check for proper drainage from your garden. According to feng shui belief, rushing water will cause your finances and higher aspirations to roll right off your roof and into the street from the roof deck. Conversely, standing water represents stagnant chi.

If you have outdoor furniture in your rooftop garden, be sure that any small sitting areas are covered with a symbolic roof such as an umbrella or a small awning to protect you from catastrophes in life. Be extra-mindful of the straight lines so apparent in most apartments, and balance them out with curved planters. Also, use window boxes with brightly colored flowers when you can, since they attract strong phoenix energy and can bring you prospects and helpful contacts. Remember, too, to use bamboo as a tree alternative in an area that is too small to grow trees in. Bamboo has terrific luck energy!

Down to Earth

Lower-level or basement-type gardens need the same kind of attention, although here you'll be paying much more attention to light. If you don't get strong enough sun rays in this kind of garden, you might want to invest in some lighting especially tailored to greenhouses. This will help your plants flourish.

If you live in an apartment and cannot have an outside garden, create a small one indoors with a few houseplants, some quality lighting, and a small Zen rock garden or fountain nearby.

E-WISDOM

The difference between a weed and a flower is a judgment.

—Zen saying

Remember that feng shui is about personal intention, and adapt its practices to your life and environment. Know that a small, simple garden will allow you to tend to a few things well, while keeping your potential for greater abundance wide open!

Seeds of Thought to Go

With all the talk about the perfect elements, plants, directions, colors, and energies, it's easy to forget that your garden also needs to have some room in it for family fun. After all, what good is having a backyard if it's only a flower museum?

Outdoor Fun

Designating the appropriate amounts of space for football, badminton, tree houses, swing sets (great movers of chi), and other fun activities will not only keep your family happily together during playtime, but it will also add to the fire element of your feng shui landscape.

SSENTIALS

Balance in the garden represents the balance of nature. Achieve it by contrasting textures, such as rough edges of rock versus smooth water in ponds or fountains. You should also be mindful of your garden's purpose: to cultivate healthy bodies, both inside and out.

Always be sure to have another designated area for entertaining, too, since occasionally you'll want others to come into your garden for a sip of lemonade or a wine spritzer. Festive outdoor lights also add flair—and a fire element—to your outdoor parties and get-togethers.

A Year-Round Retreat

The fun needn't stop when those autumn leaves start falling. For those of you who live in parts of the world where the climate changes seasonally, note that your garden is not just for you to enjoy in the spring and summertime. Each changing season brings with it a new chance for growth and positive change.

In the winter, look outside and appreciate the cycle of nature that is hidden beneath the frozen ground. In the fall, be thankful for the great beauty of the green season before, and for the harvest. Be mindful of each season and appreciate what each means in nature's cycle of change and renewal. Don't forget that winter can be an excellent time for planning next year's garden surprises.

E-WISDOM

A thing of beauty is a joy forever; its loveliness increases. It will never pass into nothingness, but still will keep a bower quiet for us, and a sleep full of sweet dreams, and health and quiet breathing.

—John Keats

No matter when or how you do it, creating the feng shui landscape experience is a creative, or yin, activity, and it can reconnect you with missing or long-forgotten parts of your soul. In your feng shui garden, you and the earth join hands to surround your home with the best of all possible energies, empowering you to be a "life-giving" or chi-filled source of the natural resources needed to achieve your goals. Connect with nature and you accept your role in the great circle of life!

How Does Your Garden Grow?

Do you have a green thumb? If you do, are you aware that there is more to a garden with good feng shui than a talent for making things grow? Find out just how strong your feng shui garden sense is by answering the following:

1. According to feng shui, what does it mean to have a healthy garden?
2. What's wrong with having an untidy garden?
3. What is the garden's main purpose?
4. What's the first step toward achieving good garden chi?
5. How can you achieve a yin-yang balance in your garden?
6. What are the five feng shui elements (and how can you represent all of them in your garden)?
7. What's the significance of color in your garden?
8. What shape should your garden be?
9. Is it all right to have structures in your garden?
10. What are "the eight enhancements" for connecting a garden with your personal energy?

Answers

1. A healthy life.
2. It can drain away the healthy chi surrounding your home.
3. To soften negative energy caused by sharp edges directed at your house.
4. Clearing space—removing weeds or debris, and even giving the area a good sweep.
5. By combining unusual shapes, orientations, structures, or arrangements containing a variety of energies. For example, combining flat land with rolling hills; stones with water; inanimate objects, such as statues, with living things, such as plants, insects, and animals.
6. The elements are fire, earth, metal, water, and wood. Trees, plants, wooden decks, and gazebos represent wood, for instance. Garden

lighting can represent fire, as can outdoor grills and clay fire pots, or even crystals and sun symbols. Lawn sprinklers, wind chimes, metal playground equipment, and metal patio furniture can represent that element. Earth is a given in a garden, but also can be represented by planters, chimes, or stepping-stones. Finally, water fountains, waterfalls, ponds, pools, and birdbaths are lovely in gardens. You even can try a mirror or a piece of glass.

7. Color, placed strategically, can have a healing power. Family, career, knowledge, fame, wealth, relationships, children/creative ideas, helpful people, and health all have representative colors and should be planted in positions that correspond with the bagua, just like furnishings inside your home.

8. Ideally, a square. If this isn't possible, say because it's more of a triangle, plant in such a way that you eliminate the sharp angles of your yard, which will make it appear square.

9. Yes. It's fine to have small greenhouses, sheds, or cottages, but keep size and location in mind. Don't allow the structure to overwhelm the landscape. At the same time, it should be large enough to do its job. Also, a small cottage or studio in your yard can be a great escape. The kids need that, too. A tree house or playhouse can be great fun and will get the kids outside more!

10. Light, color, sound, movement, life, straight lines, stillness, and mechanical devices.

Your Score

- 1–3: You need to do some reading and planning before starting your garden to ensure that you will have positive energy flow outside your home.

- 4–6: You're well on your way to a peaceful garden, but a few more ideas and a re-evaluation of whether you're following the bagua and inviting chi into your yard would help.

- 7–10: May I take a walk through your garden? What a wonderful, restful place it must be!

CHAPTER 12

Home Offices That Attract New Business

So you left the rat race and launched a business from the comfort of your own home. Now, you might want to consider applying the principles of feng shui to your office space. Do what you can to create a space that serves your "higher purpose" in life and streamlines positive energy to your wealth corner, making every project worth its weight in gold!

Beyond the Business Plan

While you've probably already devoted many weeks of attention to your business plan and everything affected by it, more than likely you haven't given as much thought to the basics of your office layout. Maybe you haven't even chosen the space for your office yet and are experiencing excess clutter on your kitchen or dining room table.

Although many great businesses have gotten their start at those tables, very few are successful if they are held back by the negative energy of clutter and misguided intention. In good feng shui, you must be as mindful of the way you treat your business as you are mindful of its proper guidance and growth into the future. Don't bog down your dreams by confining them to space that's really intended for eating, or your dreams will indeed be washed down the drain with yesterday's leftovers!

E-WISDOM

It's best to have more energy in front of your desk than behind it, if you want more business to come to you.

In five easy steps, you can put together a home office that supports and enhances your dreams, rather than suppresses them. Review and consider each step so you can start your home business moving in the right—and most auspicious—direction.

Determine the Best Workspace

Take a good, hard look at the kind of work you will be doing in your home office. Will you be conducting high-powered sales deals or low-key writing assignments? Will there be clients coming to your home office, or will you have the kind of privacy that enables you to literally work in your pajamas? An assessment of the kind of energy *you* will be expending in this space can go a long way toward helping you choose the best location for it. In feng shui, everything begins with energy!

Consider Your Options

Once you've given thought to the kind of work you'll be doing in your home office, you can start thinking about how you would best like to accomplish it. The idea here is to create a workspace that is in harmony, or in flow, with your life and your goals. Do you want to make a comfortable living in your current line of business, or do you want to shoot for the stars and become a millionaire? Every dream starts with a goal, and every feng shui assessment begins with look at your goals to determine whether each room truly supports those goals.

Place symbols of success or a list of goals in your fame/reputation corner of your home office to help you be mindful of old successes while visualizing new ones.

Which room works best for a home office? Well, it depends. If you've got a den, that's great because it is space especially designed to accommodate a home office. Easily accomplished, right? Think about where the den is in relation to the bagua: Is it located in your wealth sector? Great! If it isn't, does this mean you won't be successful? Hardly. It just means you'll need to spend more time positioning your business for its best chances of success. That requires some planning, but more than anything else, it requires mindfulness about what you want in your life and what you don't.

Consider the possible shape of your home office. Rectangular works best from a feng shui standpoint, since it allows the chi to flow freely as long as it is not interrupted by furniture. **L**-shaped offices can work, too, but be careful not to position yourself in a sharp-edged corner of the room. Beware of sharp edges, since they cut chi in a room. You can soften sharp lines and edges by adding a soft element such as a red fabric cord (which can be hung from the ceiling in front of the sharp corner) or draping fabric in front of the spot where the two sharp lines meet.

Bring Back Your Bagua

A room that is located toward the front of your home is considered in feng shui to be an auspicious or fortunate location, since chi flows in from the front of the house and has a more difficult time reaching the back. Good chi is especially important when you meet clients at your home office. If your office is actually toward the back of your home, be flexible. You can meet with your clients in another room, perhaps the room that's located in the helpful people section of your home's bagua. Regardless of what your business is, you'll want your clients to feel that they are being helped in whatever situation brings them to you.

QUESTIONS?

What if the only workspace you have is in your bedroom?
Create a small workspace using a small desk that has cabinets that close, or employ some other item (such as an oriental screen) that hides or covers your equipment when you're not using it.

Location is critical to a home business, but you can work only within the parameters of your current home. Although your bedroom is not an ideal choice for any kind of workspace in good feng shui, it still can be usable if there isn't any other room to use or if you need it to enhance your productivity. Ideally, a bedroom should be used only for sleep-related activities; a large desk with a computer and electrical cords going every which way would definitely be out of bounds. The electrical energy in the room is likely to interfere with your sleep, impacting your effectiveness and reducing your income potential. That spells certain disaster!

Perhaps most often, you work in your "official" home office space because the room has been designed with business, if not feng shui, in mind. But what about the laptop that occasionally makes its way into your bedroom? Keep it on a small computer table with a shelf that slides back under the table, under a rolltop desk, or even pack it back in its case when you are finished for the evening.

Place the table or small desk in the knowledge corner of your bedroom. Applying the bagua to your desk itself, place a photo of a mentor or someone who inspires you in the helpful people corner, and a small award or remembrance of your successes in the fame corner. Even just these few items will remind you of your journey and keep you mindful of your goals.

ESSENTIALS   Put your books and self-education resources in the knowledge corner of your home office bagua to strengthen and reinforce their power in directing your future.

You can have your office in unusual places throughout your home, as long as you don't disrupt the flow of positive energy in your workspace. Many people have outside structures such as a converted garage or small cottage that they use as a home office, and this, too, can be good feng shui. Try to keep your work life and home life as separate as you can, though, and you will find that your home business brings invigorating new energy to your home without causing a major disruption to your family's life.

Deal with Clutter—Clear Your Space

Before you start moving your office furniture around, you should do every-thing you can to start with a clean slate in your home office. That means, "Clean up the clutter—*now!*"

Buy a large box of manila file folders and some hanging files with labels, and organize your papers according to how you are most likely to use them. Break them into sensible categories, and file away as much as you can while simultaneously throwing papers you no longer need into the trash. Empty the trash regularly to keep your chi flowing in a healthy manner. Every piece of paper you keep without strong reason represents indecision and chaos.

If you feel really bogged down and perplexed by your office clutter, call in a good professional such as a feng shui consultant or an organizer. Most interior design firms know of good pros in your area who can help you deal with your clutter effectively. (For more tips on clutter and what it means from a feng shui standpoint, refer back to Chapter 2, "Slaying the Clutter Dragon").

E-WISDOM

> Keep your intentions crystal clear: Do you want an efficient, healthy, and prosperous business? Remember that whatever goes in the "In" box is what will likely come back "Out" to you.

Do space clearings on a regular basis, too, since your home office may quickly accumulate lots of unneeded or negative energy. After dealing with a negative client or prospect, clear the space immediately. Light a little lavender incense and walk around your office area to do the cleansing. You may also choose to use mineral sea salt. Sea salt carries with it the water element, as well.

To ward off unsolicited phone calls, try Caller ID and a humorous or novelty candle with a prayer to keep away telemarketers. You can sprinkle a little of the sea salt around the phone, too. Do whatever works for you, but always "clear the air," so to speak, after a negative phone call or client interaction.

Set the Stage for Success

You've cleaned up your clutter and cleared your space—now what do you do to have a home office that uses principles of good feng shui? You position your office furnishings in a way that increases your potential for success!

Start with the Big Things

The desk, which is usually your largest object anyway, is the best starting point. Curved, round, or oval desks work best for keeping chi open (especially important for creative types such as writers and graphic designers), but sharp corners on square or rectangular desks can be softened by draping small silk scarves on each end. Wooden desks activate natural chi, since wood is one of the natural elements used in feng shui.

One of the primary "rules" of feng shui is that you should never have a desk (or bed) that puts your back to the door. This is considered an extremely vulnerable position to be in, since you have no control over who comes up behind you. You will always be on guard, jumpy, or excitable if you have your desk in this position, so place it diagonally so that it faces the door (or doors) and you are always aware of everyone entering or leaving the room. Always have a clear line of vision in your home office to reduce nervous tension.

ESSENTIALS

In your home office, be sure your desk is in the wealth corner and your back is not to a door. A desk can be angled in the wealth corner if there are two doors in the room.

Metaphorically speaking, you'll want the Chinese mythical phoenix to be able to fly above your desk, so keep that area as clear as possible. Try not to place your desk against a wall, since this is considered confining and limiting to your personal chi. If there is no other place for your desk, you can keep it in such a position, but do use a feng shui cure such as a mirror or hanging crystal to help the chi to keep flowing in your workspace.

Watching the World

Facing a window can inspire you, but being surrounded by them can actually inhibit creativity. Too many windows in your home office can be distracting, so use some draperies or mini-blinds to control the amount of chi lost through such a space.

If you put your desk against a full wall of windows, with your back against the windows, you may create a feeling of having nothing solid to back yourself up. This, too, can be a vulnerable position, and vulnerability is not a valued commodity in Chinese philosophy.

If you have lots of windows in a small office space such as a sunroom, position your desk diagonally in your wealth corner, with your back facing the points where two walls meet. This small corner will create a strong sense of security in you as you joyfully pursue your work. When using you wealth corner for the "command central" of your home office, you can't go wrong!

> While natural light is a good thing, too many windows can keep your eyes outside rather than on the work at hand.

A lot of people think that placing a desk in the center of a room is a good thing, but in reality, it will create a sense of lost power or authority. The center of the bagua is represented by health and well-being, and in this negative placement of a desk, you might actually create health problems for yourself as well. Extreme Type-A individuals tend to like their desks in the center of rooms, and it's no wonder that these individuals are at higher risk for heart attacks.

FIGURE 12-1: Know Your Intentions
Although this plant is in a garden, the intention is universal. A small stone sculpture that says "Truth" is the owner's way of celebrating the power of truth in life—and business.

If you face the door head-on, you will experience the full power and force of chi as it flows into the room. This may make you feel agitated, confused, or irritable. You want to be working at your personal best, so give your home office its best potential to serve you and keep your chi as open and flowing as possible. Keep your desk away from passageways or tight spaces, since these can choke your creativity.

E-WISDOM

Create a nice, open space in your health section, or place a healthy, vibrant plant in it. This will keep your health well as you embark on your daily to-do list.

Accentuate the Positive

Once your desk is settled to its (and your) best advantage, you will need other tips for ideal placement within your home office surroundings:

- Keep a crystal bowl, plant, or small water fountain in the wealth corner of your desk or home office. These objects tend to attract or increase prosperity. An expensive, beautiful object of art will work the same way.
- Place a deep blue rug in the middle of the room—it represents the water element and will give you the feeling of gazing into the water for reflective moments or times when you need to meditate over a business decision.
- Bright red objects in the upper-left corner of your home office can increase financial success of your home-based business. Use a picture of red flowers, a red cord, or red silk in this area for good money luck.
- No place for indoor plants? Don't have a green thumb? Instead of torturing yourself, use pictures of plants in areas where you seek vibrant good health and well-being.
- Use a hanging crystal or wind chime in your fame and reputation corner. Don't use anything that's blue in color in that corner, since

blue represents water. Water in the fame quadrant of the bagua can literally drown it out.

- Place only objects that are useful or meaningful to you (and your business!) in your office. The key to home office success is creating a space where you will feel whole, inspired, comfortable, and energized. Too much clutter inhibits creativity.

Remember: Every item carries with it an energy; be sure it's an energy you really want to use before you put something new on your desk.

- If you don't have any windows in your home office, use lots of bright color in your décor. Hang unusual, interesting, and brightly colored objects on the walls wherever you can, but remember that a few nice larger items is always better than lots of little ones.
- Cover electrical wires to minimize electrical disturbance. Electricity can create a thick energy that bogs you down.
- Decorate your office in calming colors such as lavender, soft pink, or light shades of blue.
- To lessen feelings of chaos, eliminate clutter (a major and recurring problem in feng shui) and ground swirling energy with a fountain or Zen garden that will help slow your mind down.

The principles of feng shui are not only related to style and placement of your furniture and objects. Be as mindful in managing your office as you are in keeping your home. Clean computer files regularly (including cache files and hard drives), and keep one centralized planner with a place to list your professional and personal commitments and goals. Keep both your physical surroundings and filing/business systems as streamlined as possible.

Check Your Balance

Which colors are best for creating a sense of balance in the home office? It's long been known that yellow stimulates clear thinking and intelligence.

That's why so many school classrooms feature this lively color. Mental activity is especially enhanced by bright, sunshine yellow—the best choice for a home office color palette.

Color by Type

By the way, creative types also perform their specialized tasks very well in soothing tones of blue-green. They will work well to soothe you when you feel like your mind is running overtime with creative ideas. Blue-green is reflective and helps slow down rushing thoughts. Conversely, purple can stimulate creative activity when you feel you are in a creative slump.

E-WISDOM

Looking for ideas or more inspiration? Candles in your work area can shed a whole new light on things and illuminate your mind. The more blocked your mind feels, the more candles you can use to "fire up" your imagination.

Red can frighten creative types by its boldness, but sales and marketing folks find it invigorating because it represents aggressiveness in the business setting. If you're working on the edge as a sales pro, stockbroker, or manufacturer's rep, red can be an auspicious color to use in your home office. You needn't paint every wall red for it to be effective, either.

Warm, soothing orange and its related spectrum of desertlike colors can be good for teamwork and collaboration. Use this color in any rooms where you are likely to meet with others to work toward common goals.

Stay away from dark tones on your ceiling. Keep it as white and bright as possible, since the ceiling represents higher aspirations. This is especially true for attic offices—you can't get any closer to your higher aspirations than in an attic home office.

Shed a Little Light

Light also affects the balance you have in your home office. Of course, natural light is the best to have in your workspace, so windows or full-spectrum lightbulbs work best. Try to avoid using fluorescent lighting in your home office—besides reminding you of the rat race from which you recently escaped, such lighting inhibits creativity and has been known to create headaches and eyestrain. Use live plants to balance electrical energy in the room.

The Business of Balance

A good balance of yin (soft, introspective energy) and yang (bold, aggressive energy) is what you're after in your home office. Every month or so, when you have a few spare minutes, take a look around and do a quick yin-yang check. Too much of one over the other will upset your balance, creating more of the dominant force in your business.

Yin rooms are usually decorated in calm colors and feature subdued accessories and lighting. Yang office spaces have bold, sharp corners and are often very task-oriented in appearance rather than multifunctional. Offset too much yin by adding boldly colored objects on the walls and through the room. Placing live plants in the sharp corners can soften too much yang. Use the power of opposites to balance out every room in your house, not just your home office!

ssentials

Claim your space daily with an opening work meditation. Take a deep breath, plug in your feng shui or Zen fountain, pop in a calming CD with soft nature sounds, and get ready for a peacefully productive day in your "world headquarters."

For added balance to your home office, look for a nice mixture of elements that corresponds to the bagua (see Chapter 1) in each section of your room. For instance, a wind chime hung in your wealth sector works well with its corresponding element, wind. The center entrance to your home office is in your career sector, which has water as its element. So, putting a water fountain or something blue in the doorway is considered good feng shui placement.

The bagua can also be applied to your desk itself. Start with your career sector in the bottom center of your desk, closest to you. Since this area represents the beginning of your workday, you should keep it clear to keep it open to possibility throughout the day.

The relationship area in the top right corner is ideal for photos of your spouse or lover, and is also a good place for brochures and anything else you give to your clients in order to begin or build strong business relationships.

In your family/ancestral sector (middle left), you can put a photo or something of family meaning. Do you have antique tools from a family craftsman, or another item that either signifies or symbolizes a predecessor's work and success? Inspirational items, with good chi, represent positive energy and a family legacy.

E-WISDOM

Aside from the essentials like a computer and telephone, keep just a few meaningful things on your desk. When the surface and surroundings are clear, there's plenty of room for positive chi to flow!

In the wealth corner of your desk, you can put a fishbowl with three goldfish in it (to attract money luck) or you can put your accounts receivable file here. Just don't put your checkbook in this corner, since it represents money that is leaving you.

In your helpful people quadrant (bottom right corner), place your Rolodex or phone directory, or go metaphysical and place a statue of Buddha or angels. I have an angel in every helpful people corner of every room of my house, including my home office!

ESSENTIALS

Put your planner in the center of your desk, the health corner. The best way to stay healthy in business is to stay on top of things!

Your new projects files should be placed in the children section (right center). These new projects are like children: They are new and need your nurturing in order to come to fruition.

Finally, in the far center representing your fame sector, place a small award you've received, or use a crystal paperweight that reflects out future possibilities like a crystal ball.

Organizing your desk and your office according to the best feng shui principles is the clearest, most direct way to reach your business and professional potential. But don't get too bogged down in rearranging every corner of your home office in one weekend. As in nature, the process of good feng shui is one of continual evaluation and refinement—a fluid process that moves like good chi through your home, life, and surroundings. Don't feel like a failure if you can't accomplish everything you'd like to right away, there may be a good reason why now is not the best time for a radical change in your office surroundings!

Give Thanks—Trust the Process

Remember to give thanks back to the Universe for its support of your new enterprise. Give thanks for every new project, and for the support of the Universe throughout your previous ones. You can never be thankful enough for the flow of positive energy and prosperity in your life, and it's the best way to keep yourself wide open for more.

E-WISDOM

Purple is a wealth color, but it is also a power color that will help separate you from your competition. Use it in your logo or on your desk, and don't forget to add some "power colors" to your computer screen.

The key to having a strong and successful home-based business is to be sure everything is working for you and your goals, not against them. Use chi as your guide for a more happy and productive home business. Try not to get in your own way too much. If you notice yourself slipping into old bad habits (such as clutter), deal with it as soon as you can and don't be too hard on yourself. Just as in nature, every part of your life (including your business life) is governed by the unseen forces, and you must trust yourself well enough to know that you are in a constant state of change and learning.

You'll fall back into old habits but will always emerge stronger and more knowledgeable than you were before. This is a good thing for you and a great thing for your business, too!

Element-ary Tips for Home Offices

Your home office workspace should be as pleasant and inspiring as you can afford to make it. You can achieve some measure of delight in your home office by looking at the five elements as they relate to your work and surroundings.

Form Follows Function

How you set up your home office largely depends on what kind of work will go on there, that is to say, with which of the five elements your work is associated. Feng shui employs the elements of wood, fire, earth, metal, and water in achieving balance, and each element is represented in a different bagua or section of the bagua.

Ideally, your office would be located within the bagua of your home representing the element associated with your work. If that is not the case, you can arrange your furnishings and décor according to the appropriate element to achieve compatibility with your surroundings.

ESSENTIALS You can have your office in unusual places throughout your home, as long as you don't disrupt the flow of positive energy in your workspace.

Many feng shui practitioners use a luo pan (compass) or intuition to determine the elements needed to bring about balance within a building. Ideally, you are building a new home and can consult a practitioner about the best placement of your home office. However, if you do not have this opportunity, or you do not have a choice about which room will be your office, then skip this step and move on to what you can control: the furnishings and décor.

Purposeful Décor

Creative types such as writers and illustrators might want to include a tabletop fountain, or even an attractive bowl or glass of water, in their workspace since these are water activities. Creative pursuits require their practitioners to dig deep within themselves while remaining quiet and contemplative on the surface.

Other elements are associated with other professions, such as:

- **Metal**—accounting and management. Use metal art, a trophy, or a metal desk.
- **Earth**—medicine and social work. A small granite or clay sculpture or pot can represent this element.
- **Wood**—marketing, selling, and teaching. Paneling, a wooden desk and chair, or picture frames are easy to incorporate into your office.
- **Fire**—sports and public relations. A candle or two is great, especially with a stimulating scent that keeps you alert. (Use safely!)

Keep optimal direction in mind, too. Even if you can't do anything about which direction your office faces, you might be able to set up your desk in a favorable position. A feng shui practitioner can help you determine which direction is right for you.

Incorporating the five elements in some way when you decorate and arrange your workspace can boost your productivity.

Better Business Through Feng Shui

In good feng shui, you must be as mindful of the way you treat your business as you are mindful of its proper guidance and growth into the future.

- Don't bog down your dreams by confining them to kitchen or dining room space that's really intended for eating, or your dreams will indeed be washed down the drain with yesterday's leftovers!

- Assess the kind of work you will be doing and the kind of energy you will be expending in order to choose the best location for your office. Where is it in relation to the bagua? Best is in the wealth corner and/or toward the front of your home, to capture the chi flowing in from that direction.
- Clear your space! Clean up the clutter! Every piece of paper you keep without strong reason represents indecision and chaos.
- Clear your mind daily with an opening work meditation. Do space clearings on a regular basis, too. And always "clear the air," so to speak, after a negative phone call or client interaction.
- Never position your desk in such a way that it puts your back to the door. Try not to place your desk against a wall. If there is no other place for your desk, use a feng shui cure such as a mirror or hanging crystal to help the chi to keep flowing in your workspace.
- If you face the door head-on, you will experience the full force of chi as it flows into the room, which may make you agitated or irritable.
- Place only objects that are useful or meaningful to you in your office. The key to home office success is creating a space in which you feel whole, inspired, comfortable, and energized.
- The bagua can be applied to your desktop. Organize the items on it.
- Give thanks back to the Universe for its support of your new enterprise. You can never be thankful enough for the flow of positive energy and prosperity in your life—and it's the best way to keep yourself open for even more.
- Use chi as your guide for a happier and more productive business.
- If you notice yourself slipping into bad habits, like clutter, deal with it as soon as possible, but remember that achieving good feng shui is a process, much like building a business.

Positioning your home office for success and good fortune isn't brain surgery, but it does require using your brain (and intuition) to be sure you're placing everything from desk to file cabinets and bookshelves in ways that serve you rather than detract from your goals.

Using the energy of the dragon and the phoenix, you *can* beat the rat race and rise to your fullest business potential!

CHAPTER 13

How to Succeed in Business

I n Chinese astrology, the rat is considered to be very lucky in business due to its sharp wit and broad perspective. Rats are good advisors and are very good at sizing up opportunities for the future. Perhaps a large number of rats are behind the corporate trend of applying feng shui principles to the workplace.

A Competitive Advantage

Although it's been around for thousands of years and has been used in Asian businesses for centuries, the art of feng shui has only recently found its place of honor in American business. Virgin Airlines, the United Nations, Prince Charles, and Donald Trump have all used it, as did the TV series *Big Brother*. It's actually quite trendy now to have your office "feng-shui-ed," and some businesses have even paid practitioners as much as $15,000 for a three-hour "reading" of their workplace environment!

 **ESSENTIALS**

In a corporate office setting, good flow of energy is essential to worker productivity—and company profitability. Creating an open workspace can also alleviate stress, another productivity zapper.

Many businesses have used feng shui to their competitive advantage in the last few years, and with great success. One real estate company hired a feng shui consultant to look into the possible reasons why it was losing clients. The company was surprised to learn that it was because there was a long hallway leading to the office, and no method of slowing down the chi to make it seem like a welcoming walkway. The feng shui consultant advised them to place a wooden church bench along one wall and a gentle water fountain at the doorway entrance, and to hang a crystal from the middle of the hallway's ceiling. She also told them to play soft, meditative music in the hallway to further enhance a welcoming mood.

Retail establishments have used the same tips for years. On your next trip to Borders or Barne and Noble, stop for a minute to smell the coffee and listen to the music—it's all consciously aimed at making you feel comfortable enough to stay awhile . . . and staying a while at the store can mean you'll spend more than you had originally planned to, right? That's the plan, so make it your plan, too. Take a new look at your total business experience, beginning with where your office has its home.

Location, Location, Location

When you're checking out a new business location, you'll have a lot to consider. It's more than just looking at high-traffic areas or commerce centers, it's looking into the history and the lay of the land.

The Natural Landscape

Landscape design is important to the success of your business. According to many feng shui consultants, the most auspicious lots are circular or horseshoe shaped and are located near the base of a hill with elevated land on either side. Although this positioning is protective and good for home locations, if your office or business is located at the foot of a large hill, you can expect to be fighting uphill battles in keeping the business afloat year to year—at least according to Chinese philosophy.

QUESTIONS?

What is the best driveway design for a drive-through business? Although roads that lead directly into your business are not considered good in feng shui, they might work well for drive-through businesses, which are designed with rushing chi in mind.

If you can help it, try not to locate your business too close to any one particular element (especially an ocean). Facing a smaller body of water such as a pond would be a fortunate position for your business, as would a position in which you are looking down on a steady, flowing body of water (but not a fast-flowing stream, which symbolizes rushing chi). Roads in feng shui are much like rivers or streams and should, ideally, meander around your business rather than draw people directly into it.

The Neighborhood

Look for poison arrows (sharp corners) near your proposed business site before signing on the dotted line. If there are lots of poison arrows, you can still lease or purchase the site, just be sure to hire a feng shui consultant to install some necessary cures (such as a mirror that reflects the poison arrow back to its owner and away from your building, or even a metal wind chime to dissipate the negative chi). In terms of the shapes of neighboring buildings, the rooftops should ideally be varied in their height rather than all one level; such variations will help each business in the immediate vicinity maintain its unique identity.

E-WISDOM

> If you use a mirror in your business or office, be sure it doesn't reflect the "sha" or negative chi of a bathroom or staircase.

If you are considering a location that is older and has been occupied previously by other businesses, be sure to run a little background check on the site. If the previous business didn't do well, try to find out why. Address those issues first by doing a good space clearing, then by paying particular attention to the wealth section of the business's bagua. Add extra wealth cures to this corner of your business to increase its chances of success over its predecessor's.

Your Lobby: The Opening Act

Once inside, your visitors should feel welcomed and embraced by your business. It's best if your entrance faces an open area with lots of bright light, and the entry doors should be large enough to accommodate the chi moving into and out of your business each day.

Reception areas also need to be located in open, well-lit places to encourage good chi. But if the area is too open, it could allow visitors to pass by too quickly, leading to security problems. A divider would help in this situation. Conversely, many reception areas look like secretarial pools, with several straight-lined cubicles and pathways that force visitors to go through a maze of workstations before they find anyone who can tell them where they need to go in the office. This is very negative chi for a business, since your competitive edge can hinge on customer service and responsiveness.

Lost souls meandering around your office looking for a person to help them find their way is not conducive to repeat business—and many people might not try that hard even the first time. *That* is bad feng shui.

For added flow of chi in the reception area, stagger the workstations, use screens with soft fabrics rather than large cubicle walls, or place a water fountain in the wealth corner of the reception area. Not only do these "cures" seem more welcoming, they will also contribute greatly to your team's productivity, resulting in a better bottom line and lots of happy customers. Who could want more than that in business?

FIGURE 13-1: Say It with Pictures
The travel area of this room is charmed by framed photos of favorite vacation spots. Whether you use the room as a lobby or even as a casual meeting area, photos can symbolize several corners such as knowledge (awareness of the world), ancestors, or family (the importance of your business family, or your company's journey).

Cubes with a View

Let's face it, cubicles are a way of life for those who work in the halls of corporate America. While some people enjoy the denlike security of working in a small space, others wish for a workspace all their own, a place in which they can work uninterrupted on a project, and even kick the door shut for a conference or two. Of course the reality is that there are often too many workers sharing too small a space, leading to the necessary construction of cubicles.

If attitude is everything, then good feng shui will definitely improve your chances for success!

"Cubes" don't have to be confining spaces, however, especially in terms of creativity. It's all in how you approach your surroundings, and the quality of the intention behind your décor. So many cubicles are left stark by inhabitants who have never gone beyond hanging a memo on the wall, let alone given thought to placing a plant, a mirror, or anything that employs the principles of feng shui. Don't be bland; show some life and know that when you "claim" a space, you can improve your work attitude, which could also have the added bonus of helping you keep your job or even be promoted later on. Here are some tips for surviving life in the cubes:

Watch Your Back . . .

Always be sure you can see who is coming up behind you. Unfortunately, most cubicles are designed in the weakest feng shui position there is, forcing your back to its entrance. So, you'll need to devise a way for yourself to keep from being surprised. You may be interested in the Dilbert mirror that attaches to a computer and says: "Warning—Objects in the Mirror May Appear More Annoying Than They Are!" (It's okay to have a sense of humor in feng shui, you know!)

You will want to place a small mirror at an angle that will allow you to see behind you. An eye on your entrance keeps you from feeling vulnerable to potential backstabbers or even well-meaning people who could otherwise make you jump out of your chair by seeming to sneak up on you.

. . . And the Door

Make sure that you can always see an entrance. If you can't see one from where you sit, suggest to the office manager that they purchase a mirror to position on the nearest corner wall, so that everyone can see who's coming into an office and who's leaving. Such an addition is not only good feng shui, but it's becoming increasingly necessary in these days of heightened office security due to the unfortunate risk of workplace violence.

Take it personally! Make your space as homelike as possible. You'll want your cubicle to feel comfortable and welcoming to you each day when you arrive at work.

Protective Walls

If you are in direct line with a door, create a barrier. Being in the "line of fire," so to speak, will keep you always on the defensive. The lack of privacy is bound to make you feel like you're always being watched. You could do something as simple as placing a plant near the entrance of your cubicle, or even perhaps create a small screen using drapery or beads. Of course, you'll need to comply with office policy here, but there are ways around every negative situation using the Black Hat Sect of feng shui. Be solution minded! (Note: If you have a particularly nosy boss, hang a piece of stained glass with an all-seeing eye on it—your boss will get the message then for sure!)

Cubicles don't need to be oppressive, uncreative workspaces. Although they can present design and décor challenges, from a feng shui standpoint, there is nothing that cannot be corrected using cures such as small aquariums, plants, or even hanging crystals. Be sure to update your surroundings when anything about your job or the company changes (like your title due to a promotion or a new company name as a result of a merger). Do a space clearing each time!

Good Vibrations

You already know that a harmonious workplace is a productive one, but what's the best way to achieve good chi in your work environment? Actually, there are several things you can do to enhance chi and increase the sense of harmony and well-being in your office:

- **Keep up with cleanliness and clutter removal.** Don't be a clutter junkie. Hanging on to old memos, files, and messages will only hold you to the past and keep you from moving toward the future. If you work in a field where archiving is required, designate a particular place in the office for a library. Deal with your paper trails efficiently, and you'll never be left behind in the corporate dust.
- **Live in harmony with your mechanical equipment.** Fighting with inanimate objects such as computers is not good feng shui. Appreciate the items that are useful to you by showing them respect and reverence. By being good to your computer, you will help it serve you better!
- **Live in harmony with coworkers.** Keep gossip and negativity out of your work life, and you will become a conduit of good.
- **Shed some light on important matters.** Most often, offices don't lend themselves to high-quality natural lighting. Improvise by buying a good desk lamp with natural, full-spectrum lightbulbs. Such a minor change will give you the maximum amount of healthy light and will even work to improve your mood if you happen to suffer from seasonal affective disorder.

The biggest changes you can make to improve your work experience really come from within. Taking a mindful approach to your peers and your environment will improve both your attitude and your performance. Not only will you do (and feel) much better, but the good chi, and good spirits, you bring to the office will benefit everyone!

Meeting Mindfulness

Most companies' important business happens in meeting rooms or boardrooms, so pay attention to those rooms as well. In addition to the major aspects of your conference rooms (which can vary depending on their purpose), certain elements are fast and simple. Consider implementing the following:

- To encourage creativity in a brainstorming meeting, try hanging a crystal in the children/creativity corner of the boardroom's bagua to activate chi and stimulate creative thought.
- For a top-level discussion about the company's financial standing, you should focus on the wealth corner using a small water fountain during the meeting.
- Reduce interfering chi by using a room that doesn't have too many doors or windows, since both can lead to distraction, disruption, or even quarrels.

Since the boardroom is where all the action begins and ends, you'll want to do regular space clearings in this chi-filled room, especially after any major changes. You'll need to clear the energy, too, after any negative outbursts, since you won't want the negative energy of argument to linger (or spill into the next meeting).

Corner Office, Corner Seat

The president, manager, or leader should always be in the position of greatest strength at the table—most often, that's the corner facing southeast (beneficial for leadership and authority). Let each person who arrives at the table after the leader assume a position that is most comfortable for him or her. Most often, attendees will gravitate toward the spot on the table bagua that corresponds to what they most need to focus on. For instance, a timid person may instinctively choose to sit in the northwest corner since it is farthest away from the leader. This is okay because the northwest corner of the table represents communication, dignity, and respect—all things the timid worker is no doubt focusing on as areas of self-improvement. Not everyone can be a leader and sit in the southeast corner!

Circle the Wagons

If avoiding a hostile takeover is part of the meeting's agenda, you can anchor the protective elements in the room by placing potted trees in each corner—carry this through the entire office if you want. That's not a guarantee that another company won't acquire yours, but it can go a long way in protecting your collective psyche. It will also help keep morale high despite the financial climate. You don't have to believe in every single aspect of feng shui for it to have a beneficial effect.

E-WISDOM

Yellow in your office can stimulate intellectual ability, creativity, and thought. It also promotes self-discipline and follow-through, both good qualities for an employee or executive.

Brand Chi

Your business identity extends way beyond the lobby and the boardroom of your office. You display it to the whole world in the form of your logo, business card, stationery, and Web site. So often, especially with entrepreneurial startups, such identity items are an afterthought, when, combining good feng shui and business principles, they actually should come first.

Be mindful in knowing yourself and your business, then consider how you want to be seen and known for what you do. How else can you build a strong brand around your business except with a logo and its unified business identity pieces (including advertising along with the stationery, business cards, and Web site)?

More Mindful Design

Your business card, which will be seen every day by people who consider doing business with your company, can utilize feng shui for its most auspicious impact—starting with the dimensions you choose. Feng shui consultant Lillian Too uses a business card that is two inches in both width and length, which she considers the most auspicious dimensions for abundance and wealth. It must be working, since she is one of the highest-paid feng shui consultants in the world!

Logo designs that contain lots of sharp, pointed, or angular parts are generally not considered to be auspicious for business, since they, in effect, shoot poison arrows at your business (or, worse yet, at potential clients!). Use harmonious colors like black with white, green, and metallic colors, or brown with blue.

Black and red, red and orange, and black and yellow are all considered to be inauspicious business card or logo colors (although black with red could work for Chinese restaurants!). Use harmonious colors instead.

Pay attention to the balance and feel of your logo and business card design. If it's too busy, with lots of color, artwork, and words, you're bound to look scattered and unprofessional. If it's too sparse and uninteresting, you'll look like you aren't sure of yourself. Take the moderate approach and strategically place the elements on your business card, from the logo art to correct wording. If you're not sure what balance and symmetry are, hire a graphic designer to produce your business cards so they have the best chance of creating a positive picture in the minds of their recipients.

Working the Web

In terms of Web-savvy feng shui, design your Web site with the flow of chi in mind. After all, you want your prospects to be able to navigate freely and without experiencing any blockages, right? Maximize the use of your links to ensure a smooth, flowing experience from one page of your site to the next—as seamlessly as possible.

In terms of color on the Web, use bright colors balanced with white for a crisp, attractive look. Bold colors can activate chi for your Web site, as can any kind of Flash or animated images. Use animation judiciously, however, since you won't want to offend viewers with too much action—

and chi that seems to be rushing all around the Web with animated graphics or lots of links leading from your site to other places.

E-WISDOM

Purple is a wealth color, but it is also a power color that will help separate you from your competition. Use it in your logo or on your desk—and don't forget to add some "power colors" to your computer screen.

Use mindfulness and intention to move your prospects from one area of your site to another, without sending them away until they reach the end of your site (that's why so many "links" pages are the last button to click on a page). Stimulate the chi of each person who visits your site, by leading him or her through the process of viewing, page by page and image by image. Personally, I favor nice, crisp, bold images used sparingly on a page with some focused, interesting content. Too many images and too little content tells me that the company is more interested in the aesthetics of creating an image than in educating people about their intent. Why does your company exist? Whom does it serve, and how is this accomplished? Make it easy for people to do business with you by taking the time to design your site with feng shui in mind.

There are plenty of other things to take into consideration with your feng shui Web site. Here are other auspicious elements for the "well connected":

- **Simplicity.** Keeping your site simple and uncluttered is in step with one of the main principles of feng shui: eliminate clutter. Also, use all space well in your Web design; don't box in the chi by lining all of your elements against the four sides of the screen. Choose only the best links to include on your site; don't clutter pages with long lists of links just to look impressive.
- **Yin and yang.** On the well-balanced site, movement counteracts the many straight and angular lines or sharp corners produced by some designs (or the computer screen itself), but there is also a stillness

that allows the eye to focus on a particular area that feels grounded. Your logo, for example, could appear in the same area of each page in your site, or your navigational images will be consistent from one page to the next. Revamp sites with lots of straight lines to include some wavy or meandering lines to achieve balance (not to mention add great interest!). Think in terms of opposites to keep your site well balanced.

ESSENTIALS

A Web page is a sales tool for reaching the broadest possible audience. With that in mind, remember that for salespeople, red is a wonderful color: it is powerful, aggressive, and relates to the fame (and reputation!) sector of the bagua.

- **Direction.** Ideally, your site will be intuitively easy for viewers to navigate smoothly. If they feel backed into a corner on a page where they cannot move either forward or backward within your site, not only have you lost their interest on the page, but also you've probably lost them as potential customers. Customers expect easy-to-navigate sites. Using the principles of good feng shui, you should have no problem getting customers to where they want to be—both on your site and in their lives.
- **Appeal.** Your "splash" page or home page should be warm, interesting, and inviting. It can also be bold, as long as you limit the amount of color and animation on the page. In feng shui terms, the home page is the mouth of chi on the Web. If customers can't make it through the mouth, they'll never venture further than your symbolic front door.
- **Harmony.** Good harmony on your Web site, in the feng shui sense, means creating a pleasant experience—aligning yourself with harmonious relationships. You should evaluate every relationship that is key to the development, hosting, and marketing of your site. Web designers or ISPs with a bad track record are not harmonious folks to include in the development of your site. Think carefully about whom you align yourself with, even in the links you provide to other

businesses. In business, your reputation is very important and often hinges on whom you are associated with and why.

The yin and the yang of Web sites is to keep them uncluttered yet powerfully attractive, focused yet interesting, and open-ended yet well directed. Apply feng shui and you will be happy with the results!

Moving Ahead

You've applied feng shui to your tiny cubicle and meeting rooms, and even helped improve the lobby of your company. Now, how can feng shui help you climb the corporate ladder without banging your head on the crystal hanging from the glass ceiling?

Face First

Make sure you have plenty of flowing energy all around you, and that you are facing the right direction. For fame and recognition in your field, you'll want to be facing the fame section of the bagua, which would be the south wall. If you can't sit facing this direction, try placing a fiery red object (painting, flower pot, small sculpture) in this area of your office.

ESSENTIALS

If you are feeling sluggish at your desk, infuse a little energy in the form of the color red. Red is an energizing color, and since it represents the fire element, it is sure to "light a fire" under you to get you motivated!

For career advancement, try facing north so that you are activating the career section of your office bagua. If you want, you can move your computer to this area (as long as you can still see the doorway clearly) or place certificates of recognition there to show your "worth." To enhance working relationships, use the southwest corner, since it represents the relationships area of your bagua. Pictures of people shaking hands or conducting positive business deals together are good here, as are quotes about teamwork.

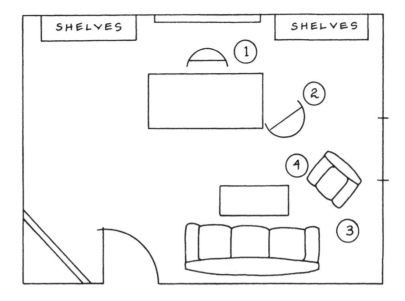

FIGURE 13-2: The Office
This plan works for most offices because it is relatively simple. 1. From behind your desk, you can see the door, yet you are not directly facing it. 2. The desk's guest chair is placed in the desk's (not the office's) wealth/ health segments, encouraging visitors who will feed the health and wealth of your business. 3. The office also has a more casual seating area in its helpful people corner, for more intimate and comfortable conversations. 4. Note that the single armchair still has a good view of the door.

Dress Your Desk

Square or rectangular desks are better for making more money; round or oval ones enhance creativity (which can get you promoted). The darker the desk, the harder it will be to get work done.

Use the bagua on your desk to its fullest advantage: Put your planner in the northwest corner of your office desk (which is a different placement than on your home desk), family photos in the family section, and whatever you most want to achieve in your fame section (i.e., a new car, a picture of someone doing the kind of work you want to do, or any other image meaningful to you with regard to your future—just use the far center of the desk). For added chi activation, hang a crystal in your fame/recognition corner, too.

Put Your Best Foot Forward

If you're making a career-advancing presentation, try to place your body in the most auspicious direction you can (i.e., in the relationship corner for a people-oriented presentation, or in the fame corner for your chance to "shine" in the spotlight). If it feels like the right position for you, it probably is.

Work from Good Intentions

Remember the "golden rule" of the Universe (also known as the Universal Law): What you put out there is what you are likely to get back. If you are constantly spreading rumors and negative things about the company or your coworkers, you can expect the Universe to keep throwing it back at you. Positive people get what they want; all they have to do is put positive intention out there, and spread the good chi. There is enough good chi for everyone, and the more you give the more you are likely to receive in the way of goodness, recognition, and abundance.

Creating a successful company or career can be easy using feng shui—just don't get too hung up on the details. Trust your intuition. Learn to go with the flow. Climb your way to the top; then stretch your wings to fly. You can do it!

Surviving the Rat Race

Be mindful of the following useful tips when using feng shui to achieve your career goals:

1. Location, appearance, and the history of your place of business are critical. Landscape design, surrounding elements—such as bodies of water or roads—sharp corners on the site, shape and height of nearby buildings, as well as the history of other businesses that may have occupied your building all play a role in the success of your business.

2. The lobby should be warm, welcoming, bright, and airy, as should the reception areas. These spaces should not be too open, however, or visitors may pass by too quickly.

3. Cubicles should be welcoming, and should reflect as much of the occupant's personal tastes as possible. Plants or feng shui articles like mirrors and crystals can help instill life and increase energy flow in the space. Make your cubicle feel a bit homelike, if you can.

4. Even in a cubicle, try to arrange things so you can see who is coming up behind you—say, by using a mirror. You may also need a mirror to help you see the entrance of the office.

5. If you are in direct line with a door, create a barrier. Being in the "line of fire," so to speak, will keep you always on the defensive. The lack of privacy is bound to make you feel like you're always being watched. You could do something as simple as placing a plant near the entrance of your cubicle, or even perhaps create a small screen using a drapery or beads.

6. Keep up with cleanliness and clutter removal. Don't be a clutter junkie. Retaining old memos, files, and messages will only keep you in the past and prevent your moving toward the future.

7. Live in harmony with coworkers. Keep gossip and negativity out of your work life, and you will become a conduit of good.

8. Consider direction, not only for office furnishings but for yourself. If you're making a presentation that is critical to your advancement, for instance, try placing your body in the most auspicious direction you can.

In general, career advancement using the principles of feng shui has to do with sending positive energy into the Universe so that it will come back to you. Work in accordance with the Universal Law: What you put out is what you are likely to receive.

CHAPTER 14
A Closer Look

Now that you are an expert on using practical feng shui to improve your home and environment, you are probably ready to go one step further in your understanding of this ancient practice. A closer look at feng shui reveals a history rich in spirituality and practicality.

How It All Began

Feng shui, or the practice of arranging possessions and surroundings so that they are in balance and harmony with the positive energy of the Universe, actually began thousands of years ago in ancient China. But in today's Western world, you would never think, as you stand in the middle of a serene feng shui garden, that this positive, energizing practice had its roots in the care of the dead.

Experts have pinpointed the beginnings of feng shui to early text references dating back to the Shang Dynasty (1766–1046 B.C.). During this time in history, royal fortune-tellers consulted the High God (Shang Di) by looking carefully at heated animal bones for telling cracks. These oracle bones directed them to the best, most auspicious sites for burial of prominent citizens.

E-WISDOM

Something mysteriously formed,
Born before heaven and earth.
In the silence and the void,
Standing alone and unchanging,
Ever present and in motion.
Perhaps it is the mother of ten thousand things.
I do not know its name.
Call it Tao.

—Tao te Ching

The ancient Chinese believed "as in death, so in life." Death was a relative state, an extended part of living that was eternally linked to life in a yin-yang band of opposing energy forces. These early feng shui practitioners believed that you could overcome your limitations by joining your energies with those of the Great Spirit, harmonizing your earthly life with the ways of the Universe.

They also wrote of the "cosmic breath," which relates to the name *feng shui* (translated as "wind and water"). The cosmic breath was the primary source of all life, of all energy, and over the years, this concept was brought down from the lofty clouds of heaven to more mundane (and understandable) earth energies like wind and water, which are the primary sources of life on earth. By bringing the cosmic down t o the practical, the concept of wind and water was made more accessible, particularly for the farmers who began using feng shui later in history.

Heaven and Earth

Feng shui, then, became a practice of balancing and harmonizing the cosmic energies with the earthly ones in order to find burial spots that offered ancestral lines the best opportunities both here and hereafter. The ancient Chinese believed strongly that in order for future generations to enjoy health, wealth, and happiness, their ancestral burial ground needed to be located in the kind of sacred ground that supported such endeavors. The simplest way for us to understand this today is to put it in terms of "good luck land" versus "bad luck land."

In its earliest forms, feng shui had three main tenets: first, that the particular orientation of tombs was as significant and important as the proper orientation of homes; second, the direction of both tomb and home was critical; and third, that astronomical and geophysical issues must be taken into consideration. Of course, the energy (or, in Chinese, chi) of the land must also be taken into account when seeking the perfect spot in which to live on the earth.

Reading the Land

Geomancy, which is the practice of divination using natural earth forms, is also a predecessor to traditional feng shui and was a natural extension of the ancestral burial practices, especially since the ancient Chinese often prayed to and included their ancestors in their daily lives.

When faced with any major decisions or life dilemmas, people called upon their ancestors in much the same way as today's psychic mediums call upon the spiritual world for assistance to the living. Like fortune-telling using natural earth elements, geomancy allowed the ancestors to speak through a person's immediate surroundings. In Chinese culture, the best luck came from creating living situations that were in harmony with one's ancestors, since it was believed that the more you honored your ancestors, the better your future would be.

In addition to using the earth in a form of ancient fortune-telling, the earliest feng shui practitioners also relied very heavily upon their own intuition in guiding royalty toward the most fortunate or auspicious use of their land. Geomancists, as they were called, would stand in the middle of a property and "feel" a connection with the land and its energies. Then, after performing a ritual and looking at each family member's birth chart, they would offer their guidance for the best positioning of the new home. In many ways, these rituals and practices live on, especially in the more intuitive schools of modern feng shui.

The Feng Shui Diaries

Feng shui has enjoyed a rich and colorful life through the red threads of Chinese history. From its secretive B.C. beginnings to modern practice worldwide, the system of creating harmony and balance in one's surroundings has grown from a class-based, aristocracy-only practice to one that all people can benefit from and enjoy.

E-WISDOM

Water is the blood and breath (chi) of the earth, flowing and communicating as if in sinews and veins . . . chi flows where the earth changes shape. The flora and fauna are thereby nourished. It flows within the ground, follows the form of the terrain, and pools where the terrain runs its course.

—from *The Book of Burial*

- **The Early Days (Post-Shang, Pre-Qin Dynasty).** Archaeologists have found evidence that the ancient Chinese chose their dwelling sites with specific features such as higher ground, peaceful surroundings, and solid foundations. During the Qin Dynasty, a practice known as "Xiangdi" began. Xiangdi was a form of land observation and appraisal. Even then, people looked to nature for a connection to the mystical nature of the Universe and, more specifically, for a correlation of sorts between the spiritual energies of nature and the fortune of man.

- **Qin/Han Dynasties.** It was during the Han Dynasty that the earliest known writings pertaining to feng shui appeared. During this era, the ancient geomancists were called in to find suitable burial grounds, using a scroll known as the "Canon of Dwellings." At that time, theory met practice to form an even more dogmatic form of feng shui practice, one that was held secret from the masses by feng shui "masters."

- **Wei Dynasty.** *The Book of Burial* was written by Guo Pu; it gave the first real definitions of feng shui. Another prominent person in feng shui history, Guang Ge was the first high-profile feng shui master and author of *Guang's Guide to the Principle of the Earth.* Feng shui was beginning to spread to the north and south of China.

- **Tang Dynasty.** The birth of the Form School of feng shui (as explained in Chapter 1) occurred at this time. Using the hills, valleys, rivers, and land formations, practitioners determined the best places for burials and for living off the land. At this point in China's history, society had changed from aristocracy to merit-based promotion. For the first time, people could move out of one class system and into another, making proper placement even more instrumental in achieving one's goals. During the Tang Dynasty, farmers began to use the practice to choose land with good feng shui. In their case, that meant land with tall mountains that shielded crops from too much wind, and ample water supplies in front of the farm to properly nourish the crops of the land. A good, healthy crop would create great abundance for a family, increasing their prosperity for generations to come.

- **Song Dynasty.** As feng shui began to enjoy its first "golden" period, two schools became apparent: the Form School, based on land formations, and the Compass School, based on more scientific and directional practice. The luo pan, or compass, began to be used by many practitioners and is still used today by some.

- **Yuan Dynasty.** The first suppression of feng shui occurs as the Mongolian rulers actively forbid any Chinese cultural practice from taking place. Since the Mongols were not Chinese, they felt vulnerable ruling China, and even persecuted practitioners who tried to preserve Chinese cultural systems, including feng shui.

Although it is often credited to China, many believe that feng shui actually began with Buddhism in India. It is possible that the practice moved across Tibet and quickly became assimilated into Chinese culture. At that point, it became mixed with folklore, philosophy, Confucianism, and Taoism. This blended heritage makes feng shui a very eclectic system of ideas, theories, and practices!

- **Ming/Qing Dynasties.** After the Mongols were defeated, there was a great revival of the Song Dynasty and interest in feng shui. Still, in spite of this resurgence, much of the purity of the original feng shui practice had been lost. During the Ming and Qing dynasties, there was much confusion about what feng shui was and how it worked. Toward the end of this period, interest in feng shui began to decline, primarily because of the confusion that too many differing opinions caused. China's Forbidden City was built during this dynasty, and it reportedly used many of the principles of good feng shui. Emperor Chien Lung, who lived in the Forbidden City during this period, enjoyed a happy and prosperous reign; coins from his period in Chinese history are considered to be lucky omens.

- **Contemporary China (1949–Present).** When the last emperor of China had been removed from power, the Communist Party was established in China and feng shui was banned in the mainland. Mao Tse Tung was strictly opposed to the practice, and reportedly feared its use by someone who might try to overthrow him. Thanks to several thousand migrating Chinese, feng shui practice continued on in Hong Kong, Taiwan, and Southeast Asia. Eventually, it spread to Western society, where it has been practiced since the mid-1970s. Hong Kong and Taiwan in particular were largely built using feng shui principles, and many say that these markets are successful today because of their attention to auspicious location and good flow of energy.

Though it has evolved and grown considerably since the early days of "ancestral land divination," feng shui as it is practiced worldwide today has still retained much of its original flavor. People may not necessarily arrange their living rooms to please or reflect their dead ancestors, but many do still find ways to incorporate personal or cultural memories of ancestors in every room of their homes. Whether it's a photograph of your grandmother in the gilded frame on the mantle in the family area of the room, or a Chinese altar with ancient ancestral artifacts, individuals still celebrate the people of the past whose fortune, good or bad, helped bring them to where they currently stand in life.

Feng Shui and "The Way"

In addition to the physical roots of feng shui, there are spiritual roots as well. The Tao (pronounced "Dow" and translated as "The Way") is a spiritual philosophy that was founded by Lao Tsu (604–531 B.C.), a contemporary of the great Confucius. It began as a combined doctrine of psychology and philosophy, then evolved into an established faith.

In the *Tao Te Ching,* Lao Tsu refers to the Tao as the path that engulfs and flows through all living and nonliving things. The Tao seeks to achieve balance and harmony in the Universe and embodies the concepts of yin and yang opposites. In essence, feng shui is based on the Taoist philosophy that everything is comprised of energy that flows through living and nonliving things.

ESSENTIALS Although it has many followers worldwide and its roots in Taoism, feng shui is not a religion. It is much more closely related to philosophy and architecture, and is often described as a system of creating harmony in one's environment.

Taoism provided a fresh perspective to Confucian thought, taking the focus on perfection one step further. Taoists believed that in order for people to evolve into superior individuals, they must learn to live in harmony with the laws of nature. Of course, living in harmony with nature is what feng shui is all about!

Although it is considered a religion, Taoism does not worship a personified deity and followers do not pray as Christians do. They seek wisdom and solutions to life dilemmas through deep inner meditation and objective outward observation.

At one time, Taoism was one of the three great religions of China, along with Buddhism and Confucianism. State support ended with the Qing Dynasty in 1911, and the Communist Party squelched religious freedom in 1949. China's cultural revolution (1966–1976) brought with it the further destruction of Taoist heritage, but there has been increasing support for religious tolerance since 1982. Today, there are nearly 20 million Taoists in the world, many of whom are based in Taiwan. Taoism has had a significant impact on Western culture, introducing such practices such as acupuncture, holistic medicine, herbalism, and meditation.

Some Taoist legacies of importance to feng shui study today include the following beliefs:

- Time is continuous and cyclical in nature.
- Yin is the breath that formed the earth, and yang is the breath that formed the heavens.
- The Tao is everywhere and can be heard by everyone for enlightenment.
- Everyone must nurture the chi that has been given to him or her by nature.
- Compassion, moderation, and humility are key to the development of virtue.

Like Buddhists, Taoists are committed to peaceful mediation and compassion for all humanity. Perhaps this is why many modern Eastern homes still have shrines dedicated to the Buddhist goddess of compassion, Kuan Yin. Often, this altar is placed in the family or children areas of the bagua, since Kuan Yin is the goddess that many Chinese traditionally prayed to for the safe delivery of children to the family. In homes where health is of concern, a Kuan Yin altar placed in the health corner is thought to appeal to the goddess's sense of mercy, compassion, and protection.

I Ching, You Ching

One day, about 3,000 years ago, the Emperor Fu Hsi was walking beside China's Yellow River when he saw a turtle emerge from the water. Since he was known for observing nature with great attention, he stood at the water's edge and watched the turtle closely. In Chinese culture, the turtle is a mystical creature whose dome of a shell represents heaven, and whose underside represents earth; in this sense, the turtle is actually symbolic of the entire cosmos.

QUESTIONS?

What are trigrams?
Trigrams are symbols that consist of a stack of three lines, either whole or broken (yin or yang). From sixty-four combinations of the whole and broken lines come the Judgements, which form the basis of the *I Ching* as a divination tool. Trigrams can be derived from divination sticks, coins, or stones.

Fu Hsi reached down, picked up the turtle, and looked closely at its back. Here is where he first saw the eight trigrams that created the foundation for the *I Ching,* or "Book of Changes." This book of ancient wisdom was passed on through the centuries and was even studied by Confucius himself, who wrote long commentaries on the topic. It was Confucius who added advice to the Judgements, and created the standards for the *I Ching* that are still basic to the divination system today.

Trigrams and Feng Shui

How does the *I Ching* relate to feng shui practice? Yin and yang are critical to the *I Ching,* and harmony with the Universe is mentioned throughout the text of the "Book of Changes." Feng shui derives much in its teachings from the wisdom of the *I Ching,* and much of feng shui's offerings are guided by the meanings attached to the trigrams.

The ultimate goal of feng shui is to aspire toward your personal best so that you can be in harmony with all of nature and the Universe. In the Compass School, the trigrams of the *I Ching* are relied on even more heavily to provide a more tangible "plan" for one's success in life. For instance, feng shui Compass School practitioners carefully calculate natal charts, numerology, and the auspicious directions associated with each person's chart in order to create the most harmonious living space for all who live in a home. To accomplish this, they must also rely on the trigrams of the *I Ching,* because they spell out in great detail which directions are best for each life endeavor.

Let the Spirit Guide You

Other schools of feng shui, like the Black Hat Sect, use the *I Ching* as more of a spiritual resource rather than a scientific one. These practitioners read the "Book of Changes" and offer advice from it when needed or appropriate to a given situation. They then proceed to help their clients with feng shui issues on an intuitive level that is rooted in Chinese philosophy but not directly dependent upon it. In other words, the Black Hat Sect, through each practitioner's private research and study into the ancient works, teaches its followers to "go with the flow" rather than get bogged down in dogma.

E-WISDOM

If you do external exercises, you must do internal exercises.

—Taoist proverb

The Form School of feng shui pays more attention to the natural earth forms and relates the *I Ching* to each land formation as a reference guide. Form School followers can choose to include the *I Ching* as part of their "land readings," but often rely on their own earthy sense of intuition, especially in helping their clients locate auspicious lots on which to build homes or businesses.

Today, the *I Ching* lives on both as a fascinating ancient text and a divination tool. In fact, there are *I Ching* tarot cards, software programs, and fortune-telling sticks that incorporate the messages of these ancient pearls of wisdom.

Such divination can provide an interesting companion activity to your feng shui endeavors, but it's important to note that the *I Ching* isn't a fortune-telling game. Rather, it's an established system of sharing wisdom through the ages in an effort to achieve human perfection. A lofty goal, to be sure, but definitely one worth pursuing!

Energy in Motion

Feng shui does not need to be limited to external surroundings. You can move energy or chi positively from within through tai chi, meditation, and qi gong.

Tai Chi

Tai chi is one of the world's most ancient and popular martial arts, and, like feng shui, emphasizes balance and harmony. Through a series of stylized movements, each with a philosophical meaning, tension is eased and the flow of positive chi through the body is enhanced to create total mind-body harmony. Tai chi is a terrific way to enhance relaxation, relieve stress, and improve concentration because when chi is flowing properly in the body, the blood flow is improved as well. Solid breathing (wind) is critical to enhancing the flow of chi.

Meditation

In meditation, breath work is also the starting point for connecting your spirit with that of the greater Universe—harmonizing your inner life with the external world around you. This is its primary similarity to feng shui. When you meditate, you are performing an "inner clearing," removing the spiritual clutter of stress, anger, and negative memories, among other things.

Removing clutter is the key starting point for feng shui, as clutter can weigh down a person and render him or her unable to rise to his or her true potential in life. Meditation elevates your inner self to allow you to see possibilities beyond the earthly or physical, and to rise to your full spiritual potential, too.

Qi Gong

Qi gong (pronounced "chi gong")is the combination of life-giving energy and physical study, practice, or exercise. It is very difficult to translate qi gong literally, as each of the two words has multifaceted meanings. However, when used together, this phrase describes a method of exercise that moves energy within the body in an effort to connect it with the cosmic forces of the Universe.

QUESTIONS?

What is the purpose of qi gong?
The practice of qi gong develops the three treasures of life: essence, energy, and spirit. Balancing these three brings balance to life.

Qi gong has a strong connection to the *I Ching* and began nearly 3,000 years ago when groups of people gathered in the fields to perform dancelike movements and animal-like postures to improve their circulation and promote good health. Today, qi gong incorporates diet and nutrition concepts into its practice for a total mind-body approach to well-being.

Like feng shui, qi gong has a long and interesting history. Qi gong enjoyed a period of religious dedication during the time of Christ, and has been heavily influenced and differentiated by Taoist, Buddhist, and Confucian followers throughout its history. Taoist followers of qi gong emphasized soft, gentle movements and relaxation with an earthy, more practical spirituality behind it. The Buddhists from India introduced more active, dynamic movements along with concentration and focus, with spiritual enlightenment as their ultimate goal. Confucians practiced qi gong in order to further themselves toward becoming "superior" persons.

Just as the secrets of feng shui were kept hidden from the masses until recently, qi gong's secrets were housed in the temples and monasteries of China until recent times. The ultimate goal of qi gong as it is practiced today is to develop the "three treasures of life": essence (jing), energy (qi or chi), and spirit (shen). In harmonizing these three treasures, one achieves balance and harmony in all of life.

ESSENTIALS

Many famous people today have used the principles of feng shui to improve their surroundings and their lives in general. Donald Trump, Madonna, Cher, Eric Clapton, Kevin Spacey, George Clooney, and Oprah Winfrey head a virtual list of "Who's Who in the Modern World of Feng Shui." You're in stellar company!

The common thread between tai chi, meditation, qi gong, and feng shui is the positive, healthy flow of energy, and perhaps a connection with the great "cosmic breath." All are concerned with moving energy in the best directions to enhance the health, wealth, and overall prosperity of each individual—and of the cosmic whole of life.

Feng Shui Today

As you can see, feng shui is so much more than the practice of moving furniture or selecting the right home site. It comes from a long, rich history full of ancient masters, scrolls of wisdom, and dogma that persists into this modern era.

When you begin to use feng shui to improve your home, life, and surroundings, you are joining forces with the combined energies of others before you, cultivating the good luck of many centuries of insight, struggle, and triumph. As you continue navigating your way along your personal path of ongoing self-improvement through feng shui, know that you have the support of thousands who have gone before you, refining the path just a little bit more with each step. May you have the blessings of the Universe in all of your life endeavors!

Feng Shui FAQs

Learning about the practice of feng shui, both from the practitioner and the consumer standpoints, is sometimes complex but always rewarding. The Feng Shui Society of the UK has graciously allowed us to share frequently asked questions from its Web site (*www.fengshuisociety.org.uk*).

Feng Shui: A Primer

As there are many misconceptions about feng shui, the first point to be addressed is "what feng shui is not."

Feng shui has been called the art of placement. This describes feng shui well, as it is an art rather than a science, a religion, a philosophy, or a belief system. In the West, feng shui is not science as its principles cannot yet be proven by scientific method. It is not a religion as, although some of its advocates may consider it part of their religious practice, it is not necessary to follow any religion to understand or practice feng shui. It's not a philosophy as it encompasses many practical tools and techniques. It is not a belief system. Asking someone if they believe in feng shui is like asking them if they believe in the weather. It's not a question of faith but a fact of life.

The Chinese have always considered that success in life is dependent upon five influences:

1. Fate, destiny, or karma
2. Lucky and unlucky eras
3. Feng shui
4. Virtue
5. Personal factors (including background, inheritance, family, and actions, education, and experience)

Whether you concur with this Chinese belief or not, it does make an important point. The first two of these influences—fate and luck—are beyond our control. Therefore, feng shui is only one of the three influences on our lives that can be controlled. Although it can be very effective, feng shui is not magic or the ultimate power tool. It cannot guarantee great wealth, health, and happiness, so beware of people who claim otherwise.

Good feng shui can simply help us to overcome difficulties during our times of bad luck, and can help us reap maximum benefits from the good times. It is generally used to increase wealth, enhance health, improve relationships, and protect against misfortune and harm.

Q How did feng shui originate?

A Feng shui is an ancient Chinese discipline dating back at least 3,000 years, although its philosophy can be traced back to the teachings of the *I Ching*—from 6,000 years ago.

Feng shui was first used to determine the best sites for tombs. Later it was used to site palaces, government buildings, and monuments, until finally whole cities were designed and built according to feng shui principles. Over time, the classical practice of feng shui developed to include detailed observation of the living world and the way in which earth's energy affects our daily lives.

Feng shui remained an integral part of Chinese culture until recent times when Western influences and Communism relegated feng shui to a more superstitious and mystical practice, and the Chinese in Hong Kong reduced its essence to helping businesses thrive.

Feng shui was devised through the cultural paradigms of China, with its unique geography and rather stable social structure, which varies little from generation to generation.

Despite these origins, however, its core truths are central to human awareness and experience. When it is stripped of culture and ritual, and synthesized with other bodies of knowledge to meet the specific requirements of culture, geography, climate, and human uniqueness, the essence of feng shui can be applied to any space and time.

Q What is feng shui?

A *Feng shui* means "wind and water," which are the two most powerful forces of nature and the fundamentals of life. The underlying principle of feng shui is to live in harmony with your environment so that the energy surrounding you works for you rather than against you.

Feng shui is a complex art involving many disciplines from site planning to psychology, based on the Chinese understanding of the dynamic flow of energy throughout the Universe.

Feng shui explains how the environment in which people live affects their lives. Beyond this, it is the art of using the environment to influence the quality of a person's life.

Ultimately, feng shui is a sound and sensible way of living with a conscious connection between our outside environment and our inner world.

Q How is feng shui used today?

A Despite the fact that the West has not had the benefit of a consistent person-to-place philosophy through the ages, many people, on discovering feng shui, recognize things that they always knew deep down to be true. Many successful people practice some form of feng shui without realizing it.

The integration of the external world and our internal environment is a cornerstone of most traditional philosophies. Indigenous people all over the world have long understood that we are not separate from our planet, our homes, or one another.

In the West we have lost this connectedness with our earth and our environment and this lack of balance is a cause of much physical, mental, emotional, and spiritual disease. Feng shui offers a means to reconnect and regain our balance, our health, and our good fortune.

Q Should I rotate my compass/bagua in the southern hemisphere?

A The jury is out on this one. Some people say, "*No*—north is north wherever you are," and others say, "*Yes*—just because the Chinese never had to do it does not mean it should be swept under the carpet now."

In reality, until feng shui can be scientifically examined, there is no acid test. "There are strong arguments on both sides and at this point in time, it would appear that the voices calling for the *no* vote have the edge in terms of decibel levels. But then again, most proponents of the *no* theory do live in the Northern Hemisphere—and if you were to ask people who have actually spent a reasonable amount of time in the Southern Hemisphere, you may get a different response.

Feng Shui: The Next Level

Q **How do I become a professional feng shui consultant?**

A There are many ways of studying feng shui. The path you take will depend on your expected outcome and the time and money you have at your disposal. If you are interested in feng shui as a hobby, and would like a simple introduction to the subject, you need do no more than read a few books and attend an introductory course. This will bring the subject alive, introduce you to other people who are at the same point of learning as yourself, and become the catalyst for you to discover that feng shui is something you wish to pursue further.

If you become passionate about feng shui, have a genuine desire to help people, and feel you have some latent aptitude in this area, you may decide to pursue a career in feng shui.

In this case, study and training are extremely important. There is nothing to prevent you from reading a couple of books, doing a one-weekend feng shui course, and setting up as a feng shui consultant the following Monday morning—and some people do. This is not recommended.

As with any other subject, the only sensible way to study is to do the groundwork, put in the hours, and apply yourself as well as you possibly can. It could take several years of study before you are competent with feng shui and handling the client relationship. Even then, there is always more to learn—feng shui is a lifetime study and the feng shui knowledge you acquire needs to be assimilated. It will take time for you to mature and develop as a consultant.

As there are currently no recognized feng shui standards, regulations, recommended courses, or certification, the onus is on the individual to approach study and practice with the utmost integrity and commitment to professionalism. To obtain a depth and breadth of knowledge, use the following checklist to assist you in your studies:

☐ **Attend courses.** Courses come in many shapes and sizes—from two-hour evening seminars to two- or three-year structured training programs. Finding the right course is a little like finding the right consultant. Ask lots of questions beforehand and, if possible, get opinions from past students. Some consultants offer training in the form of an apprenticeship scheme, which can be more flexible than other training methods, but exposes you to only one individual and his or her own style. As well as being educational and experiential, feng shui courses are great networking opportunities, and you will also learn from your fellow students.

☐ **Check the media.** Radio, television, newspapers, and magazines regularly feature feng shui. A lot of this is light-hearted and some of it dismissive, but it is useful to keep in touch with public perception of feng shui.

☐ **Business-minded feng shui.** If you set up a feng shui business, whether as a sole trader, partnership, or company, you will need to understand your responsibilities with regards to handling clients, money, tax, VAT, insurance, and possibly staff. You may want to consider advertising, marketing, and PR as well.

☐ **Mailing list management.** Many feng shui businesses and consultants have mailing lists that will keep you in touch with the courses, products, and services that they are offering. Use any other skills that you have. Many consultants find their previous skills help in their feng shui practice—architecture, interior design, astrology, landscaping, acupuncture, and so on.

☐ **Have a feng shui consultation.** If you can see a need and can justify the expense, put yourself in the client's position and engage a feng shui consultant.

☐ **Listen to cassette tapes.** These are another source of feng shui information. Tapes are either studio recorded or taped during live events, in which case they may include material not found in books.

☐ **Observe.** Feng shui is everywhere. Develop your critical feng shui faculties and next time you are out and about, or traveling overseas, use your feng shui knowledge to examine your surroundings.

☐ **Perform case studies.** You can find case studies in several places—books, magazines, the *Feng Shui Society Newsletter*. Some consultants allow students to accompany them on their consultations. Examine the birth data and floor plans, perform your feng shui analysis, and check to see how your results compare with the case study results.

☐ **Practice your feng shui skills.** Start by practicing in your own home. Then, when invited, you can help family and friends. These "consultations" will be qualitatively different from "real" consultations as you will know the individuals and homes already and you will need to suspend pre-existing judgments to perform objective analysis. The need for objectivity is one reason that consultants often don't perform their own feng shui but ask others to do it.

☐ **Read plenty of books.** If you don't want to buy an abundance of books, ask your library to order them. Feng Shui Society members can use the Society's library.

☐ **Study other energy-based healing systems.** A knowledge of space clearing or vibrational healing is useful to the study of feng shui because such knowledge includes hands-on experience of what energy feels and looks like, and how it moves. Practice chi development. Martial arts or exercise systems such as qi gong or tai chi enhance awareness of chi.

☐ **Subscribe to feng shui magazines.** Current publications give you access to up-to-date feng shui news and views, including articles, book reviews, and course details.

☐ **Use the Internet.** There is a wealth of feng shui knowledge on the Internet. It is a very interesting and useful source of information and contacts for people in the feng shui world, with plenty to offer hobbyists, students, clients, and practitioners alike. The newsgroup to start with is alt.chinese.fengshui, where you will find personal experience and opinion. Here is your opportunity to ask all the questions that have been bugging you for ages. On the World Wide Web, start at *www.fengshuisociety.org.uk* to find links to many of the best feng shui Web sites.

☐ **Watch videos.** Several feng shui videos are on the market and can bring the subject alive in a way that books cannot.

Q **How do I become a Feng Shui Society member?**

A Membership is open to everyone and not restricted to the UK. The Society's bimonthly newsletter keeps members up to date with all forthcoming events. It also includes informative articles, reviews on recent lectures and seminars, feng shui case studies, book reviews, members' questions and answers, announcements of interest to those in the feng shui world, and advertising space.

The Society provides a support network for its members through regular talks, educational programs, and informal groups that look at contemporary environmental, social, and personal issues from a feng shui perspective. There are also purely social events from time to time throughout the year. Events are held regularly at various locations throughout the UK and organized by regional groups who act as focal points for local Society member needs. Where Feng Shui Society events are open to nonmembers, members receive a discount.

To support individual learning, the Society keeps a stock of books, tapes, videos, and CDs on feng shui and related subjects, many of which can be lent to members. New products are added to the library as they are published. The Society also holds tape recordings of presentations given by visiting speakers. The library facility is not available to nonmembers. The Society does not sell feng shui products.

You may contact the Society for an application form by e-mail (ced.Jackson@fengshuisociety.org.uk) or post (Feng Shui Society, 377 Edgware Road, London W2 1BT).

Q   How do I find feng shui products?

A   If you do not have access to a local feng shui/new age/crystal shop or market, the best option is to use one of the many mail-order companies available throughout the world and on the Internet. For a list of links to online product suppliers, check the "Products," "Books," "CDs," and "Videos" sections on our links page. Feng shui magazines regularly feature product suppliers as advertisers, and these are listed in the "Magazines" section on the links page of our Web site.

Q   How can I register as a professional consultant?

A   The Feng Shui Society currently holds a register of professional feng shui consultants in the UK who have signed the Society's Code of Ethics and are insured for professional practice.

(Due to limitations of regulation and insurance coverage, the Feng Shui Society can only register consultants in the UK. For information on other resources, please refer to Appendix D.)

- Consultants should deliver a professional service—whether paid or unpaid—acting legally and honorably and upholding before the public, the dignity and reputation of feng shui and the Feng Shui Society.
- Consultants should be guided by a high level of personal integrity and compassion, never causing a client to be exploited and ensuring their confidentiality and safety, both physically and psychologically.
- It is considered important that consultants have well-developed interpersonal skills. Consultants should inspire confidence in clients and should not undermine public confidence in either their role as consultants or the work of other consultants.
- Terms of business must be made clear to the client before the commencement of the consultation. When advertising professional services, consultants should ensure accuracy and avoid exaggeration, unwarranted statements, or misleading publicity.
- Consultants may describe themselves as "Registered Consultant of the Feng Shui Society" for publicity and on business stationery.
- The Feng Shui Society requires notification of any dispute or claim made against the consultant, in their professional capacity, at the time of, or during the period of, their registration with the Society.

Q **How do I find and choose a feng shui consultant?**

A If you feel your feng shui requirements exceed your capabilities, or you would like the insight of an expert, you should consider hiring a profess-ional feng shui consultant. As a feng shui consultation can represent a significant cost in terms of time, money, and effort, it pays to find the right consultant for the job.

There are no nationally recognized qualifications in feng shui. This is an important point that needs repeating. You will find consultants with all manner of certificates and paper-based qualifications but, in all instances, these certificates are provided by the person running the course, and as such, have not been independently validated as being indicative of any particular level of training, skill, or experience. That is not to say that the consultant is not skilled or experienced, or that the course is not valuable, simply that the certificate is not proof of this.

You will need to assess the consultant in some other way. If you do not have a word-of-mouth recommendation from someone that you trust, you are advised to telephone a number of consultants and "interview" them on the telephone. To do this properly, you must speak directly to the consultant that you would be working with, not an assistant, colleague, or agent.

Feng shui agents will generally take a percentage of the consultation fee. This may be up to 30 percent. So, not only is it sensible to choose a consultant by speaking to them directly, it may also be cheaper.

Here is a selection of questions for you to pick from. Don't be afraid to press the consultant, as you can look elsewhere. If the consultant answers your questions with language or terminology you don't understand, ask for clarification.

- *Are you a registered consultant of the Feng Shui Society?* Generally, a registered consultant is preferable, but there may be a good reason for not being registered.
- *How did you get into feng shui?*
- *When did you start your feng shui training, with whom did you train, and for how long?* There will be huge variation here. Read the section on studying feng shui to get more information about feng shui training.
- *How long have you been practicing, as opposed to training? How many consultations have you done?*
- *Can you provide me with marketing material or examples of your work?*
- *What type of clients do you have? For example, do you specialize in homes, businesses, hotels, retail outlets, or gardens?*
- *Do you have testimonials or references from your clients?* This is optional as some clients and consultants are happy providing references, and others aren't.
- *What type of feng shui do you practice? Do you consider feng shui to be a science, an art, a therapy, a religion, a philosophy, and*

why? There are no right or wrong answers here. This question will tell you about the consultant's approach and whether his or her style will suit you or not.

- *What services and products do you offer?* There is a long list of possibilities—feng shui, space clearing, astrology, geopathic stress treatment, and so on. Some consultants may have related experience such as acupuncture, shiatsu, architecture, or interior design.
- *What format does a consultation take?* Try to find out what to expect in advance. How much do you charge, and on what basis—by the hour, a flat fee, according to the number of rooms in the property, or by measurement of the floor space?
- *What does the fee include—preparation, on-site work, off-site work, materials, traveling? Are there any additional or hidden costs? What kind of follow-up service do you offer? Will any charge be made for follow-up work?*
- *Do you provide a written report, and if not, why not?* Some consultants may suggest you take your own notes or tape-record the consultation.
- *Do you have public liability or professional indemnity insurance?*
- *If I am not happy with the outcome of the consultation, what will you do?*

The way that the consultant answers your questions is as important as the answers that you receive. Even if you are unsure about some of the information and its implications, you will be able to make a good assessment of the consultants when you have spoken to several of them, and can compare their answers. If you are still unsure, contact the Feng Shui Society for advice.

During this interview, you will be testing the consultant's interpersonal skills and professionalism. Ensure that there is no language barrier. Use your intuition when judging the consultant. Think of the qualities that you require in someone to whom you will be turning for help with issues of a personal nature. Does the consultant seem sympathetic, open, confident, caring, trustworthy, patient, warm?

If you have had an unsatisfactory previous experience with feng shui, or have heard a horror story from one of your friends, then ask the consultant specific questions about your concerns, to ensure you avoid a repeat of the negative experience.

Finally, it is very important that you are clear about what you want from the consultation, that your expectations are realistic, and that you will act reasonably with the advice that you are given. The clearer you are about what you would like to achieve and the more involved you become, the more likely you are to achieve successful results. It is also a good idea to involve other family or business members as much as possible.

The most successful consultations are partnerships between client and consultant, but remember that you, the client, make all the decisions and are ultimately responsible for whatever happens in your home, your business, or your life. The consultant is only an adviser, and you are free to accept or disregard the advice as you see fit.

Q **What can I expect from a feng shui consultation?**

A A feng shui consultation generally involves preparation, a site visit, and follow-up by mail, phone, fax, e-mail, and/or a return visit. Many consultants provide a written report and detail can vary from one sheet to sixty. Some consultants require the client to take their own notes, and some will allow the consultation to be recorded electronically.

As fees and services vary widely, it is a good idea to ask your consultant to detail exactly what you will be getting for your fee so that reasonable comparisons can be made among consultants. Read the section on choosing consultants for more detail.

Prior to the on-site visit, the consultant may ask questions about the property and occupants or require a questionnaire to be completed. You are likely to be asked to provide dates of birth and information about the age of the building and any renovations that have taken place. Scale plans of the building are extremely useful but can be drawn up during the visit if necessary.

During the site visit, the consultant will walk through the property, "reading" the space and relating it to the lives and fortunes of the occupants. It isn't necessary for all of the occupants to be present during the visit—although one occupant will need to be there to answer questions—and it is most effective if the property is presented in its usual condition, rather than dressed up for the occasion!

Once the consultant has a good understanding of the client's requirements and preferences, advice and recommendations can be given for changes in placement, lighting, color, and other interior design elements, in order to create the environment that most effectively facilitates the client's desired outcomes. Some consultants may delay offering any advice until after the visit.

The client is generally free to take notes or record the visit as it progresses. If you are receiving a detailed report, it should cover all of the recommendations made at the time of the visit, and be supplemented by the appropriate calculations and analysis. The report should be dispatched shortly after the visit and the consultant should be able to provide an additional copy should it be necessary.

Consultants should aim to stay within the limits of your aesthetic and financial parameters, so beware of consultants who are unable to make recommendations on this basis. Also, although consultants may offer to provide recommended feng shui products, you should feel under no pressure to purchase on the spot, and hard-sell techniques often do not go hand-in-hand with professional integrity.

After the consultation, you may be free to contact the consultant with questions or for further advice and generally feedback is greatly appreciated.

Most consultations cost several hundred dollars, and take between one and three hours. As consultants vary in their charges, it is a good idea to discuss (and understand) your cost in advance, and payment is generally due in full at the time of the visit.

Consultations by mail, fax, and e-mail—using diagrams, photographs, or video—can often be arranged, if required. It is also possible to obtain consultations—particularly those with an astrological bias—on the Internet.

Although some distant evaluations of this type can be limited in scope, but not necessarily in effectiveness, these types of consultations can be less effective than site visits. In some instances, they are absolutely no more than "play feng shui"—and they are often priced accordingly.

Q ## What are the types of feng shui?

A Imagine that you want to engage an interior designer to redesign your home. You think carefully and come up with a concept that you feel will work for you. You are able to convey, in some detail, the type of interior you are looking for. Perhaps it's minimalist chic, with cool colors—blues, grays, some silver and chrome—sleek lines, hidden lighting, and no soft fabrics or carpets. You speak to several interior designers, perhaps going on the recommendation of a friend, and eventually you find the person that you trust to turn your dream into a reality. They complete their work and your home is transformed.

What would have happened if you had engaged a different interior designer? Would they have created an identical home for you? Of course not. They would have interpreted your ideas in a similar but different way. The effect would have been the same but the details would have been different. In fact it would be impossible to find two interior designers who would deal with your requirements in an identical way. It is the same with feng shui.

There are many different approaches to the practice of feng shui. Although the principles underlying these approaches are the same, their application can vary widely from one teacher or practitioner to another. There are many different feng shui tools and techniques and different circumstances require the use of different tools and techniques.

The most useful way of looking at this is to consider that there is no right or wrong way of practicing feng shui. There are only different ways. If you decide to study further, in time, you will find a way that suits you.

As soon as you read books on feng shui, you will find that they differ, and often contradict each other. It is best to read as widely as you can, because eventually you will be able to discern what feels right to you.

There are several reasons why feng shui practice varies so much. First, feng shui developed over thousands of years and in several areas of the world. Many techniques were developed to deal with different situations and lifestyles. For example, feng shui as practiced in rural China is different from the feng shui used in very densely populated Hong Kong. Also, as their skill and experience increased, feng shui masters developed their own techniques, based on their own observations. Today, in the West, feng shui is still adapting and developing.

The main approaches to feng shui follow. Most Western practitioners develop their own style by taking selectively from these main approaches. Some practitioners even "brand" their own style and a new feng shui "school" is born.

- **Traditional/classical/authentic feng shui.** Form School and Compass School feng shui are two types of traditional feng shui. Form School examines shapes and symbolism in the environment without reference to compass directions. Compass School utilizes the compass, pa kua, lo shu, and feng shui formulae. This type of feng shui is most popular amongst Chinese practitioners, many of whom may consider it a science. Critics find it obscure, culturally inappropriate, or too literal.
- **Black Hat Sect/Tantric/Buddhist feng shui.** Developed in the United States fifteen years ago by Thomas Lin Yun, Black Hat Sect is a hybrid of Tibetan Buddhism, Taoism, and feng shui, simplified for Western tastes. This type of feng shui is hugely popular, particularly in the United States, and practitioners are often Buddhist or adopt Buddhist rituals and ceremonies into their practice.
- **Intuitive/modern/applied feng shui.** This type of feng shui is an interpretation of traditional feng shui adapted for the West. It strips out Chinese culturally specific symbolism and superstition, and instead uses equivalent devices more appropriate to modern, Western lifestyles and tastes. This type of feng shui is widely used in the UK and most media coverage is of this type. It can be very practical and pragmatic but sometimes becomes overlaid with "new age" spirituality or mixed up with "pop" psychology.

To sum up, there is no such thing as generic feng shui. Although there are many similarities, everything you read or hear is coming from a particular style or mix of styles. These approaches aren't inherently right or wrong—good or bad—but some will be more appropriate for you than others.

A Feng Shui Plan

You've learned so much—now apply it! Using the following grids, and the bagua on page 64, consider changing your home or office with mindful intentions. Use a pencil (and additional graph paper, if necessary) to sketch out a basic floor plan for either your whole home or a specific room. Then, arrange the sample furnishings until you find a design that works best for you—before you start moving furniture!

Office

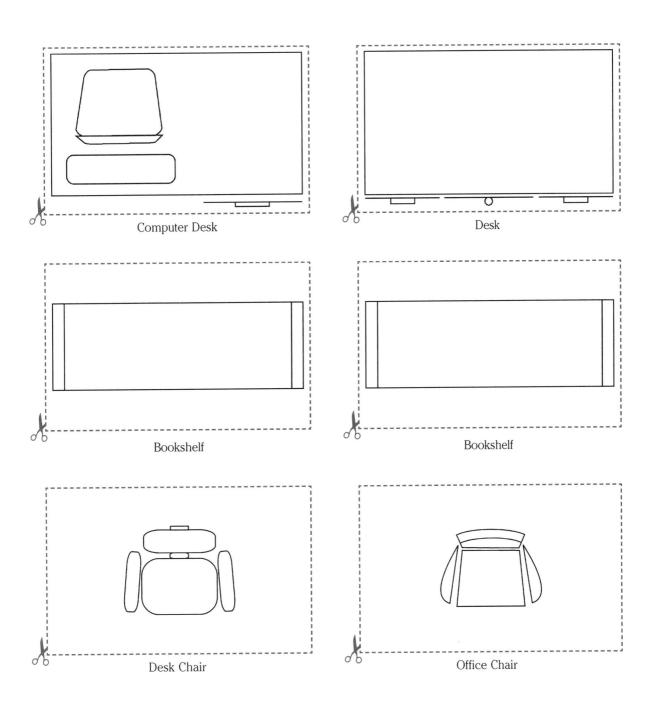

Computer Desk

Desk

Bookshelf

Bookshelf

Desk Chair

Office Chair

Bedroom

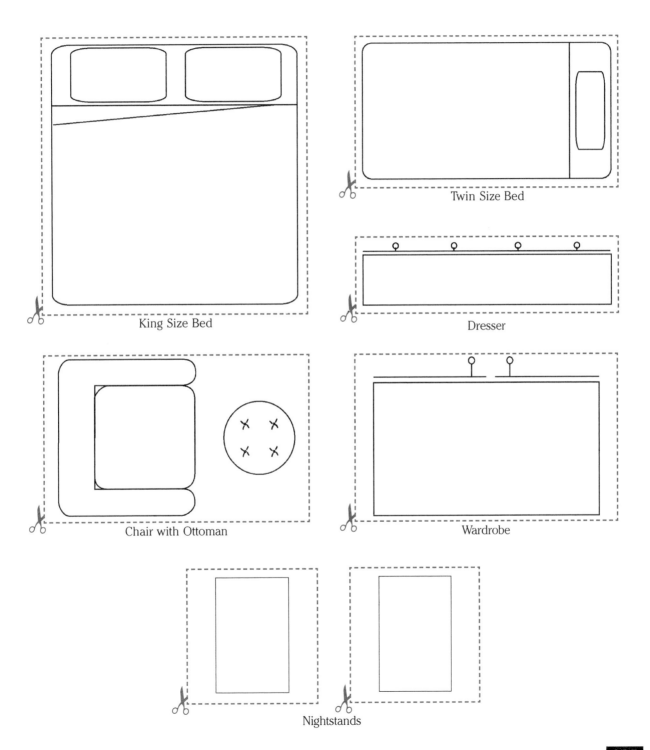

King Size Bed

Twin Size Bed

Dresser

Chair with Ottoman

Wardrobe

Nightstands

Dining Room

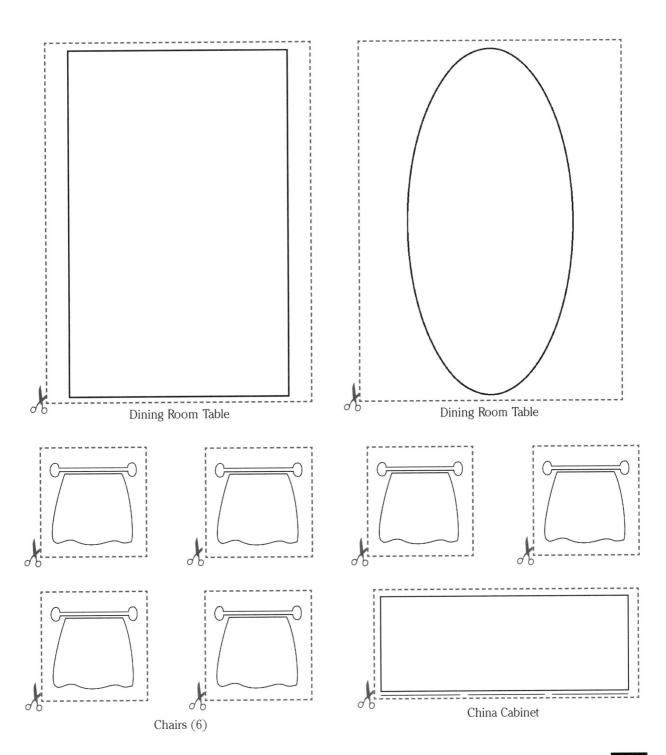

Dining Room Table

Dining Room Table

Chairs (6)

China Cabinet

Living Room

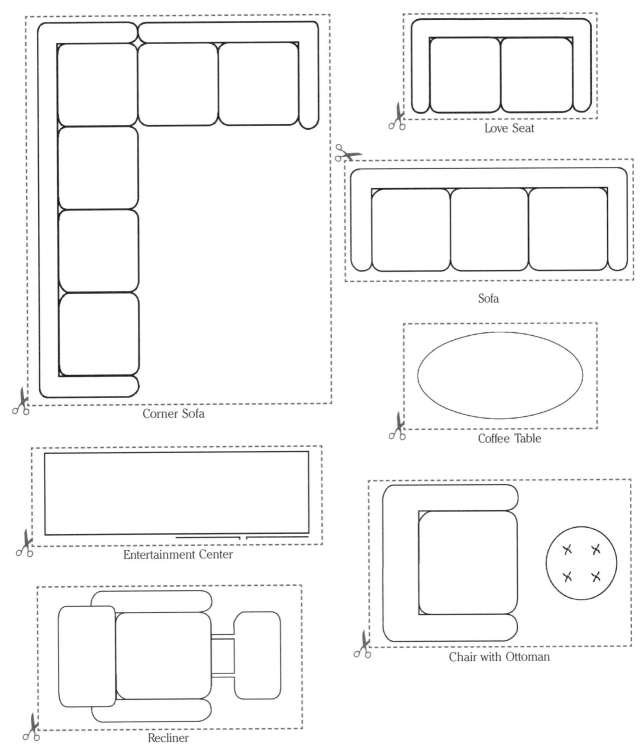

Love Seat

Sofa

Corner Sofa

Coffee Table

Entertainment Center

Chair with Ottoman

Recliner

APPENDIX C
Sign Finder

I n Chinese astrology, each lunar year has a corresponding animal and element, which repeat according to a sixty-year cycle. Knowing which element corresponds to your birth date will help you apply certain feng shui practices to your best advantage (as noted in Chapter 1). Use the following chart to determine your sign and element.

LUNAR YEAR	ELEMENT/ANIMAL
January 24, 2001–February 11, 2002	Metal Snake
January 27, 1941–February 14, 1942	
February 5, 2000–January 23, 2001	Metal Dragon
February 8, 1940–January 26, 1941	
February 16, 1999–February 4, 2000	Earth Rabbit
February 19, 1939–February 7, 1940	
January 28, 1998–February 15, 1999	Earth Tiger
January 31, 1938–February 18, 1939	
February 7, 1997–January 27, 1998	Fire Ox
February 11, 1937–January 30, 1938	
February 19, 1996–February 6, 1997	Fire Rat
January 24, 1936–February 10, 1937	
January 31, 1995–February 18, 1996	Wood Pig
February 4, 1935–January 23, 1936	
February 10, 1994–January 30, 1995	Wood Dog
February 14, 1934–February 3, 1935	
January 23, 1993–February 9, 1994	Water Rooster
January 26, 1933–February 13, 1934	
February 4, 1992–January 22, 1993	Water Monkey
February 6, 1932–January 25, 1933	
February 15, l991–February 3, 1992	Metal Goat
February 17, 1931–February 5, 1932	
January 27, 1990–February 14, 1991	Metal Horse
January 30, 1930–February 16, 1931	
February 6, 1989–January 26, 1990	Earth Snake
February 10, 1929–January 29, 1930	
February 17, 1988–February 5, 1989	Earth Dragon
January 23, 1928–February 9, 1929	
January 30, 1987–February 16, 1988	Fire Rabbit
February 2, 1927–January 22, 1928	
February 9, 1986–January 28, 1987	Fire Tiger
February 13, 1926–February 1, 1927	
February 20, 1985–February 8, 1986	Wood Ox
January 25, 1925–February 12, 1926	

LUNAR YEAR	ELEMENT/ANIMAL
February 2, 1984–February 19, 1985	Wood Rat
February 5, 1924–January 24, 1925	
February 13, 1983–February 1, 1984	Water Pig
February 16, 1923–February 4, 1924	
January 25, 1982–February 12, 1983	Water Dog
January 28, 1922–February 15, 1923	
February 5, 1981–January 24, 1982	Metal Rooster
February 8, 1921–January 27, 1922	
February 16, 1980–February 4, 1981	Metal Monkey
February 20, 1920–February 7, 1921	
January 28, 1979–February 15, 1980	Earth Goat
February 1, 1919–February 19, 1920	
February 7, 1978–January 27, 1979	Earth Horse
February 11, 1918–January 31, 1919	
February 18, 1977–February 6, 1978	Fire Snake
January 23, 1917–February 10, 1918	
January 31, 1976–February 17, 1977	Fire Dragon
February 3, 1916–January 22, 1917	
February 11, 1975–January 30, 1976	Wood Rabbit
February 14, 1915–February 2, 1916	
January 23, 1974–February 10, 1975	Wood Tiger
January 26, 1914–February 13, 1915	
February 3, 1973–January 22, 1974	Water Ox
February 6, 1913–January 25, 1914	
February 15, 1972–February 2, 1973	Water Rat
February 18, 1912–February 5, 1913	
January 27, 1971–February 14, 1972	Metal Pig
January 30, l911–February 17, 1912	
February 6, 1970–January 26, 1971	Metal Dog
February 10, 1910–January 29, 1911	
February 17, 1969–February 5, 1970	Earth Rooster
January 22, 1909–February 9, 1910	
January 30, l968–February 16, 1969	Earth Monkey
February 2, 1908–January 21, 1909	

LUNAR YEAR	ELEMENT/ANIMAL
February 9, 1967–January 29, 1968	Fire Goat
February 13, 1907–February 1, 1908	
January 21, 1966–February 8, 1967	Fire Horse
January 25, 1906–February 12, 1907	
February 2, 1965–January 20, 1966	Wood Snake
February 4, 1905–January 24, 1906	
February 13, 1964–February 1, 1965	Wood Dragon
February 16, 1904–February 3, 1905	
January 25, 1963–February 12, 1964	Water Rabbit
January 29, 1903–February 15, 1904	
February 5, 1962–January 24, 1963	Water Tiger
February 8, 1902–January 28, 1903	
February 15, 1961–February 4, 1962	Metal Ox
February 19, 1901–February 7, 1902	
January 28, 1960–February 14, 1961	Metal Rat
January 31, 1900–February 18, 1901	
February 8, 1959–January 27, 1960	Earth Pig
February 18, 1958–February 7, 1959	Earth Dog
January 31, 1957–February 17, 1958	Fire Rooster
February 12, 1956–January 30, 1957	Fire Monkey
January 24, 1955–February 11, 1956	Wood Goat
February 3, 1954–January 23, 1955	Wood Horse
February 14, 1953–February 2, 1954	Water Snake
January 27, 1952–February 13, 1953	Water Dragon
February 6, 1951–January 26, 1952	Metal Rabbit
February 17, 1950–February 5, 1951	Metal Tiger
January 29, 1949–February 16, 1950	Earth Ox
February 10, 1948–January 28, 1949	Earth Rat
January 22, 1947–February 9, 1948	Fire Pig
February 2, 1946–January 21, 1947	Fire Dog
February 13, 1945–February 1, 1946	Wood Rooster
January 25, 1944–February 12, 1945	Wood Monkey
February 5, 1943–January 24, 1944	Water Goat
February 15, 1942–February 4, 1943	Water Horse
January 27, 1941–February 14, 1942	Metal Snake

APPENDIX D

Resources for Further Study

N ow that you have made the decision to apply the principles of feng shui to your life, you may want to study the subject further. Whether you are interested in a deeper understanding of feng shui practices and Chinese wisdom, or simply another point of view, the following books, software, and feng shui organizations will help you to keep your intentions clear.

Books

Beattie, Antonia, with Rosemary Stevens. *Using Feng Shui* (Barnes & Noble, 2000). Nice, simple guide to the basic principles of feng shui.

Biggs, Jane Butler. *Feng Shui in 10 Simple Lessons* (Watson-Guptill Publications, 1999). Accessible guide with several question-and-answer sessions throughout. Very helpful to beginners.

Biggs, Jane Butler. *The Feng Shui Directory* (Watson-Guptill Publications, 2000). Handy guide divided with tabs by life intentions (health, wealth, career, etc.).

Brown, Simon. *Practical Feng Shui* (Ward Lock, 1997). Rich with diagrams and color photographs, this easy-to-understand book will help the novice to get started.

Carter, Karen Rauch. *Move Your Stuff, Change Your Life: How to Use Feng Shui to Get Love, Money, Respect and Happiness* (A Fireside Book, Simon & Schuster, 2000). Considered highly accessible and written in very modern, Western terms, this book is either loved or hated by anyone interested in feng shui. Still, I think it is an easy way to get one's chi flowing in the right direction.

Chin, R.D. *Feng Shui Revealed: An Aesthetic, Practical Approach to the Ancient Art of Space Alignment* (Clarkson Potter/Publishers, 1998). This book, with its lush photographs and captivating illustrations, offers a more detailed look at feng shui applications in very real settings.

Chuen, Master Lam Kam. *The Feng Shui Handbook* (Gaia, 1995). Simple guide to getting started with feng shui.

Chuen, Master Lam Kam. *The Personal Feng Shui Manual: How to Develop a Healthy and Harmonious Lifestyle* (Henry Holt & Company, 1998). Very accessible book that spends a lot of time sharing the nuances of Chinese wisdom (astrology, I Ching, etc.).

Collins, Terah Kathryn. *Home Design with Feng Shui* (Hay House, 1999). Color, easy-to-read book alphabetized and with tabs for easy reference. A great start!

Dexter, Rosalyn. *Chinese Whispers: Feng Shui* (Random House, 1999). Dexter designed this book herself, and it is a lovely work of art. But besides that, it also offers poetic glimpses into the wisdom and philosophy behind the art of feng shui.

Fontana, David, Ph.D. *Discover Zen: A Practical Guide to Personal Serenity* (Chronicle Books, 2001). Practical guide with rich, pastel illustrations that make you want to be more Zenlike in everything you do.

Gerecht, Hope Karan. *Healing Design: Practical Feng Shui for Healthy and Gracious Living* (Journey Editions, 1999). This well-organized and richly illustrated book offers plenty of food for thought not found in other books on feng shui.

Hale, Gill. *The Feng Shui Garden: Design Your Garden for Health, Wealth and Happiness* (Storey Books, 1998). Lovely photographs in this book make you wish you had a bigger yard—or more room to make a total feng shui statement inside and out. Recommended reading for those with a green thumb.

📖 Henwood, Belinda, and consultant Howard Choy. *Feng Shui: How to Create Harmony and Balance in Your Living and Working Environment* (Storey Books, 1997). Simple and easy to understand, this little guide will answer some basic questions about the practice of feng shui.

📖 Hyder, Carole J. *Wind and Water: Your Personal Feng Shui Journey* (The Crossing Press, 1998). Lovely and spiritually uplifting book that offers wisdom for everything you are likely to do along your path on your feng shui journey. I love this book!

📖 Karcher, Stephen L., and Rudolph Ritsema. *I Ching* (Element Books, 1994). Basic guide covering the history and wisdom of the *I Ching*.

📖 Kennedy, David. *Feng Shui Tips for a Better Life* (Storey Books, 1998). Want to use feng shui to get more out of life? This book will be for you.

📖 Kingston, Karen. *Clear Your Clutter with Feng Shui* (Broadway Books, 1999). A godsend for those who are bound by clutter. Remove the obstacle of clutter in your life, but start the process by reading this book. An absolute must. I read it on an airplane to Chicago, and my life hasn't been the same since.

📖 Kingston, Karen. *Creating Sacred Space with Feng Shui* (Broadway Books, 1997). Inspiring guide to creating a space that matters versus placing matter in your space.

📖 Lambert, Mary. *Clearing the Clutter* (Barnes & Noble, 2001). A great beginning guide for those just starting, but for more depth, see Karen Kingston's book on clutter.

📖 Linn, Denise. *Feng Shui for the Soul* (Hay House, 1999). This book offers more of a metaphysical approach to feng shui, but it is a welcome and spiritually uplifting one, to be sure. I especially like the way Linn weaves ancestral energies into the feng shui mix.

📖 Linn, Denise. *Sacred Space Clearing and Enhancing the Energy of Your Home* (Rider, 1995). Fantastic book about what it means spiritually to be rid of unwanted or negative energies.

📖 Linn, Denise. *Space Clearing A–Z: How to Use Feng Shui to Purify and Bless Your Home* (Hay House, 2001). This A–Z guide features handy tabs to help you learn how to put the practice of space clearing to practical use. The house blessings are especially helpful.

📖 Linn, Denise. *Space Clearing: How to Purify and Create Harmony in Your Home* (Contemporary Books, 2000). A terrific explanation of what space clearing is and how purification can bring about harmony in your home—and life.

📖 Mah, Adeline Yen. *Watching the Tree: A Chinese Daughter Reflects on Happiness, Tradition and Spiritual Wisdom* (Broadway Books, 2001). This book contains a chapter or two on chi and feng shui, in the eyes of a Chinese woman who now lives in the Western world of California. Very insightful.

📖 Post, Stephen. *The Modern Book of Feng Shui: Vitality and Harmony for the Home and Office* (Dell Publishing, 1998). This book offers a wealth of interesting tidbits about feng shui, and is suitable for the beginner.

Reid, Lori. *The Complete Book of Chinese Horoscopes* (Barnes & Noble, 1997). A colorfully illustrated guide to all the personality traits, characteristics, and compatibilities of each Chinese astrological sign. Great fun for the whole family.

Rossbach, Sarah, and Master Lin Yun. *Feng Shui Design: The Art of Creating Harmony for Interiors, Landscape and Architecture* (Viking/Penguin Putnam, 1998). A must for anyone interested in feng shui, especially the Black Hat Sect. Master Yun is the originator of that sect.

SantoPietro, Nancy. *Feng Shui: Harmony By Design*; foreword by Professor Lin Yun (Perigee Books, 1996). Very helpful book with plenty of real-life examples, including feng shui for the apartment.

Simons, T. Raphael. *Feng Shui Step By Step* (Crown Trade Paperbacks, 1996). From an informational standpoint, this book is helpful. The illustrations are very basic, however, and not as interesting.

Spear, William. *Feng Shui Made Easy* (Thorsons, 1995). Just what this book says it is, this book will be considered helpful to the uninitiated.

Stasney, Sharon. *Feng Shui Chic: Stylish Designs for Harmonious Living* (Sterling Publishing Company, 2000). This well-designed book, complete with its fabulous photographs of homes you wish you lived in, offers much in the way of concrete detail and real-life examples. One of the best books out there on the topic of modern feng shui.

Tan, Situ. *Best Chinese Idioms* (Hai Feng Publishing Company, 1986). Want to learn some of the famous Chinese sayings to impart their wisdom on your family and friends? Try this book.

Tanahashi, Kazuaki, and Tensho David Schneider. *Essential Zen* (Castle Books, 1994). Very insightful, interesting book on the practice of Zen meditation.

Thompson, Gerry. *Feng Shui Astrology for Lovers* (Sterling Publishing Company, 1998). Okay, so this is a little out of the feng shui realm—but you can learn a lot about what to put in your relationship corner if you want to attract a certain type. What's wrong with that?

Too, Lillian. *The Complete Illustrated Guide to Feng Shui Gardens* (Element Books, 1998). Beautifully illustrated and full of tips, this is an insightful book.

Too, Lillian. *The Fundamentals of Feng Shui* (Element Books, 1999). Full of cures, enhancements, and tips galore, this book will either be very helpful or put you into "feng shui overload" with the hundreds of things you can do to improve your life. My advice: Use the tips you need most now, and leave the rest for a time when you most need them.

Too, Lillian. *Lillian Too's Chinese Wisdom* (Cico Books, 2001). Fascinating guide to the history and background behind many Chinese traditions and pearls of wisdom.

Too, Lillian. *Lillian Too's Little Book of Feng Shui At Work* (Element Books, 1999). Handy guide to keep in your desk drawer for those spare moments when you can practice feng shui from your cubicle.

Too, Lillian. *Networking* (Element Books, 1997). Another great little feng shui book for business concerns.

Tsu, Lao. *Tao Te Ching* (Wildwood House Ltd., 1992). The Tao is essential reading for anyone interested in feng shui. It is one of the main foundations of this ancient practice.

Webster, Richard. *101 Feng Shui Tips for the Home* (Llewellyn, 1998). Helpful and full of great and practical tips.

Wei, Wu. *I Ching Wisdom* (Power Press, 1994). I just open this book daily to whatever it wants to teach me.

Wing, R.L. *The Illustrated I Ching* (HarperCollins, 1987). The *I Ching* is a wonderful Chinese divination tool, and this book makes it easy to implement it into your life.

Wydra, Nancilee. *Feng Shui for Children's Spaces: A Parent's Guide to Designing Environments in Which Children Will Thrive* (Contemporary Books, 2001). Accessible and easy to incorporate into your family's life, no matter how busy you are.

Wydra, Nancilee. *Feng Shui Goes to the Office* (Contemporary Books, 2000). If I could only have one feng shui book in my office, this one would be it. A fantastic and helpful guide to implementing the practice of feng shui into modern, Western business.

Wydra, Nancilee. *Feng Shui: The Book of Cures* (Contemporary Books, 1993). Have problems with a missing corner in your living room? How about a front entrance with a straight path to the door? This book will prescribe the perfect feng shui antidote.

Organizations

Feng Shui Across America/Feng Shui Consultant Trainings
7609 New Utrecht Avenue
Brooklyn, NY 11214
Phone (718) 256-2640
E-mail: *nsanpietro@aol.com*

Feng Shui Guild
1919 8th Street
P.O. Box 850
Boulder, CO 80306
Phone (303) 444-1548

Feng Shui Institute International
7547 Bruns Court Canal
Winchester, OH 43110
Phone (614) 837-8370
Fax (614) 834-9760
E-mail: *fengshuimastersl@aol.com*

The Feng Shui Institute of America
P.O. Box 488
Wabasso, FL 32970
Phone (561) 589-9900
Fax (561) 589-1611

Feng Shui Warehouse
P.O. Box 6689
San Diego, CA 92166
Phone (800) 399-1599 or (619) 523-2158
Fax (800) 997-9831 or (619) 523-2165

Worldwide Lin Yun Educational Foundation
1896 Lexington Avenue
San Mateo, CA 94402

Yun Lin Temple Feng Shui Master Lin Yun
2959 Russell Street
Berkeley, CA 94705
Phone (510) 841-2347

Software

Dragon Dance: A Guide to Life, Love, and Fortune Through Chinese Astrology. CD audiobook/reference booklet. Magnolia Films, 1999.

Feng Shui: Change Your Surroundings and Transform Your Life. CD-ROM. COMPUworks/The WizardWorks Group, Inc., 1998.

▣ *Feng Shui: Music for Feng Shui and relaxation.* CD. The Mind Body & Soul Series, New World Music Inc., 1998.

▣ *Lillian Too's Feng Shui Space Clearing.* Multimedia CD. World of Feng Shui (*wofs.com*), 2000.

Web Sites

⌨ *www.bartlettdesigns.com* Articles and a great bagua diagram at Feng Shui master Stanley Bartlett's site.

⌨ *www.bloomington.in.us/~9harmony/* Nine Harmonies School of Feng Shui, founded by Carol Bridges. School and registration information.

⌨ *www.fengshuiguild.com/* The Feng Shui Guild's Web site, primarily for practitioners.

⌨ *www.fengshui-magazine.com* The online home of Britain's Feng Shui for *Modern Living* magazine. Informative articles.

⌨ *www.fengshui2000.com* The official site of the International Feng Shui Research Design Centre.

⌨ *www.fsgreetings.com* Free and fun feng shui e-greetings to send and receive. Created with World of Feng Shui (*www.wofs.com*).

⌨ *www.geofengshui.com* GEO—Geomancy/Feng Shui Education Organization's online information center.

⌨ *www.qi-journal.com Qi: The Journal of Traditional Eastern Health & Fitness.*

⌨ *www.raymond-lo.com* Hong Kong-based Raymond Lo's feng shui sit, with information and a list of his services.

⌨ *www.spaceclearing.com* Karen Kingston's Space Clearing site, where you can learn about her philosophies and even become certified as a space clearing practitioner.

⌨ *www.spiritweb.org/feng-shui.html* Informative articles by Jenni Liu.

⌨ *www.windwater.com* The Feng Shui Institute of America's online home.

⌨ *www.wofs.com* Lillian Too's official Web site, with lots of good information and several places to buy feng shui tools and accessories.

⌨ *www.wsfs.com* Founded by Terah Kathryn Collins and Jonathan Hulsh, this is the Western School of Feng Shui.

APPENDIX E
Glossary

As you continue reading about feng shui practices, you will also continue to learn about related topics, religions, philosophies, and traditions. The following terms are used (and defined) in varying detail both in the text and in the glossary. For more in-depth information, please refer to any of several recommended feng shui resources.

"absent" space—An area of the bagua that is not represented by a room in your home. It's also referred to in feng shui as a "missing" corner.

ancestors—In Chinese culture, honoring ancestors is very important in maintaining good health and prosperity of the family. Ancestors are represented in the family corner of the bagua, which is on the middle left side of the octagon.

bagua—An octagon that represents the nine intentions of your life. It is used as an "energy" road map used to help direct more positive energy to specific areas of your life. For instance, if you want to enhance your career, you could use the bagua to determine the career area of your home, then use the principles of feng shui to maximize your opportunities. In this sense, it can be a manifestation tool.

Buddhism—A school of spiritual thought based on the teachings of the Buddha, who believed that we all possess the ability to reach a state of Complete Understanding of nature, our lives, and the Universe. In Buddhism, enlightenment can be reached by releasing our earthly, mundane attachments in favor of higher spiritual thought. Much of feng shui (particularly in the Black Hat Sect) is based on the teachings of Buddhism.

career—The area of the bagua that represents your career. Located in the front middle of the bagua. Most people enter their homes in the career sector of the bagua. Associated with the water element.

chi—Often called *qi*. The invisible life force, or life energy, that the Chinese believe moves about in and around our bodies and environments.

children—The area of the bagua that represents children and creativity. Located in the middle right area of the bagua. Associated with the metal element.

Chinese zodiac—A popular and ancient method of astrology that explores the meanings, relationships, and synergies of twelve animal signs: rat, ox, tiger, rabbit, dragon, snake, horse, sheep, monkey, rooster, dog, and pig.

Compass School—The Compass School of feng shui uses the compass to determine auspicious directions for energy. It is a highly intellectual versus intuitive school of feng shui thought.

Confucianism—The teachings of fifth-century Chinese philosopher Confucius. These pearls of timeless wisdom refer mostly to moral conduct and ethical behavior.

cure—When a negative position is encountered in feng shui, a cure can remedy the problem by reversing or redirecting the energy into a positive flow. For instance, if there is blocked chi in your doorway, you can hang a crystal to get the energy moving. There are nine basic remedies in feng shui.

destructive cycle—Sometimes called the "reductive" cycle. Used to reduce the power of a dominating element. Each phase of this cycle reduces or minimizes the next phase.

dragon—This animal of the Chinese zodiac represents east energy and the wood element.

earth element—In feng shui, earth is one of the five elements that affect our lives. It is associated with relationships, resourcefulness, and earth colors.

east energy—This energy propels us into action.

fame—The area of the bagua that represents fame and reputation. Located in the rear middle of the bagua. Associated with the fire element and the color red.

family—The area of the bagua that represents your family. Located in the front middle left side of the bagua. Associated with the colors blue and green.

feng shui—The traditional Chinese system of placement, harmony, and balance within the environment. The goal of feng shui is to achieve harmony with chi, or the universal life force. Literally translated, *feng* *shui* means "wind and water," symbolic of the movement of energy.

fire—Represents enlightenment and vision of self. One of the five elements, fire is associated with colors such as red and orange and with southern direction.

five elements—In feng shui, there are five elements: earth, wood, metal, water, and fire. These are symbolic of the seasons and have both creative and destructive cycles.

five senses—To achieve balance in feng shui, it is best to appeal to as many of your five senses (taste, touch, smell, sound, and sight) as possible in each room. Often, as we enhance a room's energy with wonderful items that appeal either visually, as with art, or to our sense of smell, as with potpourri, we forget that the other senses need attention as well. Best to balance them in as many rooms as possible.

Form School—The primary school of feng shui thought, based on the ancient Chinese need to maximize the lay of the land. Much attention is paid to topography of the land in this school of feng shui.

health—The area of the bagua that represents the health of yourself and your family. Located in the center of the bagua.

helpful people—The area of the bagua that represents the people who help you advance in your life. Located in the bottom right of the bagua. This is also commonly called the travel corner as well, and is associated with Heaven and the colors white, gray, and black.

house blessing—A ceremonial method of enhancing a space and endowing it with the strongest potential for good luck. Usually performed after a space clearing.

I Ching—Ancient Chinese divination system, also known as the "Book of Changes." Much of feng shui theory is based on the *I Ching*.

intention—An aim that guides an action and gives it purpose and meaning.

knowledge—The area of the bagua that represents knowledge and self-growth. Located in the bottom left side of the bagua. The colors associated with the knowledge corner include black, blue, and green.

Lao Tsu—Chinese philosopher credited with writing the *I Ching,* or "Book of Changes," on which much of feng shui is based.

luo pan—This is the name given to the feng shui compass used to determine proper flow or direction of energy in your home or surroundings.

marriage—The area of the bagua that represents marriage and important relationships. Located in the rear right corner of the bagua. This is the corner where you'd most want pairs of things, to symbolize love and partnership. Associated colors are red, pink, and white.

metal—One of the five elements in feng shui. Metal represents structure and strength, but also creativity and recreation. Colors associated with the metal element include white, gold, and silver.

"mouth" of chi—In feng shui, the main entrance to your home is considered the "mouth" or opening of chi. It allows energy to come in from the front door, then directs chi through your home.

mudra—A series of symbolic postures and hand movements used in Hinduism to represent different stages along the path to enlightenment.

north energy—In feng shui, energy from the north brings quiet, meditation, and stillness. Here, we can be introspective and nourish our selves.

phoenix—A bird of great power, associated with southern energy and the fire element.

poison arrow—Any sharp corner or straight object from which chi is bounced at an angle. If you have such a situation inside or outside your home, a feng shui cure is recommended, since poison arrows are considered to be bad luck or negative energy.

productive cycle—In this cycle of the five elements, water nurtures wood, which feeds fire, which makes earth, which creates metal, which holds water. Each phase of the cycle enhances the next.

qi—Another spelling of *chi,* which is the invisible energy or life force that is within us and all around us.

qi gong—Literally, "energy cultivation." Refers to exercises that improve health and longevity as well as increase the sense of harmony within oneself and in the world. There are thousands of such exercises.

smudge stick—a tightly wrapped bundle of healing and spiritual herbs, used (with intention!) to clear or cleanse a space of negative energy.

snake—Represents a central energy and is associated with the element of earth.

south energy—Changeable, unpredictable, and enlivening energy.

space clearing—In feng shui, a ceremonial method of removing negative energy in a room or structure and replacing it with a healthy flow of positive energy. Often involves walking through the structure with a smudge stick or lavender incense. A space clearing should be performed after any major change in the energy of a room (i.e., after an argument, redecorating, or remodeling).

tai chi—The ancient Chinese practice of meditation in movement. Through a series of flowing movements and positions, tai chi has been proven to help lower blood pressure, and it promotes relaxation, harmony, and balance in mind, body, and spirit. In many ways, tai chi is like feng shui for the body, since it emphasizes fluidity of good energy or chi.

Taoism—Sometimes called Daoism, this philosophy relies on intuition and the belief that we are one with nature.

tiger—Associated with western energy and the metal element.

tortoise—This animal in feng shui symbolizes the energy of the north and the water element.

trigram—Most frequently associated with the *I Ching,* a trigram is a three-tiered set of broken and unbroken lines that symbolize the yin and yang that create all things and situations in life.

water—Another of the five elements, water represents contemplation, reflection, and solitude. It is associated with blue, black, and the north.

wealth—The area of the bagua that represents wealth and prosperity. Located in the rear left corner of the bagua. This is where you might position your desk if you have a home office, or where you would hang a crystal to activate wealth energy in your home. Coordinating colors include blue, purple, and bluish red.

west energy—Relaxing, creative yin energy.

white tiger—Any tree, bush, building, fence, or landform located to the right of your home or business.

wood—Represents growth, personal development, and the generation of new ideas or plans. Associated with green and the east. Wood is also one of the five elements.

yang—Creative, dynamic energy. Often perceived as active and masculine energy. Yang and yin are complementary opposites.

yin—Receptive, feminine energy that is seen by many as passive and soft. Yin and yang are complementary opposites.

Zen—A movement of Buddhism that emphasizes enlightenment through meditation and intuition. The Black Hat Sect of feng shui relies heavily upon these principles.

Index

THE EVERYTHING SERIES!

BUSINESS & PERSONAL FINANCE

Everything® Budgeting Book
Everything® Business Planning Book
Everything® Coaching and Mentoring Book
Everything® Fundraising Book
Everything® Get Out of Debt Book
Everything® Grant Writing Book
Everything® Homebuying Book, 2nd Ed.
Everything® Homeselling Book
Everything® Home-Based Business Book
Everything® Investing Book
Everything® Landlording Book
Everything® Leadership Book
Everything® Managing People Book
Everything® Negotiating Book
Everything® Online Business Book
Everything® Personal Finance Book
Everything® Personal Finance in Your
        20s & 30s Book
Everything® Project Management Book
Everything® Real Estate Investing Book
Everything® Robert's Rules Book, $7.95
Everything® Selling Book
Everything® Start Your Own Business Book
Everything® Time Management Book
Everything® Wills & Estate Planning Book

COOKING

Everything® Barbecue Cookbook
Everything® Bartender's Book, $9.95
Everything® Chinese Cookbook
Everything® Chocolate Cookbook
Everything® College Cookbook
Everything® Cookbook
Everything® Dessert Cookbook
Everything® Diabetes Cookbook
Everything® Easy Gourmet Cookbook
Everything® Fondue Cookbook
Everything® Grilling Cookbook

Everything® Healthy Meals in Minutes
        Cookbook
Everything® Holiday Cookbook
Everything® Indian Cookbook
Everything® Low-Carb Cookbook
Everything® Low-Fat High-Flavor Cookbook
Everything® Low-Salt Cookbook
Everything® Meals for a Month Cookbook
Everything® Mediterranean Cookbook
Everything® Mexican Cookbook
Everything® One-Pot Cookbook
Everything® Pasta Cookbook
Everything® Quick Meals Cookbook
Everything® Slow Cooker Cookbook
Everything® Soup Cookbook
Everything® Thai Cookbook
Everything® Vegetarian Cookbook
Everything® Wine Book

HEALTH

Everything® Alzheimer's Book
Everything® Anti-Aging Book
Everything® Diabetes Book
Everything® Hypnosis Book
Everything® Low Cholesterol Book
Everything® Massage Book
Everything® Menopause Book
Everything® Nutrition Book
Everything® Reflexology Book
Everything® Stress Management Book

HISTORY

Everything® American Government Book
Everything® American History Book
Everything® Civil War Book
Everything® Irish History & Heritage Book
Everything® Middle East Book

HOBBIES & GAMES

Everything® Blackjack Strategy Book
Everything® Brain Strain Book, $9.95
Everything® Bridge Book
Everything® Candlemaking Book
Everything® Card Games Book
Everything® Cartooning Book
Everything® Casino Gambling Book, 2nd Ed.
Everything® Chess Basics Book
Everything® Crossword and Puzzle Book
Everything® Crossword Challenge Book
Everything® Cryptograms Book, $9.95
Everything® Digital Photography Book
Everything® Drawing Book
Everything® Easy Crosswords Book
Everything® Family Tree Book
Everything® Games Book, 2nd Ed.
Everything® Knitting Book
Everything® Knots Book
Everything® Motorcycle Book
Everything® Online Genealogy Book
Everything® Photography Book
Everything® Poker Strategy Book
Everything® Pool & Billiards Book
Everything® Quilting Book
Everything® Scrapbooking Book
Everything® Sewing Book
Everything® Woodworking Book
Everything® Word Games Challenge Book

HOME IMPROVEMENT

Everything® Feng Shui Book
Everything® Feng Shui Decluttering Book, $9.95
Everything® Fix-It Book
Everything® Homebuilding Book
Everything® Landscaping Book
Everything® Lawn Care Book
Everything® Organize Your Home Book

All Everything® books are priced at $12.95 or $14.95, unless otherwise stated. Prices subject to change without notice.

EVERYTHING®
KIDS' BOOKS

All titles are $6.95

Everything® Kids' Animal Puzzle & Activity Book
Everything® Kids' Baseball Book, 3rd Ed.
Everything® Kids' Bible Trivia Book
Everything® Kids' Bugs Book
Everything® Kids' Christmas Puzzle & Activity Book
Everything® Kids' Cookbook
Everything® Kids' Halloween Puzzle & Activity Book
Everything® Kids' Hidden Pictures Book
Everything® Kids' Joke Book
Everything® Kids' Knock Knock Book
Everything® Kids' Math Puzzles Book
Everything® Kids' Mazes Book
Everything® Kids' Money Book
Everything® Kids' Monsters Book
Everything® Kids' Nature Book
Everything® Kids' Puzzle Book
Everything® Kids' Riddles & Brain Teasers Book
Everything® Kids' Science Experiments Book
Everything® Kids' Sharks Book
Everything® Kids' Soccer Book
Everything® Kids' Travel Activity Book

KIDS' STORY BOOKS

Everything® Bedtime Story Book
Everything® Bible Stories Book
Everything® Fairy Tales Book

LANGUAGE

Everything® Conversational Japanese Book (with CD), $19.95
Everything® French Phrase Book, $9.95
Everything® French Verb Book, $9.95
Everything® Inglés Book
Everything® Learning French Book
Everything® Learning German Book
Everything® Learning Italian Book
Everything® Learning Latin Book
Everything® Learning Spanish Book
Everything® Sign Language Book
Everything® Spanish Grammar Book
Everything® Spanish Phrase Book, $9.95
Everything® Spanish Verb Book, $9.95

MUSIC

Everything® Drums Book (with CD), $19.95
Everything® Guitar Book
Everything® Home Recording Book
Everything® Playing Piano and Keyboards Book
Everything® Reading Music Book (with CD), $19.95
Everything® Rock & Blues Guitar Book (with CD), $19.95
Everything® Songwriting Book

NEW AGE

Everything® Astrology Book
Everything® Dreams Book, 2nd Ed.
Everything® Ghost Book
Everything® Love Signs Book, $9.95
Everything® Meditation Book
Everything® Numerology Book
Everything® Paganism Book
Everything® Palmistry Book
Everything® Psychic Book
Everything® Reiki Book
Everything® Spells & Charms Book
Everything® Tarot Book
Everything® Wicca and Witchcraft Book

PARENTING

Everything® Baby Names Book
Everything® Baby Shower Book
Everything® Baby's First Food Book
Everything® Baby's First Year Book
Everything® Birthing Book
Everything® Breastfeeding Book
Everything® Father-to-Be Book
Everything® Father's First Year Book
Everything® Get Ready for Baby Book
Everything® Getting Pregnant Book
Everything® Homeschooling Book
Everything® Parent's Guide to Children with ADD/ADHD
Everything® Parent's Guide to Children with Asperger's Syndrome
Everything® Parent's Guide to Children with Autism
Everything® Parent's Guide to Children with Dyslexia
Everything® Parent's Guide to Positive Discipline

Everything® Parent's Guide to Raising a Successful Child
Everything® Parent's Guide to Tantrums
Everything® Parent's Guide to the Overweight Child
Everything® Parenting a Teenager Book
Everything® Potty Training Book, $9.95
Everything® Pregnancy Book, 2nd Ed.
Everything® Pregnancy Fitness Book
Everything® Pregnancy Nutrition Book
Everything® Pregnancy Organizer, $15.00
Everything® Toddler Book
Everything® Tween Book
Everything® Twins, Triplets, and More Book

PETS

Everything® Cat Book
Everything® Dachshund Book, $12.95
Everything® Dog Book
Everything® Dog Health Book
Everything® Dog Training and Tricks Book
Everything® Golden Retriever Book, $12.95
Everything® Horse Book
Everything® Labrador Retriever Book, $12.95
Everything® Poodle Book, $12.95
Everything® Pug Book, $12.95
Everything® Puppy Book
Everything® Rottweiler Book, $12.95
Everything® Tropical Fish Book

REFERENCE

Everything® Car Care Book
Everything® Classical Mythology Book
Everything® Computer Book
Everything® Divorce Book
Everything® Einstein Book
Everything® Etiquette Book
Everything® Great Thinkers Book
Everything® Mafia Book
Everything® Philosophy Book
Everything® Psychology Book
Everything® Shakespeare Book

RELIGION

Everything® Angels Book
Everything® Bible Book
Everything® Buddhism Book
Everything® Catholicism Book

All Everything® books are priced at $12.95 or $14.95, unless otherwise stated. Prices subject to change without notice.

Everything® Christianity Book
Everything® Jewish History & Heritage Book
Everything® Judaism Book
Everything® Koran Book
Everything® Prayer Book
Everything® Saints Book
Everything® Torah Book
Everything® Understanding Islam Book
Everything® World's Religions Book
Everything® Zen Book

SCHOOL & CAREERS

Everything® After College Book
Everything® Alternative Careers Book
Everything® College Survival Book, 2nd Ed.
Everything® Cover Letter Book, 2nd Ed.
Everything® Get-a-Job Book
Everything® Job Interview Book
Everything® New Teacher Book
Everything® Online Job Search Book
Everything® Paying for College Book
Everything® Practice Interview Book
Everything® Resume Book, 2nd Ed.
Everything® Study Book

SELF-HELP

Everything® Dating Book
Everything® Great Sex Book
Everything® Kama Sutra Book
Everything® Self-Esteem Book

SPORTS & FITNESS

Everything® Fishing Book
Everything® Fly-Fishing Book
Everything® Golf Instruction Book
Everything® Pilates Book
Everything® Running Book
Everything® Total Fitness Book
Everything® Weight Training Book
Everything® Yoga Book

TRAVEL

Everything® Family Guide to Hawaii
Everything® Family Guide to New York City, 2nd Ed.
Everything® Family Guide to RV Travel & Campgrounds
Everything® Family Guide to the Walt Disney World Resort®, Universal Studios®, and Greater Orlando, 4th Ed.
Everything® Family Guide to Washington D.C., 2nd Ed.
Everything® Guide to Las Vegas
Everything® Guide to New England
Everything® Travel Guide to the Disneyland Resort®, California Adventure®, Universal Studios®, and the Anaheim Area

WEDDINGS

Everything® Bachelorette Party Book, $9.95
Everything® Bridesmaid Book, $9.95
Everything® Creative Wedding Ideas Book
Everything® Elopement Book, $9.95
Everything® Father of the Bride Book, $9.95
Everything® Groom Book, $9.95
Everything® Mother of the Bride Book, $9.95
Everything® Wedding Book, 3rd Ed.
Everything® Wedding Checklist, $9.95
Everything® Wedding Etiquette Book, $7.95
Everything® Wedding Organizer, $15.00
Everything® Wedding Shower Book, $7.95
Everything® Wedding Vows Book, $9.95
Everything® Weddings on a Budget Book, $9.95

WRITING

Everything® Creative Writing Book
Everything® Get Published Book
Everything® Grammar and Style Book
Everything® Guide to Writing a Book Proposal
Everything® Guide to Writing a Novel
Everything® Guide to Writing Children's Books
Everything® Screenwriting Book
Everything® Writing Poetry Book
Everything® Writing Well Book

We have Everything® for the beginning crafter!
All titles are $14.95.

Everything® Crafts—Baby Scrapbooking
1-59337-225-6

Everything® Crafts—Bead Your Own Jewelry
1-59337-142-X

Everything® Crafts—Create Your Own Greeting Cards
1-59337-226-4

Everything® Crafts—Easy Projects
1-59337-298-1

Everything® Crafts—Making Cards with Rubber Stamps
1-59337-299-X

Everything® Crafts—Polymer Clay for Beginners
1-59337-230-2

Everything® Crafts—Rubber Stamping Made Easy
1-59337-229-9

Everything® Crafts—Wedding Decorations and Keepsakes
1-59337-227-2

Available wherever books are sold!
To order, call 800-872-5627, or visit us at *www.everything.com.*
Everything® and everything.com® are registered trademarks of F+W Publications, Inc.